REGENTS CRITICS SERIES

General Editor: Paul A. Olson

BEN JONSON'S LITERARY CRITICISM

Other volumes in the Regents Critics Series are:

Joseph Conrad on Fiction
Edited by Walter F. Wright

Critical Writings of Ford Madox Ford
Edited by Frank MacShane

Literary Criticism of George Henry Lewes
Edited by Alice R. Kaminsky

Literary Criticism of Alexander Pope
Edited by Bertrand A. Goldgar

Literary Criticism of Edgar Allen Poe
Edited by Robert L. Hough

Russian Formalist Criticism: Four Essays
Translated with an introduction by
Lee T. Lemon and Marion J. Reis

Literary Criticism of William Wordsworth
Edited by Paul M. Zall

Shelley's Critical Prose
Edited by Bruce R. McElderry, Jr.

Literary Criticism of John Dryden
Edited by Arthur C. Kirsch

Literary Criticism of Sir Philip Sidney
Edited by Lewis Soens

*The Author's Craft and Other Critical Writings
of Arnold Bennett*
Edited by Samuel Hynes

Literary Criticism of Oscar Wilde
Edited by Stanley Weintraub

Literary Criticism of James Russell Lowell
Edited by Herbert F. Smith

Ben Jonson's Literary Criticism

Edited by

JAMES D. REDWINE, JR.

UNIVERSITY OF NEBRASKA PRESS · LINCOLN

Copyright © 1970 by the University of Nebraska Press
All Rights Reserved
Standard Book Number 8032–0450–7
Library of Congress Catalog Card Number 71–76737

Regents Critics Series

The Regents Critics Series provides reading texts of significant literary critics in the Western tradition. The series treats criticism as a useful tool: an introduction to the critic's own poetry and prose if he is a poet or novelist, an introduction to other work in his day if he is more judge than creator. Nowhere is criticism regarded as an end in itself but as what it is—a means to the understanding of the language of art as it has existed and been understood in various periods and societies.

Each volume includes a scholarly introduction which describes how the work collected came to be written, and suggests its uses. All texts are edited in the most conservative fashion consonant with the production of a good reading text; and all translated texts observe the dictum that the letter gives life and the spirit kills when a technical or rigorous passage is being put into English. Other types of passages may be more freely treated. Footnoting and other scholarly paraphernalia are restricted to the essential minimum. Such features as a bibliographical check-list or an index are carried where they are appropriate to the work in hand. If a volume is the first collection of the author's critical writing, this is noted in the bibliographical data.

PAUL A. OLSON

University of Nebraska

Contents

INTRODUCTION   xi

I.   THE ART OF CRITICISM: GENERAL TREATISES
Timber, Or Discoveries   3
Horace His Art of Poetry   41

II.   THE FUNCTIONS OF A POET AND A CRITIC
Poetry and Study   57
On the Dignity of Poetry   57
The Court as Fountain of Manners and Artistic Eidolon to
    the Land   58
The True Critic and Poet   59
The True Critic and Poet: A Summary   60
On the Dignity of Poetry   60
Poetry's Memorializing Function   61
The Patron, the Poet, and Poverty: Virgil and Horace   62
The Great Tradition: The Training of a Poet   64
Knowledge and Criticism   65
The Office of a Poet: The Poet as Cook   66
The Office of a Poet   68
The Functions of the Critic: The Kinds   69

III.   COMICAL SATIRE
The Character of a Perfect Satirist   75
The Poet as Censor and Satirist: The Humours Metaphor and
    Old Comedy   75
The Humourist as Vicious Man: Envy   82
The Comical Satirist's Full Stage   83
The Satirist's Objects and the Application of Satire   84
The Superiority of Comical Satire to New Comedy   85
The Violent and Painful in Comedy and Comical Satire:
    The Epitasis   85
The Comical-Satire Stage Purge   86

The Comical-Satire Catastrophe: A Defense of the Decorum
of a Scene 87
The Application of Satire: The *Every Man Out* Epilogue to
the Audience 88
Jonson's Satiric Muse: The Profound, Actionless Play 89
Satiric Indignation and Human Responsibility 90
The Comical Satirist's Function and the Court's Response 91
Satiric Exposure and the Humanistic Ideal 92
The Satirist's Sentence, the Vicious Man's Self-Punishment,
and the End of Satire 94
Envy and the Comical Satirist 95
The Enemies of Satire 95
The History of Satire and the Satirist's Role 98
Realism and Satire 101
Satire and Libel—the Distinction 102
Satire of Persons and Satire of Vice: The Uses of Historical
Models and Authorial Responsibility 102

IV. COMEDY

Reason and the Humours 113
The Discipline of Poetry and Comedy 113
The Laws of Comedy Restored: *Volpone* 117
The Universal, the Particular, and the Application of Models 118
The Law of Stagecraft: Comedy as a Realistic Moral Mirror 119
The Comic Fiction as Argumentum and Its Relation to the
Function of Comedy 120
On Obscenity in Comedy 121
Laughter and Shame in Comedy 121
Comedy: The Argumentum 121
Comic Structure: The Epitasis and the Catastrophe 122
A Good Play 122
Comedy: Comic Structure and Its Purpose 125
Comic Types and the Epitasis and Catastrophe 127
Masque Elements in Comedy 131

V. TRAGEDY

The Laws of Tragedy and the Tragic Aesthetic 135
Fear and Tragedy 136

Pity and Fear   136
History and Plays   139

VI. MASQUE

The Requirements of Masque Symbology   143
The Meaning of Masque: The Soul and Body of Symbol   143
Allegory and Masque: Reason and the Humours   144
The Function of Masque as Tribute   146
The Antimasque, Function and Conception: *The Masque
   of Queens*   147
The Art of Hinting Allegory: *The Masque of Queens*   148
The Historical and the Moral: Their Fusion in Masque   149
The Antimasque   149
The Quarrel with Inigo Jones   150

VII. CONTEMPORARY POETS AND PLAYWRIGHTS

On Kyd's *Spanish Tragedy*   155
The Conventions of the Popular Stage: Its Specious Rhetoric   155
The Contemporary Abuse of Satire   159
The Italians and the English   162
In Defense of Fletcher's *Faithful Shepherdess*   163
Beaumont   164
On Plagiarism and the Writing of Plays   164
Shakespeare   165
Richard Brome   167
Joseph Rutter   168
Of Ancients and Contemporaries   169

VIII. CONTEMPORARY ACTORS AND AUDIENCES

The Audience as Stage Critic   179
The Derivative and the Revived and the Audience as Stage
   Critic   179
The Popular Theater and Popular and Cavalier Critics   180
The State of Dramatic Art: The Polished and the Copious   182
The Artist and the Audience Again   183
Edward Alleyn   184
Salomon Pavy   184
The Popular Stage and the Artist: The Audience as Critic   185

Comic Types and the Popular Audience: The Audience as
   Critic   189
The Audience of the Play *The New Inn*   192
The Artist and Popular Taste   193
The Audience of the Play   193
The Audience of Plays: Final Statement   194

SELECTED BIBLIOGRAPHY   197
ACKNOWLEDGMENTS   198
INDEX   199

Introduction

"Dryden," said Dr. Johnson, "may be properly considered as the father of English criticism, as the writer who first taught us to determine upon principles the merit of compositions."[1] Perhaps, but Ben Jonson was the first to *try* to teach us to determine upon principles the merit of compositions; and he seems to have believed, toward the end of his career, that he had been successful. Other important writers and critics believed so too. As Rymer was to note: "At this time with us many great Wits flourished, but *Ben Johnson*, I think, had all the Critical learning to himself; and till late years *England* was as free from Critics as it is from *Wolves*."[2]

Jonson believed his task as a critic to be profound and revolutionary. "I take this labour in teaching others, that they should not be always to be taught," he says in *Discoveries*.

> ... Yet with this purpose, rather to show the right way to those that come after, than to detect any that have slipp'd before by error, and I hope it will be more profitable. For men do more willingly listen, and with more favour, to precept, than reprehension. Among diverse opinions of an Art, and most of them contrary in themselves, it is hard to make election; and therefore, though a man cannot invent new things after so many, he may do a welcome work yet to help posterity to judge rightly of the old. [See p. 18.]

He waged a long, hard campaign against what he conceived to be the critical ignorance of his age, using any and every weapon that came to hand as his campaign progressed. He not only expounded and defended critical theories in prologues and epilogues, he also made his

1. "Dryden," in *Lives of the English Poets*, ed. Birbeck Hill (3 vols.; Oxford: Clarendon Press, 1905), I, 410.
2. "Preface to the Translation of Rapin's Reflections on Aristotle's Treatise of Poesie," in *Critical Essays of the Seventeenth Century*, ed. J. E. Spingarn (3 vols.; Oxford: Clarendon Press, 1908), II, 164.

characters discuss plays and play-making; his criticism appears in poems, epigrams, and dedicatory verses. His letters, personal, dedicatory, and those addressed "To the Reader," usually contain interesting critical remarks, as do Drummond's notes on his informal conversation.

Jonson, with the possible exception of his lost dialogue commentary on Horace's *Ars Poetica*, did not attempt to write a systematic and thoroughgoing essay on criticism. In the absence of such an essay, an analysis of the material that has come down to us must serve as a poor substitute—just how poor, we shall unfortunately never know. If his criticism appears in a variety of places, it also appears in a variety of guises: as an ardent defense of poesy, an attack on contemporary abuses, a philosophical discourse on some aspect of theory, an outraged defense of a particular work, a satire on contemporary audiences, an *apologia pro vita sua*, or an appeal to the authority of one or more of the ancients. The temptation will be, no doubt, to furnish more synoptic order and unity than the spreading critical material can rightly bear—to find complexity where there is only self-contradiction. Not only does Jonson's dramatic criticism from *Volpone* onward contradict much that went before; within the later criticism itself he occasionally proposes irreconcilable theories. One must try to penetrate the accidental complexities of his criticism and, reducing the whole to its essential parts, present in an orderly manner whatever real complexity there is.

THE POET

In Jonson's great tribute to Shakespeare (p. 167), the proverb "The poet is born, not made" becomes "For a good Poet's made, as well as born." The idea comes up time and again in his criticism. He does not hesitate to say that the *sine qua non* is genius. Poets are not born every year as are mayors and sheriffs. Most often, though, he introduces genius only to argue that genius alone is not enough. The second and equally important requisite for the good poet is art: "skill, or Craft of making" (p. 29). To have natural wit or genius without art is to have the bow without the string.

Jonson has much more to say about art than genius. Nature, for better or for worse, is in the hands of the gods; art is pre-eminently the care of men and critics. A poet is not born with art; art must be got with much study and hard work at the craft. Such was the burden of a life-long Jonsonian jeremiad, and his contemporaries must have seen early that he could be as outspoken, as stubborn, and as mono-maniacal as any Old Testament prophet. In *Discoveries*, he catalogues the requisites of a good poet—genius, exercise, imitation,[3] and study. The perfect fruition of these is art. He puts it as succinctly as he can (p. 32): art is "an accession, or conformation of Learning, and Discipline." Art is not separate and distinct from nature, exercise, imitation of other poets, and study. It is rather the sum of these.

The first element of art is learning. Jonson usually insists upon both the importance of learning and the danger of relying too heavily upon it. He could boast to Drummond that "he was better versed & knew more in Greek and Latin than all the poets in England and quintessenced their brains" (p. 175); but he could also warn in *Discoveries* that the ancients "went before us; but as Guides, not Commanders" (p. 4). He had no trouble in distinguishing, in theory at least, between learning and pedantry.

The second element of art is discipline, hard and painstaking work at the difficult craft of poetry. He places even more emphasis on art as discipline than he does on art as learning. If he complains often and at length about the poor state of the contemporary stage, it is the contemporary want of the discipline of art which provokes his pro-foundest scorn. The letter which prefaces the quarto of *The Alchemist* is typical. About twenty years later, in some commendatory verses which he wrote for Brome's *The Northern Lass*, he is more scornful than ever about those "presumers on their own Naturals":

> Now each Court-Hobby-horse will wince in rhyme;
>   Both learned, and unlearned, all write *Plays*.
> It was not so of old: Men took up trades
>   That knew the Crafts they had been bred in, right.
>
> [p. 167]

3. Jonson's definition of "imitation" in *Discoveries* is a nonce definition of one of the requisites of the good poet: "to be able to convert the substance, or Riches of another *Poet*, to his own use." This definition should be (but almost never is) quoted only with the strictest care for its context. It has nothing to do with Jonson's con-ception of mimesis in the usual sense of that term.

Finally, in *Discoveries*, he virtually quotes from the *Alchemist* letter: "*But* the Wretcheder are the obstinate contemners of all helps, and Arts" (p. 11).

It may or may not be accidental that this *Discoveries* attack on contemners of art follows hard upon his well-known attack on incipient Bardolatry. As every schoolboy knows, Jonson opined to Drummond that "Shakespeare wanted Art" (p. 170). Jonson had seemed to reverse this criticism in his tribute in the Shakespeare folio, but in *Discoveries* he comes full circle; apparently, even Shakespeare (Jonson would have, reluctantly, granted one the "even") ought to have sweated more at the Muses' anvil. The spontaneous overflow of a powerful imagination must be controlled—regulated by art; sometimes Shakespeare's genius overpowered his art. Jonson suggests with what is, for him, something like humility that a discriminating critic would not seize upon Shakespeare's "artlessness" as a point of praise. To the degree that Shakespeare wanted art, to that degree he needed pardon, not praise.

On the one hand, then, Jonson conceives of art as the true poets' knowledge of and ability to apply the rules and precepts of their craft. To the degree that poets lack this knowledge and ability, their work will be spurious and ephemeral. On the other hand, art is the rules and precepts themselves, the laws which the good poet must study and apply.

THE LAWS

Over the years commentators have enjoyed citing fragments of Jonsonian criticism to prove that his attitude towards poetic laws was romantic or classical—depending upon the commentator's own predilections. Seizing on the *Every Man Out* induction (p. 81), one critic observes: "In the struggle between the law of writ and the liberty, the liberty gained the day; and when Ben Jonson is reached, classical learning itself is won to the Romantic Drama."[4] Another commentator, familiar with later pronouncements in Jonson's criticism, puts Jonson in "the true classical tradition."[5]

4. R. G. Moulton, *The Ancient Classical Drama* (Oxford: Clarendon Press, 1890), pp. 434–435.

5. T. W. Baldwin, *Shakspere's Five-Act Structure* (Urbana: University of Illinois Press, 1947), pp. 327–329.

Here as elsewhere, one should probably be careful to distinguish between the pre-*Volpone* and the post-*Volpone* criticism. The importance of the *Volpone* criticism (pp. 113–118) can scarcely be stressed too often—it marks a turning point in the development of Jonson's critical theory. Up to the time he wrote *Volpone*, his attitude toward the so-called laws would seem to be one of respectful independence. In the induction to *Every Man Out*, for instance, Cordatus lectures Mitis and the audience on the subject of comic laws (p. 81). He concludes that "strict and regular forms" derived from the practice of the ancients "are too nice observations . . . which the niceness of a few (who are nothing but form) would thrust upon us." The ancients themselves "augmented . . . with all liberty. I see not then, but we should enjoy the same licence, or free power, to illustrate and heighten our invention as they did." One would hardly have predicted on the basis of this initial pronouncement that Jonson would one day see fit to boast that he had taught his age the comic laws (p. 167). The "strange Muse" of comical satire doubtless demanded at least as much independence of the strict forms as had the Muses of the ancients. Nevertheless, from *Volpone* onward, when Jonson turns from comical satire to "quick *comedy*, refined,/As best Critics have designed" (p. 117), "licence, or free power, to illustrate and heighten our invention" is more likely to be attacked as a dangerous tendency of an illiterate age than to be defended on the grounds of classical precedent. In the dedicatory epistle to *Volpone* (p. 113), Jonson states categorically that henceforth it will be his endeavor to "raise the despis'd head of poetry again, . . . restore her to her primitive habit, feature, and majesty." Throughout, it is the "liberty" or "licence" of contemporary poetry that he attacks most bitterly. And in the *Volpone* prologue, three of Mitis' "too nice observations" are brought forth as necessary elements ("needful rules") of "quick comedy" (p. 118).

Jonson did not suddenly, in 1606, surrender all critical independence; even in the *Volpone* prologue he indicates that there are rules and rules; he will observe the "needful" ones. Still, the weight of his later criticism is squarely behind critical authority as opposed to "liberty." To be sure, *Discoveries* is sometimes quoted to show Jonson's independence of the laws:

> I am not of that opinion to conclude a *Poet's* liberty within the narrow
> limits of laws, which either the *Grammarians,* or *Philosophers* prescribe.
> For, before they found out those Laws, there were many excellent Poets,
> that fulfill'd them. Amongst whom none more perfect than *Sophocles,*
> who liv'd a little before *Aristotle.*   [p. 34]

However, in its *Discoveries* context, this paragraph is actually subordinated to the one which immediately follows it:

> But, whatsoever Nature at any time dictated to the most happy, or long
> exercise to the most laborious; that the wisdom, and Learning of *Aris-*
> *totle,* hath brought into an Art: because, he understood the Causes of
> things: and what other men did by chance or custom, he doth by reason;
> and not only found out the way not to err, but the short way we should
> take, not to err.   [p. 34]

The effect and apparently the intention of these paragraphs is to
point up the great authority of the laws as codified by the greatest of
the ancient critics—as a guide, of course, not as a commander.

Jonson never mistakes a pedantic adherence to the laws for art,
then; but his emphasis from *Volpone* onward is on the necessity for
laws. As he observed the contemporary world of letters, especially the
drama, he fancied that he saw the ravages of ignorance and license,
not of pedantry, and he set out to teach his age the remedy—poetic
laws, the "good grace of everything in his kind" and the "strict and
regular forms."

STYLE

Regular form is partly a matter of sense of style—style as a moral
matter. In an elaborate analogy in *Discoveries,* Jonson, following
Vives, demonstrates how style may be likened to the body of a man.
Like a man, style has its stature, figure and feature, skin, flesh, blood,
and bones. The high, low, and middle styles of traditional rhetoric
may be likened to a man's stature:

> Some men are tall, and big, so some Language is high and great.
> . . . Some are little, and Dwarves: so of speech it is humble, and low,
> the words poor and flat. . . . The middle are of a just stature. There the
> Language is plain and pleasing; even without stopping, round without
> swelling; all well-turn'd, compos'd, elegant, and accurate. . . . And

according to their Subject, these styles vary, and lose their names: For
that which was even, and apt in a mean and plain subject, will appear
most poor and humble in a high Argument.   [p. 24]

The ideal style is of a just stature; there are no absolute criteria—the
subject dictates stylistic level. As Jonson remarks elsewhere in *Discoveries* (p. 18), "And though a man be more prone, and able for one
kind of writing, than another, yet he must exercise all. For as in an
Instrument, so in style, there must be a Harmony, and consent of
parts." In another passage (p. 22), "As it is a great point of Art,
when our matter requires it, to enlarge, and veer out all sail; so to
take it in, and contract it, is of no less praise when the Argument doth
ask it."

After stature comes the "figure and feature" of syntax: "that is,
whether it be round, and straight, which consists of short and succinct
Periods, numerous, and polish'd; or square and firm, which is to have
equal and strong parts, everywhere answerable, and weighed" (p.
25). Jonson does not seem to express a preference. The contrast here
is between the baroque style and the Ciceronian style, and he implies
that, in syntax as in stylistic level, a writer must be prepared to fit his
style to his matter. Jonson is not so much interested in converting
writers to the baroque camp as in encouraging them to work hard at
perfecting all styles in the service of decorum.[6]

After figure and feature comes the "skin, and coat"—that other
part of syntax "which rests in the well-joining, cementing, and coagmentation of words; when as it is smooth, gentle, and sweet; . . .
not horrid, rough, wrinkled, gaping, or chapp'd" (p. 25). Earlier in
Discoveries (p. 23), he had observed that "the congruent, and harmonious fitting of parts in a sentence, hath almost the fast'ning, and
force of knitting, and connection: As in stones well squar'd, which

6. Morris Croll, "Attic Prose," *Studies in Philology*, XVIII (April 1921), 133,
names Jonson as one of the "anti-Ciceronian leaders" in England. And Jonas
Barish, *Ben Jonson and the Language of Prose Comedy* (Cambridge: Harvard University
Press, 1960), pp. 41–89, demonstrates in detail the accuracy of Croll's observation
as it applies to Jonson's stylistic practice. On the other hand, Jonson's criticism of
style is only moderately anti-Ciceronian, if that. For a treatment of Jonson's theory
and practice of the "plain style" in his nondramatic poetry, see Wesley Trimpi,
Ben Jonson's Poems: A Study of the Plain Style (Stanford: Stanford University Press,
1962).

will rise strong a great way without mortar." The last quotation suggests the syntax of the baroque period;[7] the first does not rule out the well-joined syntax of the Ciceronian period. Again, the theory seems eclectic.

Having moved from stylistic levels down through aspects of syntax, he concludes his analogy between writing and the body by showing how words are to style as flesh, blood, and bone are to men (p. 25). The "flesh" of style is periphrasis—in excess it becomes mere corpulence.The "blood and juice" is propriety, harmony, "the phrase neat and picked." Where blood is wanting,

> the Language is thin, flagging, poor, starv'd, scarce covering the bone; and shows like stones in a sack. Some men, to avoid Redundancy, run into that; and while they strive to have no ill blood, or Juice, they lose their good. There be some styles, again, that have not less blood, but less flesh, and corpulence. These are bony, and sinewy. . . .[8]   [p. 25]

The analogy asserts that style is not an ornamental garment for the body of thought; it is the incarnation of thought, the body of which thought is the vital form and life-giving soul. The analogy should be juxtaposed with the earlier, explicit statement in *Discoveries* (p. 20):

> *Speech* is the only benefit man hath to express his excellency of mind above other creatures. It is the Instrument of *Society*. Therefore, *Mercury*, who is the President of Language, is called *Deorum hominumque interpres* [Interpreter of gods and men]. In all speech, words and sense, are as the body, and the soul. The sense is as the life and soul of Language, without which all words are dead.

"Sense," Jonson explains in the same passage, "is wrought out of experience, the knowledge of human life, and actions, or of the liberal Arts." It is the intimate soul-body relation between sense and lan-

---

7. See Morris Croll, "Baroque Style," in *Studies . . . in Honor of Frederick Klaeber*, ed. Kemp Malone and M. B. Ruud (Minneapolis: University of Minnesota Press, 1929), pp. 455–456, on baroque "loose" style: "The syntactic connections of a sentence become loose and casual; great strains are imposed upon tenuous, frail links"—or upon no links at all, Jonson might add.

8. See Croll, "Baroque Style," pp. 432–434, on the baroque "curt" style: "The period consists, as some of its admirers were wont to say, of the nerves and muscles of speech alone." It is not clear whether Jonson means to praise the "bony, and sinewy" style—probably not.

guage which makes it mandatory that a writer exercise all styles as propriety, verisimilitude, or decorum demands. It is because words are not mere clothing but the very incarnation of sense that Jonson insists that words "are to be chose according to the persons we make speak" (p. 20). Decorum of style, like decorum of characterization, is an ethical as well as an aesthetic principle.

When Drummond comes to catalogue Jonson's "Censure of the English Poets" (p. 170), the first censure that he mentions is that "Sidney did not keep a Decorum in making everyone speak as well as himself." A writer who makes all of his creations speak as well (or as badly) as himself abandons one of the most powerful moral instruments of his craft. "Language," says Jonson (p. 24)

> most shows a man: speak that I may see thee. It springs out of the most retired, and inmost part of us, and is the Image of the Parent of it, the mind. No glass renders a man's form, or likeness, so true as his speech.

Earlier in *Discoveries,* he writes:

> Wheresoever, manners, and fashions are corrupted, Language is. It imitates the public riot. The excess of Feasts, and apparel, are the notes of a sick State; and the wantoness of language, of a sick mind. [p. 13]

Moral corruption is reflected not only in what a man says but also in the way in which he says it—thus the grave error of those writers who do not keep a decorum in making all of their characters speak as well as themselves.[9]

A second requisite for style, as important as decorum for Jonson's theory, is perspicuity. He remarks (p. 19) that a writing style should be neither dry and empty nor involuted and overornamented, though "that is worse which proceeds out of want, than that which riots out of plenty." Jonson's position that overornamentation can be remedied—but poverty of invention cannot—is clearly no plea for sterile correctness. Jonson's characteristic animadversions on the stylistic excesses of his contemporaries are "remedies" of "fruitfulness"; he has nothing to say to the sterile pedestrian because he knows that he cannot help poverty of wit with advice.

9. Jonson's criticism of style sometimes suggests the "ornamental" conception. See the excerpts from *Timber, or Discoveries,* ll. 116–123 and 1881–2030 (pp. 4, 20–24).

Jonson's Virgil prescribes "fair abstinence" as the cure for the too fruitful in style Crispinus-Marston. This Jonsonian Virgil would have a style that is "sound and clear." Such is the counsel of perfection; one should not expect such art to be appreciated by the multitude:

> For they commend Writers, as they do Fencers, or Wrestlers; who if they come in robustuously, and put for it with a great deal of violence, are receiv'd for the braver fellows: . . . . I deny not, but that these men, who always seek to do more than enough, may sometime happen on something that is good, and great. . . . It sticks out perhaps, and is more eminent, because all is sordid, and vile about it. . . . There is a great difference between those, that (to gain the opinion of Copy) utter all they can, however unfitly; and those that use election, and a mean.
>
> [p. 182]

Jonson liked this considered statement so well that he quoted it twice in *Discoveries* (pp. 9, 12). In *Discoveries*, too, he observes: "Pure and neat Language I love, yet plain and customary. A barbarous Phrase hath often made me out of love with good sense; and doubtful writing hath rack'd me beyond patience" (p. 20). The perspicuous style may "differ from the vulgar somewhat," but it may not "fly from all humanity, with the *Tamerlanes*, and *Tamer-Chams* of the late Age." It is, as Jonson says in the *Every Man in* prologue (p. 119), "language, such as men do use," a definition which he expands in *Discoveries* (pp. 20–21).

The true artificer will see that style reflects character and embodies the soul. The style everywhere violent cannot reflect anything but violence of character; and if the style flies from all humanity, can it reflect character at all?

DRAMA: THE PLOT

Characters talk in an action, and the action determines how they should talk. When Jonson speaks of "plot" (or "argument" or "fable"), he may be talking about a temporal-causal abstraction from human experience, which one may call the action, the fiction, the story; or he may be talking about an artistic abstraction from this story, an abstraction of the abstraction, the *imitation* of the action, which one may call the structure. There is the action, and there is the imitation of that action. In *Discoveries* (p. 37), Jonson makes explicit some such distinction (though without the jargon) when he likens the writing of a play to the building of a house. The selection of well-appointed grounds and goodly raw materials is to the action as the actual labor of landscaping and construction is to the imitation of the action. Jonson's views on the "one, entire, and perfect Action" which the play must set forth will be examined a little later, in the discussion of the unities. Here the subject is Jonson's theory of action in the second sense, his theory of dramatic structure—the way a dramatist turns the events he chooses into a play.

The heritage of Renaissance critics on the subject of dramatic structure was a divided one. It had been one of the primary accomplishments of Jonson's critical predecessors that they had integrated the five-act structure prescribed by Horace in the *Ars Poetica* with Donatus' threefold division of comedy into *protasis, epitasis,* and *catastrophe.* According to this synthesis, Acts I and II comprise the *protasis* (the beginning of the action, the presentation of characters, and the occasion of the argument); Acts III and IV, the *epitasis* (the perturbation and entangling of the argument); and the *summa epitasis* (at once the height of perturbation and the occasion of the solution) follows, usually in Act V, in which case the remainder of Act V contains the *catastrophe* (the sudden conversion of affairs to a happy ending).[10]

The Renaissance synthesis of Horace and Donatus clearly lies behind some of the most important of Jonson's pronouncements on dramatic structure. But whatever his dramatic practice, all that can be said positively regarding his criticism is that Jonson does not get around to discussing the particulars of plot construction until late in his career. When he does get around to it, he couches his discussion as a matter of course in terms of the traditional formula.

10. See Baldwin, *Shakspere's Five-Act Structure,* pp. 228–251 and 294–296. See also Marvin Herrick, *Comic Theory in the Sixteenth Century* (Urbana: University of Illinois Press, 1950), pp. 89–129; and René Wellek and Austin Warren, *Theory of Literature* (New York: Harvest Books, 1956), p. 218.

Jonson's first unmistakable citation of the laws of plot structure occurs in *The New Inn*.[11] In the synopsis of the plot which he prefixed to the printed play, he reveals, whether consciously or unconsciously, that he is very much aware of the traditional synthesis: "Here begins, at the *third Act*, the *Epitasis*, or business of the Play. . . . The fifth and last *Act* is the *Catastrophe*, or knitting up of all" (p. 122). It is just because the allusions do not call attention to themselves that one supposes that the terms were employed (and, by the judicious men to whom they were addressed, read) as a matter of course.

Perhaps Jonson decided that it was the inability of the vulgar audience to recognize an artistically constructed plot when they saw one that had caused the failure of *The New Inn*. For whatever reasons, in the choruses of *The Magnetic Lady* it is the chore of Probee and the author's boy to teach the ill-informed Damplay the intricacies of dramatic structure. The chorus at the end of Act I opens:

> BOY. Now, Gentlemen, what censure you of our *Protasis*, or first *Act*?
> PRO. Well, *Boy*, it is a fair Presentment of your *Actors*. And a handsome promise of somewhat to come hereafter.

Probee's definition of the *protasis* is lost upon the critical Damplay, who unwisely tries conclusions with the author's boy:

> DAM. But, there is nothing done in it, or concluded: Therefore I say, no Act.
> BOY. A fine piece of Logic! Do you look, Mr. Damplay, for conclusions in a *Protasis*? I thought the law of *Comedy* had reserv'd 'hem to the *Catastrophe*: and that the *Epitasis*, (as we are taught) and the *Catastasis*, had been intervening parts, to have been expected. But you would have all come together, it seems: The Clock should strike five, at once, with the Acts.   [p. 126]

Thus the author's boy names as the consecutive parts of comic structure the *protasis*, the *epitasis*, the *catastasis*, and the *catastrophe*. The *protasis*, which Probee defines as the presentation of the actors and the promise of things to come, actually takes not one but two acts, as is clear from the boy's remark in the chorus that concludes Act II: "Let

11. Baldwin, *Shakspere's Five-Act Structure*, p. 317, says that Jonson knew of it as early as *Every Man Out*. Does Jonson allude to the *catastasis* in the chorus following Act IV (p. 86)?

us mind what you come for, the *Play*, which will draw on to the
Epitasis now" (p. 129). The *epitasis*, which Jonson has defined in the
synopsis of *The New Inn* as the business or busy part of the play, concludes with Act IV, as is clear from the boy's remark in the chorus
that ends Act IV: "Stay, and see his last *Act*, his *Catastrophe*" (p. 130).
This is precisely the synthesis already described.

But the author's boy introduces a fourth term, *catastasis*. The term
comes from Scaliger's *Poetica*:

> Catastasis is the full vigor and crisis of the play, in which the intrigue is
> embroiled in that tempest of chance, into which it has been drawn.
> Many do not mention this part, but it is necessary.[12]

Scaliger does not localize the *catastasis* in the five-act structure; he
says only that it falls between the *epitasis* and the *catastrophe*. But if
Scaliger's *catastasis* is simply the *summa epitasis* of the traditional formula, one would expect it to fall in Act V, immediately before the
catastrophe. A remark of the author's boy in the chorus at the end of
Act IV of *The Magnetic Lady* (p. 130) suggests that Jonson so localizes
the *catastasis*. Damplay says:

> Why, here his *Play* might have ended, if he would ha' let it; and have
> spar'd us the vexation of a *fifth* Act yet to come, which everyone here
> knows the issue of already, or may in part conjecture.

"Stay, and see his last *Act*, his *Catastrophe*," the boy counters, and then
adds:

> . . . how he will perplex that [the auditors' expectation], or spring some
> fresh cheat, to entertain the *Spectators*, with a convenient delight, till
> some unexpected, and new encounter break out to rectify all, and make
> good the Conclusion.

This final entanglement of the knot of the *epitasis* or business of the
play, this "fresh cheat," is apparently Jonson's *catastasis*, the final
turbulence from which springs the reversal that rectifies all, the *catastrophe*. No one previously seems to have recognized that Jonson is
actually defining *catastasis* at this point; nor, for that matter, does

12. J. C. Scaliger, *Poetices libri septem* (1561), pp. 14–15; quoted by Baldwin,
Shakspere's Five-Act Structure, p. 295.

anyone seem to have noticed how similar is Dryden's definition of *catastasis* in his *Essay of Dramatic Poesy*:

> Secondly, the Epitasis, or working up of the plot; where the play grows warmer, the design or action of it is drawing on, and you see something promising that it will come to pass. Thirdly, the Catastasis, or counter-turn, which destroys that expectation, embroils the action in new difficulties, and leaves you far distant from that hope in which it found you; as you may have observed in a violent stream resisted by a narrow passage,—it runs round to an eddy, and carries back the waters with more swiftness than it brought them on.[13]

Whether earlier critics would have recognized their theories in Jonson's discussion of *catastasis* is uncertain. But it is clear enough that Jonson begins with the traditional, somewhat abstract synthesis of Horace and Donatus and turns it into a workable formula for plot construction. In Acts III and IV, the *epitasis*, the business, is carried forward, the knot of the complication is tied. But it is clear from the remarks of Damplay, Probee, and the author's boy that Act IV, the latter part of the *epitasis*, does not simply pull tighter the knots tied in Act III. Act IV must also show or adumbrate some conclusions ("everyone here knows the issue . . . already, or may in part conjecture," says Damplay at the end of Act IV of *The Magnetic Lady*), though these conclusions are neither the ultimate ones (the *catastasis* will perplex them, as the boy points out) nor very satisfactory ones (Probee suggests to Damplay that the issue adumbrated in Act IV is at best "dull, flat, and unpointed"). Consequently, the function of Act V is twofold: first, it subverts the false conclusions insidiously provoked in Act IV by springing a "fresh cheat," the *catastasis*; second, it exposes the "fresh cheat" and rectifies all, making good the true and satisfactory conclusion, the *catastrophe*.

CHARACTERIZATION

Everyone knows that an action requires characters; and whereas we have touched on Jonson's theory of character in the discussion of style, we have not got to its heart: the moral basis of the "humours"

13. "An Essay of Dramatic Poetry," in *Essays of John Dryden*, ed. W. P. Ker (2 vols.; Oxford: Clarendon Press, 1900), I, 44–45.

theory of characterization. To turn to Jonson's theory of dramatic characterization is to turn to his theory of "humours." This is a turn most students of Jonson can no longer take without distinct feelings of nausea. Scholarship on the subject of Jonsonian humours is voluminous, boring, and largely misleading. (Readers may wish to consult an earlier study of mine [14]; what follows is a summary of some of its conclusions.)

The two most popular explanations of Jonson's humours have been that they constitute a *psychology*, and that they constitute Jonson's version of aesthetic *decorum*. But what the commentators have not made sufficiently clear is that, in the Renaissance, "psychology" and even "decorum" were moral subjects. Lily B. Campbell reminds us that "no modern psychologist has more strenuously insisted upon the fundamental relationship between body and mind or body and soul than did the moral philosophers of the sixteenth and seventeenth centuries in England" and that, following Cicero's lead in *De Officiis*, "decorum was in drama not a law of aesthetic theory but a law of moral philosophy."[15]

One book of Renaissance "psychology" Jonson almost certainly knew—Thomas Wright's *The Passions of the Minde in Generall*. Written in 1597–1598, pirated in 1601, published by Wright himself in 1604, Wright's anatomy of the mind is pre-eminently a moral study. The authorized version opens with Jonson's own verse tribute to the author and the book (p. 113). Wright on the passions sounds very much like Jonson on humours:

> He that loveth, hateth, or by any other passion is vehemently possessed, judgeth all things that occur in favour of that passion, to be good and agreeable with reason, . . . for in very deed, while the Passion is afloat, the execution & performance thereof, is conformable and very convenient unto our beastly sensual appetite, . . . but men having united in the same sensitive soul, reason and discourse, are bound, . . . to repress and resist such unreasonable and beastly motions.[16]

14. "Beyond Psychology: The Moral Basis of Jonson's Theory of Humour Characterization," *ELH*, XXVIII (December 1961), 316–334.

15. *Shakespeare's Tragic Heroes* (Cambridge: The University Press, 1930), pp. 79, 98. See also Herrick, *Comic Theory*, p. 131.

16. Thomas Wright, *The Passions of the Mind in General*, 4th ed. (London, 1621), p. 49. I have not been able to consult earlier editions.

Wright observes that passions engender humours; humours breed passions. As Jonson's spokesman Asper points out in the induction to *Every Man Out* (p. 78), one of the effects of a humour is that it draws the passions all to run one way. And in his masque *Hymenaei*, Jonson creates a symbolic antimasque in which the "four untempered *Humours* . . . with their wild *affections*" issue forth "out of a *Microcosm*, or *Globe*, (figuring Man)" and threaten to disrupt the sacred rites of marriage (p. 144). Hymen explains the symbolism:

> The four untempered *Humours* are broke out
> And, with their wild affections, go about
> To ravish all Religion. If there be
> A Power, like REASON, left in that huge Body,
> Or *little world of Man*, from whence these came,
> Look forth, and with thy bright and numerous flame
> Instruct their darkness, make them know, and see,
> In wronging these, they have rebell'd 'gainst thee.

At this, Reason, "seated in the top of the *Globe* (as in the brain, or highest part of Man)," spoke, and "the *Humours* and *Affections* [Passions] sheathed their swords, and retired amazed."

Wright's definition of passions—"They are called perturbations, for that . . . they trouble wonderfully the soul, corrupting the judgment & reducing the will, inducing (for the most part) to vice, and commonly withdrawing from virtue, and therefore some call them maladies or sores of the soul"—will serve as a definition of Jonsonian humours *without the slightest alteration*. One need only compare Jonson's characterization of humorous men (p. 93): "Their wills consume / Such powers of wit, and soul, as are of force / To raise their beings to eternity." The real subject of Jonson's theory of humours is neither psychology nor aesthetics, but moral goodness. As Jonson pointed out quite early in his career, in *Every Man Out* (p. 79),

> . . . my strict hand
> Was made to seize on vice, and with a grip
> Squeeze out the humour of such spongy natures,
> As lick up every idle vanity.

A Jonsonian humour is not simply an abnormal psychological condition; ultimately, it is that evil moral condition that occurs when man's carnal appetite gains ascendency over reason. It is not so much a state of sickness as, Jonson says, of "sacrilege" (p. 93).

Jonson's basic definition of humours in the induction to *Every Man Out* (p. 78) gives us to know that he is not interested only in humours in the strictest sense. Asper's division is threefold: There are genuine humour characters, there are characters who abuse the word "humour" by reducing it to fashionable and meaningless jargon, and there are characters who affect humours, ignorantly attributing petty whims, quirks, or idiosyncrasies to their "humours." Significantly, Asper's definition of comical satire—a mirror wherein the times' deformities are anatomized in every nerve and sinew—follows hard upon his threefold division of humours. He means primarily "humourous" deformities, the three general types which he has just delineated. All three sorts of "humorists" people the comical satires; Jonson's concern in the comical satires is to expose a variety of "humorists"—their style.

But characterization, humorous or otherwise, does not long remain at the center of Jonsonian comedy. With the appearance of *Volpone*, Jonson dedicates himself to the task of writing "quick comedy, refined, / As best Critics have designed"; and the best critics had placed plot at the center of the drama. From *Volpone* onward, Jonson's criticism is taken up increasingly with problems other than characterization. Nevertheless, in two separate pieces of his later criticism Jonson alludes to characterization, and when he does so he alludes to "humours" as a matter of course. If his theory of characterization changes after the early comical satires, there is no evidence for it in his criticism.

In the prologue to *The Alchemist* (p. 118), he says:

> Our *Scene* is London, 'cause we would make known,
>   No country's mirth is better than our own.
> No clime breeds better matter, for your whore,
>   Bawd, squire, impostor, many persons more,
> Whose manners, now call'd humours, feed the stage:
>   And which have still been subject, for the rage
> Or spleen of *comic*-writers.

"Manners, now call'd humours" may seem to modern readers an off-hand repudiation of the earlier theory of humours, but to Jonson's contemporaries the equation of "humours" and "manners" would have seemed precise and apt. The relevant *O.E.D.* definition of "manners" is "conduct in its moral aspect; also, morality as a subject of study; the moral code embodied in general custom or sentiment."

Much later, in the induction to *The Magnetic Lady*, Jonson again refers to characterization, and again characterization means "humours . . . or manners":

> The Author, beginning his studies of this kind, with *Every Man in His Humour*; and after, *Every Man out of His Humour*; and since, continuing in all his Plays, especially those of the *Comic* thread, whereof the *New-Inn* was the last, some recent humours still, or manners of men, that went along with the times, . . . hath phant'sied to himself, in *Idea*, this *Magnetic Mistress*. . . .   [p. 124]

All of Jonson's plays, especially (but perhaps not exclusively) the comical satires and the comedies, have been "humour plays." That is, there has been a continuity of characterization if not of form in all of Jonson's plays.

Jonson's theory of characterization begins and ends with humours. This should not be surprising. Renaissance theorists were unanimous in saying that decorum is based in good part upon moral philosophy, and decorum is nowhere more important than in characterization. Cicero had observed that the source of decorum is nothing more nor less than moral goodness, and Horace's interpreters invariably pointed to *Ars Poetica*, lines 309–322, as an authoritative description of decorum, a passage which begins by saying that the source and font of writing well is moral philosophy (that is, Socratic literature); the passage concludes by saying that a play which is marked by sententious moral passages and pictures of manners or characters rightly drawn is sometimes better received, even if it lacks charm and force of art, than are sonorous trifles void of thought. In Jonson's own translation of the passage, Horace's classical pronouncement on decorum as rooted in moral philosophy becomes a defense of Jonsonian humours; Jonson's rendering concludes:

> For sometimes,
> A Poem, of no grace, weight, art, in rhymes,
> With specious [*i.e.*, fair] places, and *being*
>   *humour'd right*,
> More strongly takes the people with delight,
> And better stays them there, than all the fine noise
> Of verse mere-matterless, and tinkling toys.
>
> [p. 51]

In Jonson's hands, the sense of decorum begins with the author's capacity for reason and in the moral philosophy of Socrates; it ends in his own kind of characterizations of men according to their passions (or humours)—their departures from what makes sense morally. Socrates is more relevant to Jonson's theory of characterization than is Galen,[17] right reason and strength of will more relevant than black bile or phlegm. How else could characterization serve "the principal end of *poesy*," which, as Jonson says in the *Volpone* epistle, is "doctrine [teaching] . . . to inform men in the best reason of living"? It seems improbable that Jonson would have thought there might be something doctrinally edifying about soma-psychotic automata.

DRAMA: THE UNITIES

To return to "action" in our first sense—that is, the events selected for rendering in the play—Jonson is concerned for the connections among them. Dryden may have been the first English critic to employ the term "the three unities." Jonson does not use the term "unities" for principles of plotting, preferring "rules" or, more often, "laws"; and there is no real evidence in his criticism that he conceives of the laws of time, place, and action as a special or sacrosanct trinity. In all of his allusions to them, he isolates three for special mention only

17. It will seem strange to some readers that a discussion of Jonsonian humors affords no charts and the like of black bile, blood, yellow bile, and phlegm (cold and dry, hot and moist, hot and dry, and cold and moist) and the like. Such things are touched upon at a distance in the induction to *Every Man Out*, but only in order to be dismissed: "Now thus far/ It may, by *Metaphor*, apply itself/ Unto the general disposition:/ As when some one peculiar quality/ Doth so possess a man, that it doth draw/ All his affects, his spirits, and his powers,/ . . . all to run one way." Contemporary ideas about pathology serve as a "*Metaphor*"—a vehicle the tenor of which is Jonson's moral conception of human character.

once, in the *Volpone* prologue (p. 117): "The laws of time, place, persons he observeth, / From no needful rule he swerveth." Even here it would seem that he is naming three laws *inter alia*, and he does not mention the most important of the three unities, the unity of action (the law of "persons" is presumably the "law" that stems from Aristotle's *Poetics* V.1 and V.4, where Aristotle says that comedy is an imitation of characters of a lower type, tragedy an imitation of characters of a higher type). Hence to discuss Jonson's theory of the three unities would be an anachronism; however, his theories as to how time, place, and action should be handled in a drama may be conveniently discussed together.

In *Discoveries*, Jonson includes a long discussion of the unity of action; otherwise he does not discuss the unities in any great detail, but from *Volpone* onward, takes them for granted. The *Alchemist* prologue touches on the unity of place: "Our *Scene* is London" (p. 118); the *Every Man in* prologue attacks those would-be poets whom art and nature have abandoned in an attack which is a catalogue of crimes against verisimilitude, of which crimes the violation of the unities, especially the unities of time and place, are the outward and visible signs (p. 119); and much later, the author's boy, in the chorus which follows the first act of the *Magnetic Lady*, attributes the transgressions against the unities to the benighted tastes of the penny groundlings and to such poetasters as cater to their tastes (p. 126). The author's boy is certainly ridiculing failures to observe the unities of time and place; he probably means to ridicule lack of unity in the action too. He defends such unity in the chorus which follows Act III (p. 129), and his defense there should be contrasted with his author's earlier defense of the *catastrophe* with *deus ex machina* which ends the first version of *Every Man Out* (p. 87). The law of time, for Jonson, requires that the action imitated must take place within one day; *Volpone* (which Jonson cites as a play which follows the law) begins at sunrise and ends before sunset. In the prologue to *The Sad Shepherd* (p. 69), he again states specifically that the legitimate scope of the action is "one day's chance," and in *Discoveries*, he stipulates that the action of a comedy or tragedy must grow until necessity brings about a conclusion, though it must not exceed "the compass of one Day" (p. 39). By the law of place, he apparently does not mean to prescribe one *mise en scène*; *Volpone*, which he says observes the unity of place, takes place in four distinct locales but all within the city of Venice. He was not so much interested in fixing one set limit to dramatic place as in pointing up the ludicrous lack of verisimilitude manifest in those plays which wafted the auditor over land and sea.

Though the unity of action is touched upon in the *Volpone* prologue and subsequent critical pronouncements, one would be hard put to deduce any significant theory from the brief references. Fortunately, it is treated at length in *Discoveries*, where Jonson begins his discussion by defining the word "poet" in Aristotelian terms:

> He is call'd a *Poet*, not he which writeth in measure only; but that feigneth and formeth a fable, and writes things like the Truth. For, the Fable and Fiction is (as it were) the form and Soul of any Poetical work, or Poem.   [p. 28]

The fable, in a succinct paragraph, is also given an Aristotelian definition:

> The Fable is call'd the *Imitation* of one entire, and perfect Action; whose parts are so joined, and knit together, as nothing in the structure can be changed, or taken away, without impairing, or troubling the whole; of which there is a proportionable magnitude in the members.
>   [p. 38]

The action imitated must be the right size: "*Whole*, we call that, and perfect, which hath a *beginning*, a *mid'st*, and an *end*. . . . Too vast oppresseth the Eyes, and exceeds the Memory: too little scarce admits either." It, following Aristotle (Heinsius on Aristotle, actually), may be as great as the causal sequence, the "events" (governed by necessity or probability), require and no greater. Vague prescriptions perhaps, but prescriptions which every playgoer has muttered to himself on occasion.

Jonson goes on to point out that unity of action is a complicated, not a simple, matter: a complexity of parts must be joined to one end if there is to be true unity. The actions of one man are not a unified whole action: even the epic poet, the magnitude of whose fable's scope is far greater than that of the dramatic poet, pretermits those actions of Ulysses or Aeneas which do not tend to one and the same end (Virgil does not relate all the actions of Aeneas, "but that one thing, *how he came into Italy*"), and the strong implication of Jonson's remarks on the dramatic fable is that those plays which bring children to manhood, depict long wars, and transport the auditors overseas for good measure scarcely restrict themselves to the scope of the epic fable, let alone the dramatic.

Jonson seems to have found in Heinsius' redaction of Aristotle a succinct statement of what he had been suggesting about the dramatic fable all along. That all the parts must fit the complex unity of the fable, he had intimated in the *Volpone* prologue; that the fable must be of a just magnitude, he had suggested in his attacks on the sprawling plots perpetrated by his contemporaries (see, for instance, the *Every Man in* prologue); that this just magnitude is limited by the auditors' powers of apprehension and retention, he had insinuated as early as *Every Man Out* (where Cordatus is made to base his qualified approval of the unity of place on an unqualified disapproval of those authors whose undisciplined shifts of the scene "outrun the apprehension of their auditory"). It was not for his new and striking insights into the dramatic fable that Jonson took the trouble to translate Heinsius. Quite the contrary.

Drama: The Spectacle

"The Spectacle," says Aristotle in *Poetics*, VI.19, "has, indeed, an emotional attraction of its own, but, of all the parts, it is the least artistic, and connected least with the art of poetry. . . . The production of spectacular effects depends more on the art of the stage machinist than on that of the poet."[18] Jonson's estimate of dramatic spectacle is somewhat lower even than Aristotle's. He alludes to the subject some twelve different times in his criticism.

Volpone, for instance, is introduced by a prologue that is careful to point out that "your rout" will look in vain for the vulgar but typical spectacular effects of the other plays of the day:

> Yet, thus much I can give you, as a token
>   Of his play's worth, no eggs are broken;
> Nor quaking custards with fierce teeth affrighted,
>   Wherewith your rout are so delighted;

18. All translations of Aristotle are from S. H. Butcher, *Aristotle's Theory of Poetry and Fine Art*, 4th ed. (New York: Dover Publications, 1951).

Nor hales he in a gull, old ends reciting,
  To stop gaps in his loose writing;
With such a deal of monstrous, and forc'd action:
  As might make Bet'lem a faction. . . .   [p. 117]

These lines recall the more famous ones from the *Every Man in* prologue (p. 119), where Jonson's famous definition of comedy underscores accurately and succinctly the irrelevance of the age's ludicrous use of spectacle—ludicrous and, ultimately, dangerous, as Jonson implies in the letter which he prefixed to the quarto version of *The Alchemist*:

TO THE READER

IF thou beest more, thou art an understander, and then I trust thee. . . . Beware at what hands thou receiv'st thy commodity; for thou were never more fair in the way to be coz'ned (than in this Age) in *Poetry*, especially in Plays: wherein, now, the Concupiscence of Dances, and Antics so reigneth, that to run away from Nature, and be afraid of her, is the only point of art that tickles the *Spectators*. . . .   [p. 182]

In order to teach and delight, comedy must imitate "deeds, and language, such as men do use." In so far as spectacle merely subverts verisimilar imitation—as when dramatists "with three rusty swords, / And help of some few foot-and-a-half-foot words, / Fight over *York*, and *Lancaster's* long jars" (p. 119)—the effect may be merely ludicrous. But when spectacle actually replaces deeds such as men do use —as when Shakespeare introduces a masque into the action of *The Tempest* or a clownish dance of rustics into *The Winter's Tale*—the very heart of drama is violated: the imitation is no longer of nature. Jonson's was a losing battle, of course. The demand for spectacle in the drama was on the rise, and English dramatists—some of whom were among Jonson's greatest admirers—were not slow to satisfy the demand in spite of his strictures. In retrospect, his deep-seated suspicion of spectacle seems clairvoyant, though one supposes that not even he foresaw the day when *Macbeth* would be successfully staged with the "concupiscence of *Jigs* and *Dances*," or the day when Pepys would say of a performance of his own *Catiline* that it was not diverting, "though most fine in clothes; and a fine scene of the Senate, and of a fight, that ever I saw in my life"![19] He could not have foreseen these abominations, but perhaps he did see that the battle was almost lost.. *A Tale of a Tub*, probably one of the last plays that Jonson wrote, not only provides a masque for the gapers but also calls attention to the fact in the epilogue (p. 13). The epilogue is disdainful but resigned:

> This Tale of me, The *Tub* of *Totten-Court*,
> A *Poet*, first invented for your sport.
> . . . .
> Got *In-and-In*, to get you in a *Masque*:
> That you be pleas'd, who come to see a *Play*,
> With those that hear, and mark not what we say.
> Wherein the *Poet's* fortune is, I fear,
> Still to be early up, but never the near'.

COMEDY

Jonson speaks of comedy or the drama in general as an art of imitation; he also speaks of comedy or drama in general as an art of achieving effects in an audience: of comedy as an art of teaching, or delighting, or moving, or a combination. And he would have been an unusual Renaissance critic indeed if he *had* clearly and consistently separated mimetic and pragmatic theories of comedy.[20] Whether he ever made a rigid separation between the two is problematic; and he certainly failed to separate them in many crucial passages, passages in which the fusion of the two is explicit and complete. The fusion seems to change imitation from an end to a means: the poet imitates in order to teach delightfully:

> *Poetry*, and *Picture*, are Arts of a like nature; and both are busy about imitation. . . . For they both invent, feign, and devise many things, and accommodate all they invent to the use, and service of nature. Yet of the two, the Pen is more noble, than the Pencil. For that can speak to the Understanding; the other, but to the Sense. They both behold pleasure, and profit, as their common object. . . .   [p. 15]

19. See Hazelton Spencer, *Shakespeare Improved: The Restoration Versions* (Cambridge: Harvard University Press, 1927), p. 160, and Samuel Pepys, *The Diary*, ed. H. B. Wheatley (8 vols.; New York: Harcourt, Brace and Co., 1926), VIII, 171–172, entry for December 19, 1668.

20. I borrow the terms and their usage from M. H. Abrams, *The Mirror and the Lamp* (New York: Norton Library Edition, 1958). See especially pp. 14–17.

There are similar fusions of the mimetic and pragmatic theories of comedy throughout the criticism, and it seems clear that this fusion constitutes the foundation of Jonsonian criticism of the drama.

The mimetic theory of drama has it that the drama imitates some aspect of the universe. Aristotle said that the drama imitates men in action, such elements as character and thought being subsidiary to action. Speaking in *Discoveries* of the magnitude and compass of the fable, epic or dramatic, Jonson invokes the Aristotelian dicta: "For, the Fable and Fiction is (as it were) the form and Soul of any Poetical work or *Poem*" (p. 28); "So that by this definition we conclude the fable, to be the *imitation* of one perfect, and entire Action" (p. 38).

Aristotle is not usually so clearly seen in Jonson's criticism. Even when Jonson is discussing comedy as a mode of imitation, he tends to wander from Aristotelian precision if not from Aristotelian orthodoxy; nor is it always easy to know whether it is the precision or the orthodoxy that is wanting. Nevertheless, many of Jonson's critical statements do seem to parallel or complement the Aristotelian passages quoted from *Discoveries*.

The Aristotelian affinities are real, and they deserve special study; but there is another strain in Jonson's mimetic criticism, a strain that does not seem to have a clear parallel in Aristotle. One way to put it is to say that Jonson tends to demand that the universal which comedy imitates wear a realistic contemporary guise. At one level of meaning in *Poetaster*, when Demetrius attacks Horace, the audience is supposed to know that Dekker is attacking Jonson. There is an element of truth in Dekker's attack, the point being (presumably) that anything that Dekker attacks cannot be all bad: "HORACE! he is a mere spunge; nothing but humours, and observation; he goes up and down sucking from every society, and when he comes home, squeezes himself dry again" (p. 102). "Observation" of contemporary society does, at any rate, go hand in hand with Jonson's conception of imitation. To say this is to say simply that Jonson conceived of comedy as the imitation of certain types of men acting according to the laws of probability or necessity, but that Jonson conceived of these types of men as products of the poet's observation of contemporary society and contemporary manners.

The pragmatic theory of comedy has it that comedy achieves certain effects in an audience and tends to judge its value according to its success in achieving that aim. Thus, in *Discoveries* (p. 14), Jonson observes that poetry *teaches* its audience about the good life, and *persuades* men, leads them to good actions. In connection with this latter element, the persuasive, another comment in *Discoveries* is particularly relevant:

> The *Poet* is the nearest Borderer upon the Orator, and expresseth all his virtues, though he be tied more to numbers; is his equal in ornament, and above him in his strengths. And, (of the kind) the Comic comes nearest: Because, in moving the minds of men, and stirring of affections (in which Oratory shows, and especially approves her eminence) he chiefly excells.   [p. 33]

One reason that poetry excels other "learnings" is that it persuades men to live the good life, and comedy excels other poetic kinds in this respect, at least, for it persuades best. Generally, however, Jonson emphasizes the persuasive power of comedy rather less than its instructive power.

Besides teaching and persuading or moving, comedy has a third way of achieving effects in its audience: it delights. Surprisingly enough, there are a number of critical passages in Jonson which do not indulge in the Renaissance habit of turning Horace's idea that pleasure is the aim of poetry into a didactic theory of pleasurable teaching. In the first *Epicoene* prologue (p. 183), an unusual document on more than one count, Jonson writes a rather specific defense of comedy on no grounds other than that it affords pleasure to everyone. The prologue to *The New Inn* resumes the analogy between the poet and the cook who furnishes a dish for every palate (p. 193). Finally, in *The Magnetic Lady* (p. 128), Damplay and the audience are given a lecture the Horatian orthodoxy of which Horace himself could not have outdone:

> If I see a thing vively [vividly] presented on the *Stage*, that the Glass of custom (which is *Comedy*) is so held up to me, by the Poet, as I can therein view the daily examples of men's lives, and images of Truth, in their manners, so drawn for my delight, or profit, as I may (either way) use them: . . . will I, rather (than make that true use) hunt out the *Persons* to defame, by my malice of misapplying?

Though he often ignored or distorted (in the Renaissance way) the Horatian view that pleasure is the end of comedy, it is clear enough that Jonson understood it.

By isolating certain of Jonson's critical remarks, one might make out a case for Jonson's being a mimetic critic; by isolating others, a case for his being a pragmatic one. At the heart of his theory is the fusion of the two: Comedy imitates nature in order to teach delightfully. Imitation was especially in danger of getting short shrift in Renaissance criticism, though it got lip service enough. In Jonson, imitation comes to life as a genuine critical principle. Perhaps as good an example as any of the way the fusion works in Jonsonian theory is the prologue to *The Alchemist*. Here Jonson observes that it is contemporary London that breeds the manners, humours, vices which he imitates, and that he imitates them in order to correct, to cure, to remedy:

. . . .
Our *Scene* is *London*, 'cause we would make known,   [5]
  No country's mirth is better than our own.
No clime breeds better matter, for your whore,
  Bawd, squire, impostor, many persons more,
Whose manners, now call'd humors, feed the stage:
  And which have still been subjects, for the rage   [10]
Or spleen of *comic* writers. Though this pen
  Did never aim to grieve, but better men;
However the age he lives in, doth endure
  The vices that she breeds, above their cure.[21]
But, when the wholesome remedies are sweet,   [15]
  And, in their working, gain, and profit meet,
He hopes to find no spirit so much diseas'd,
  But will, with such fair correctives, be pleas'd.
For here, he doth not fear, who can apply.
  If there be any, that will sit so nigh   [20]
Unto the stream, to look what it doth run,
  They shall find things, they'd think, or wish, were done;
They are so natural follies, but so shown,
  As even the doers may see, and yet not own.
            [p. 118]

21. The syntax is confusing here. See p. 118, footnote 9.

This is an important document in Jonson's criticism, and it repays close study. Correctives tend to be harsh and, by definition, unpopular. Comedy is first and foremost a corrective, but it is a "fair corrective." Comedy is a pleasing corrective (l. 18) because it does not imitate particulars (l. 19), but rather imitates natural follies (l. 23). The particular individual need not feel *publically* exposed (l. 24)! On the other hand, the manners or humours of contemporary London are Jonson's subject matter (l. 5) and are ectypes of the subject matter of all comic writers (ll. 10–11). Jonson seems to be saying something like this: Comedy is a pleasing corrective because, despite its contemporaneousness, it does not imitate the particular but rather penetrates the particular manners, humours, vices of contemporary London (or Athens, or Rome) in order to reveal the underlying universal that masquerades in these contemporary guises—namely, natural human folly. The implication is that the spectators, at least the best ones, have only to see the natural folly that underlies contemporary manners in order to mend their own lives accordingly. As a matter of fact, this theory of comic correction is explicitly and elaborately propounded in *Cynthia's Revels* (p. 93). Jonson's most famous prologue, in the folio version of *Every Man in* (p. 119), also bears all of the marks of the Jonsonian fusion.

One final point. The conclusions of the *Every Man Out* induction, the *Volpone* prologue, and the *Every Man in* prologue all propose laughter, some kind of laughter, as an effect to be achieved by true comedy. Though Jonson dismisses scurrilous laughter in *Discoveries* (p. 36), he evidently conceived of right laughter in comedy as being intimately connected with comedy's corrective power, a sort of comic catharsis, a purgation of the stupidity which custom induces. Such a theory is implied in most of Jonson's allusions to laughter. The theory is more than implied in the chorus at the end of Act I of *The Magnetic Lady*, where the author's boy explains to Damplay, who desires "miracles" and "Hokos-pokos," that true comedy imitates the ridiculous without going "beyond nature" (that is, shows an image of the times) and culminates in the audience's right laughter, a laughter which foments stupidity itself, bringing it to a head, bursting it, and leaving behind healthy brains (p. 122). In another Jonsonian metaphor, comedy lifts the mask of custom from the face of vice and reveals man enamored of a very ugly face, so that even as we laugh we are freed of custom's blinding spell.

COMICAL SATIRE

Of his fourteen extant plays "of the *Comic* thread," Jonson called three—*Every Man Out, Cynthia's Revels,* and *Poetaster*—"comical satires"; the others he called simply "comedies." He was not given to employing critical terms loosely; he meant to distinguish between dramatic forms. As *Every Man Out* is about to begin, Jonson's spokesman, Cordatus, explains that the play we are about to see is "strange, and of a particular kind by itself, somewhat like Old Comedy: a work that hath bounteously pleased me, how it will answer the general expectation, I know not" (p. 81). "Old Comedy" had the same meaning in sophisticated Renaissance criticism that it has in ours; the term referred to Greek comedy of the type Aristophanes wrote, a type that Scaliger and other critics pointed to as the prototype of formal Roman satire, especially the Juvenalian kind.[22] And Old Comedy was, of course, contrasted with the New Comedy of Menander and Plautus and Terence. Jonson himself glosses "Old Comedy" in unmistakably traditional terms in his farewell to comical satire, the "Apologetical Dialogue" (p. 108), when, responding to the accusation that he rails, he says:

> If all the salt in the old *comedy*
> Should be so censur'd, or the sharper wit
> Of the bold *satire*, termed scolding rage,
> What age could then compare with those, for buffoons?
> What should be said of *Aristophanes*?
> *Persius*? or *Juvenal*? whose names we now
> So glorify in schools, at least pretend it.

Every Man Out is to be something like the comedy of Aristophanes, which is something like the formal satire of Juvenal.

22. See O. J. Campbell, *Comicall Satyre* (San Marino: Huntington Library Publication, 1938), pp. 3–8. Renaissance views of Old Comedy stem largely from Horace, *Satires*, I.iv. A good discussion of Horace's views of Old Comedy is B. L. Ullman, "Horace on the Nature of Satire," *Transactions and Proceedings of the American Philological Association*, XLVIII (1917), 111–132. Much of Jonson's criticism of comical satire is translated or adapted from Horace on satire, not Horace on comedy!

To Scaliger and Puttenham, the Old Comedy was distinguished primarily by two characteristics: its harsh *personal* correction and its intimate connection with formal satire. Thus, Puttenham sketches the history of comedy from satire, "solitary speeches and recitals of rebuke," through Old Comedy, "which followed next after the Satire, & by that occasion was somewhat sharp and bitter after the nature of the Satire, openly & by express names taxing men more maliciously and impudently than became," but which never meddled "with any Princes' matters nor such high personages," to New Comedy, "more civil and pleasant a great deal, and not touching any man by name, but in a certain generality glancing at every abuse."23 In the induction to the first of his three comical satires, *Every Man Out*, Asper, who represents Jonson, the perfect poet, or both, defines comical satire in a torrent of metaphors:

> Well I will scourge those apes:
> And to these courteous eyes oppose a mirror,
> As large as is the stage, whereon we act:
> Where they shall see the time's deformity
> Anatomiz'd in every nerve, and sinew,
> With constant courage, and contempt of fear.

[p. 78]

The scourge, the mirror, and the anatomy were, of course, favorite metaphors of the satirists. Jonson uses the mirror analogue throughout his criticism of comedy, but the scourge and the anatomy are primarily analogues for formal satire—that is, thoroughgoing, systematic exposure and ridicule rather than incidental derision. The metaphors reveal one good reason why Jonson insists that comical satire is like Old Comedy—it is very close to formal satire. And Asper's opening critical tirade sets forth another affinity between comical satire and the Old Comedy, their common willingness to expose the evil of individuals:

> . . . and with a whip of steel,
> Print wounding lashes in their iron ribs.
> I fear no mood stamp'd in a private brow,
> When I am pleas'd t'unmask a public vice.

23. "The Arte of English Poesie," in *Elizabethan Critical Essays*, ed. G. Gregory Smith (2 vols.; Oxford: Clarendon Press, 1904), II, 33–34.

I fear no strumpet's drugs, nor ruffian's stab,
Should I detect their hateful luxuries:
No broker's, usurer's, or lawyer's gripe,
Were I dispos'd to say, they're all corrupt.
I fear no courtier's frown, should I applaud
The easy flexure of his supple hams.

. . . .

... not one of these but knows his works,
Knows what damnation is, the devil, and hell,
Yet, hourly they persist, grow rank in sin.

Asper's poet must seize upon and expose vice where he finds it and create a literary milieu such as would make it clear that anyone who feared to be exposed on the stage should shun vice. Asper has rejected New Comedy, Terence's or Shakespeare's—its impersonal correction, "more civil and pleasant a great deal."

With the *Volpone* prologue, Jonson makes his peace with New Comedy; he had for some time been careful to point out that comical satire's "strange Muse" "shuns the print of any beaten path; / And proves new ways to come to learned ears" (p. 90). With *Volpone*, he turns to quick comedy as best critics have designed.

TRAGEDY: "THE OFFICES OF A TRAGIC WRITER"

Jonson thought highly of his two tragedies, confidently calling *Catiline* "a legitimate Poem" despite its poor reception in the "Jig-given times" of 1611, and introducing *Sejanus* in 1605 with a preface anything but apologetic (although the play had been violently received at the Globe in 1603). The *Sejanus* preface (p. 135), notes that *Sejanus* does not observe the strict "Laws of *Time*," which state that the action must fall within the compass of a day, and that it does not have a "proper Chorus," a lack which Jonson was to remedy in *Catiline*. But the "other offices of a *Tragic* writer" Jonson claims to have faithfully fulfilled: truth of argument, dignity of persons, gravity and height of elocution, fullness and frequency of *sententiae*.

The *Sejanus* preface is quite conventional. As Spingarn points out,[24] three points of distinction between comedy and tragedy which

24. *A History of Literary Criticism in the Renaissance*, 2d ed. (New York: Columbia University Press, 1908), pp. 66–67.

carried over from the Middle Ages through the Renaissance were that the subjects of tragedy are generally historical rather than invented ("truth of Argument"), that the characters in tragedy are kings, princes, or great leaders rather than humble persons and private citizens ("dignity of Persons"), and that the style and diction of tragedy are elevated and sublime, not humble and colloquial ("gravity and height of Elocution"). One may compare Jonson's "fullness and frequency of Sentence," or *sententiae*, with Spingarn's summary of Scaliger and Minturno:

> For Scaliger the moral aim of the drama is attained both indirectly, by the representation of wickedness ultimately punished and virtue ultimately rewarded, and more directly by the enunciation of moral precepts throughout the play. With the Senecan model before him, such precepts (*sententiae*) became the very props of tragedy. . . . Minturno points out that these *sententiae* are to be used most in tragedy and least in epic poetry.

By "truth of Argument" Jonson has been said to mean more than "that the argument of a Tragedy must . . . be drawn from history," and to mean in addition that "the argument of a tragedy must be historically verifiable—in the main outline and even in . . . insignificant details."[25] The interpretation is attractive; it fits Jonson's dramatic practice in tragedy; it invites us to observe Jonson silently and secretly wrenching a conventional law of tragedy to his individual, unconventional purposes. But Jonson knew as clearly as do we the difference between history and tragedy, and when he mentions "truth of Argument" as one of the universal offices of the tragic writer, we ought not to assume that he means anything more than what any learned reader of the day would have understood—that is, that tragedy gives one a historical argument capable of being presented with verisimilitude. Jonson himself carefully distinguishes between "truth of Argument" and "integrity in the *Story*." The latter he discusses separately with specific reference to his own tragedy *Sejanus* (and the printed version at that, apologizing, in his fashion, for the footnotes). He speaks of his own fear and hatred of "those

25. J. A. Bryant, Jr., "The Significance of Ben Jonson's First Requirement for Tragedy: 'Truth of Argument,' " *Studies in Philology* (April 1952), 203. This is a helpful study, but I trust that the distinction at issue is not a mere quibble.

common Torturers, that bring all wit to the Rack"—men who had found political allegory lurking in every literary treatment of persons of dignity. "Integrity in the *Story*"—detailed, scholarly, historical fact accurately documented—is Jonson's own unique and extreme version of "truth of Argument"; and all that Jonson claims for this integrity is that it may save him from the malicious "applications" of contemporary allegorists. (Drummond was to note cryptically: "He was called before the Council for his *Sejanus*"!) "Truth of Argument" does not necessarily entail absolute and meticulous historical accuracy; that it might is obvious.

Aristotle, whose ghost Jonson is said to disturb by his observations on truth of argument, observes: "And even if he chances to take an historical subject, he is none the less a poet; for there is no reason why some events that have actually happened could not conform to the law of the probable and possible, and in virtue of that quality in them he is their poet or maker." Jonson made Aristotle's permission into his own precept; "integrity in the *Story*" as he practices it is a perfect example of imitation and study as he describes these requisites of the good poet in *Discoveries* (pp. 31–32).

Implicit in the *Sejanus* preface, with its emphasis on truth, dignity, eloquence, and sententiousness, is the belief that the ends of tragedy, like those of comedy, are to teach and delight. In *Discoveries* (p. 36), he is explicit: "The parts of a Comedy are the same with a *Tragedy*, and the end is partly the same. For, they both delight, and teach." The tragic poet is to "feign a Commonwealth" with "truth of Argument, dignity of Persons, gravity and height of Elocution, fullness and frequency of Sentence" in order to delight and to render all virtues loved and all of their contraries hated. On the other hand, Jonson's observation in *Discoveries* is that the ends of comedy and tragedy are only *partly* the same. Significantly, he goes on immediately in the same passage to discuss and discriminate between right and wrong types of comic laughter, a discussion opening with a statement sometimes misleadingly taken out of context: "Nor, is the moving of laughter always the end of Comedy." What is meant, the context reveals: that man is wrongheaded who thinks comedy inferior to tragedy because it creates laughter. For rightly understood and used, such laughter is potent, potent to please and improve. "Partly the same"—comedy and tragedy each have their peculiar generic ends: the generic end of Jonsonian comedy is right laughter, leading to a fomenting and a healthy brain. And the generic end of Jonsonian tragedy?

If Jonson knew anything about Aristotle and his Renaissance interpreters, the end of tragedy should be emotive and cathartic— the exciting (raising, moving, stirring) and purging (tempering, rectifying, exercising, hardening, expiating, purifying) of the passions (affects, affections, emotions), especially those of pity (commiseration) and fear (terror, horror, admiration). Jonson *did* have some such Aristotelian conception of the end of tragedy, though historians of English criticism have been as one in lamenting that none of his extant criticism deals with the function of tragedy, the tragic catharsis. The ends of comedy and tragedy are the same; they are to teach and delight—presumably through their moral fables with their "proper embattaling" of "all virtues, and their Contraries" and through their pleasing artistry and pleasurable imitations of nature. The ends are different only in so far as, in addition to teaching and delighting (or, as it sometimes seems, *by way of* most effectively teaching and delighting) each also moves and purges in its own characteristic way various of the passions.

Comedy not only moves, persuades, convinces; it also excites or stirs the emotions. In the *Discoveries* discussion of the Poet and the Orator (p. 33), the context shows clearly enough that Jonson's interest in the emotive side of the drama, the "stirring of affections," does not necessarily have to derive from Aristotelian sources. If sources were needed, Ciceronian sources would have done well enough. To be sure, Aristotle observes of *dianoia*: "Under Thought is included every effect which has to be produced by speech, the subdivisions being,—proof and refutation; the excitation of the feelings, such as pity, fear, anger, and the like; the suggestion of importance or its opposite." This parallels Jonson's "moving the minds of men" and "stirring of affections." But so do passages in the works of Cicero, who observes not only that the end of oratory is "to prove, to please and to sway or persuade,"[26] but also that "a narration is delightful

26. *Orator* xxi.69. Translated by H. M. Hubbell (Loeb Classical Library; London, 1952).

moreover which has surprises, suspense, and unexpected issues, mingled with human emotions, dialogues between persons, grief, rage, fear, joy, and desire."[27] Likewise, there are interesting parallels in Quintilian, who points out that mimesis may be counted "among the devices which serve to excite the gentler emotions,"[28] and he distinguishes between comic and tragic emotions with some care:

> The more cautious writers . . . therefore explain *pathos* as describing the more violent emotions and *ethos* as designating those which are calm and gentle: in the one case the passions are violent, in the other subdued. . . . I cannot better indicate the nature of the difference than by saying that *ethos* rather resembles comedy and *pathos* tragedy. For *pathos* is almost entirely concerned with anger, dislike, fear, hatred, and pity.[29]

Comedy, then, not only moves the minds of men to embrace virtue; it also excites the passions of men—the "gentle passions" and also love, hate, jealousy, mirth, rage, melancholy, avarice, riot, fear, and every other "*perturbation in common life.*" The stirring of passions may be good in itself—that may be the meaning. Or is it that to stir the passions is automatically to purge or rectify them? Or is it that the stirring of affections is part and parcel of the suasive tug toward virtue which manifests itself in action—praxis: "If thou would'st have me weep, be thou first drown'd / Thy self in tears, then me thy loss will wound, / *Peleus*, or *Telephus*"? As Quintilian says, the tragic emotions may command and disturb; the comic emotions are subdued—they persuade. One thing is manifestly clear, at any rate: the emotive element is a cardinal one in Jonson's theory of comedy. But equally clearly Jonson's emphasis on the emotive element belongs traditionally, in Renaissance poetics, to tragic and not to comic theory. Even when Renaissance critics rely primarily upon the rhetoricians for their emotive theories, they typically conflate rhetorical theories of the role of the emotions in oratory with Aristotle's theory of their role in tragedy. And if they discuss the passions in rhetorical terms, they do so under the impression that they are discussing the poetics of

27. *De Partitione Oratoria* ix.32. Tr. by H. Rackham (Loeb Classical Library; London, 1948).

28. *Institutio Oratoria* IX.ii.58. Tr. by H. E. Butler (Loeb Classical Library; London, 1920).

29. *Ibid.*, VI.ii.8–20.

tragedy—one thinks of Sidney and of Minturno, who taught him and who observes that the function of the tragic poet "is nothing other than to . . . teach, delight, and move so that he purges the passions from the minds of the spectators."[30] "As to . . . the affections, which are *especially mine*," Sforza Oddi has Tragedy say to Comedy, "with what authority do you so often usurp them, and by usurping them strive to make your dramas almost tragic?"[31]

One could find no better illustration of the primacy of comedy in Jonson's criticism than his unparalleled claims for the emotive superiority of comedy over the other poetic kinds, including tragedy. Still, his obvious knowledge of and interest in the emotive element of drama reflected in his criticism of comedy renders his supposed indifference to the emotive element in tragedy inconceivable. The *Discoveries* passage already discussed, for instance, begins explicitly as a comparison of poet and orator, but it quickly becomes an implicit comparison of comic and tragic poet. And in this comparison, "stirring of affections" per se is not an issue. Rather, given the emotive content of both comedy and tragedy, the question becomes one of variety: Comedy alone expresses "*so many, and various* affections of the mind"; there is "*no perturbation in common life*" which is not stirred in comedy. But though it be granted that to claim all of the passions for comedy is not to deny some of the passions to tragedy, the original question remains: What is the generic end of Jonsonian tragedy? The answer is given in the concluding scene of *Sejanus*. Jonson apologized for the lack of "a proper *Chorus*" in *Sejanus*, but there is in it a chorus of sorts: the noble, feckless Roman trio—Arruntius, Lepidus, and Terentius. They, with the Nuntius, take over the final scene and, chorus-like, discuss the meaning of the preceding action; like Jonson's comic choruses, this one seems to be characters criticizing the action part of the time and part of the time critics characterizing the imitation of the action. With "fullness and frequency of Sentence" they point Jonson's moral. They do so in such a way as to recall Aristotle on the end of tragedy: the stirring of pity and fear. The passage in the *Poetics* is well known: "Tragedy, then, is an imitation of an action

30. *L'Arte Poetica* ii,76, trans. Alan Gilbert, *Literary Criticism: Plato to Dryden* (New York: American Book Co., 1940), p. 289.
31. Quoted in Gilbert, *Literary Criticism*.

that is serious, complete, and of a certain magnitude; . . . through pity and fear effecting the proper purgation of these emotions."

The chorus of the final scene of *Sejanus* (p. 136), opens (ll. 833–864):

ARRUNTIUS, NUNTIUS, LEPIDUS, TERENTIUS.

More of *Sejanus?*   NUN. Yes.   LEP. What can be added?
We know him dead.   NUN. Then, there begin your pity.
There is enough behind, to melt ev'n *Rome*,
And *Caesar* into tears: (since never slave
Could yet so highly' offend, but tyranny,
In torturing him would make him worth lamenting.)
A son, and daughter, to the dead *Sejanus*,
(Of whom there is not now so much remaining
As would give fast'ning to the hangman's hook)
Have they drawn forth for farther sacrifice;
Whose tenderness of knowledge, unripe years,
And childish silly innocence was such,
As scarce would lend them feeling of their danger:
The girl so simple, as she often ask'd,
Where they would lead her? for what cause they dragg'd her?
Cried, *she would do no more. That she could take
Warning with beating.* And because our laws
Admit no virgin immature to die,
The wittily, and strangely cruel *Macro*,
Deliver'd her to be deflowr'd, and spoil'd,
By the rude lust of the licentious hangman,
Then, to be strangled with her harmless brother.
LEP.   O, act, most worthy hell, and lasting night,
   To hide it from the world!   NUN.   Their bodies thrown
Into the *Gemonies*, (I know not how,
Or by what accident return'd) the mother,
Th'expulsed *Apicata*, finds them there;
Whom when she saw lie spread on the degrees,
After a world of fury on her self,
Tearing her hair, defacing of her face,
Beating her breasts, and womb, kneeling amaz'd,
Crying to heaven, then to them. . . .

"For pity," says Aristotle, "is aroused by unmerited misfortune." The belaboring of pity in Jonson's final *Sejanus* chorus is not merely

accidental. The deliberate dwelling upon emotive detail owes little
to the poet's sense of the "integrity in the Story" (the carefully
described picture of the distraught mother in *Sejanus*, for instance, is
far from Dio's laconic note, "His wife Apicata was not condemned,
to be sure, but on learning that her children were dead and after
seeing their bodies on the Stairs she withdrew and composed a statement regarding the death of Drusus. . . . This document she forwarded
to Tiberius and then committed suicide"[32]). We are in the presence of a scene almost wholly calculated to arouse pity. That tragic
pity depends rather heavily on choral sentence may not please modern readers, but even here Jonson makes legitimate Renaissance use
of the sentence. As Minturno advises, "The sentence . . . serves also
to awaken in the mind fear, pity, wrath, envy, and other passions, to
amplify and increase what of itself does not appear marvelous."[33]

The final chorus of *Sejanus* begins with "pity" and "tears." It closes
with choral observations on the horrible career of Jonson's protagonist, Sejanus. Again, the emphasis is not accidental. *Sejanus* concludes:

> LEP. How fortune plies her sports, when she begins
>   To practice them! pursues, continues, adds!
>   Confounds, with varying her empassion'd moods!
> ARR. Do'st thou hope, Fortune, to redeem thy crimes?
>   To make amends, for thy ill placed favours,
>   With these strange punishments? Forbear, you things,
>   That stand upon the pinnacles of state,
>   To boast your slippery height; when you do fall,
>   You pash your selves in pieces, ne'er to rise:
>   And he that lends you pity, is not wise.
> TER. Let this example move the 'insolent man,
>   Not to grow proud, and careless of the gods:
>   It is an odious wisdom, to blaspheme,
>   Much more to slighten, or deny their powers.
>   For, whom the morning saw so great, and high,
>   Thus low, and little, 'fore the 'even doth lie.

"This do we advance as a mark of Terror to all *Traitors*, & Treasons," Jonson points out at the conclusion of his description of "The
Argument" in the 1605 quarto of *Sejanus*, "to show how just the

---

32. See W. D. Briggs (ed.), *Sejanus* (Boston: Belles-Lettres Series, 1911), p. 288.
33. *L'Arte Poetica* iv.282, trans. Gilbert, *Literary Criticism*, p. 294. *Cf.* Aristotle
Poetics xix.1.

Heavens are in pouring and thund'ring down a weighty vengeance
. . ." (p. 136). Jonson had an un-Aristotelian preference for villainous
tragic protagonists. He was probably well advised to "amplify and
increase" through choral sentence "what of itself did not appear
marvelous"—so as to arouse tragic terror. As Aristotle observes,
"Fear is aroused not by the downfall of the utter villain but by the
misfortune of a man like ourselves."[34] Aristotle, in saying that
tragedy's function is to raise and purge pity and fear, doubtless meant
to define *one simultaneous function*; but his Renaissance interpreters
assumed that he meant to define *two separate functions*: pity might be
raised without fear, fear without pity; and each separate affection
carried its separate catharsis. The disjunction is obvious in the
Sejanus chorus, and the confusion did not stop with Jonson. Dryden's
discussion of the tragic function in his preface to *Troilus and Cressida*
is especially interesting in this connection:

> I hasten to the end or scope of Tragedy, which is, to rectify or purge
> our passions, fear and pity.
>
> To instruct delightfully is the general end of all poetry. Philosophy
> instructs, but it performs its work by precept; which is not delightful, or
> not so delightful as example. To purge the passions by example, is
> therefore the particular instruction which belongs to Tragedy. Rapin, a
> judicious critic, has observed from Aristotle, that pride and want of
> commiseration are the most predominant vices in mankind; thus, to cure
> us of these two, the inventors of Tragedy have chosen to work upon two
> other passions, which are fear and pity. We are wrought to fear by their
> setting before our eyes some terrible example of misfortune, which hap-
> pened to persons of the highest quality; for such an action demonstrates
> to us that no condition is privileged from the turns of fortune; this must
> of necessity cause terror in us, and consequently abate our Pride. But
> when we see that the most virtuous . . . are not exempt from such mis-
> fortunes, that works us to be helpful to, and tender over the distressed;
> which is the noblest and most god-like of moral virtues.[35]

34. But Aristotle would doubtless have understood the Renaissance critics'
reasons for failing to follow him here; see *Poetics* xviii.5–6, where he discusses the
tragedies of Agathon: "In his Reversals of the Situation, however, he shows a
marvellous skill in the effort to hit the popular taste,—to produce a tragic effect *that
satisfies the moral sense*. This effect is produced when the clever rogue, like Sisyphus, is
outwitted, *or the brave villain defeated*" (italics mine).

35. In *Essays*, I, 209–210.

Dryden might be glossing the final scene of *Sejanus*. The example of Sejanus's downfall, so Arruntius insists, ought to purge pride by exciting fear or terror (whoever lends pity to the likes of Sejanus "is not wise"). The example of the slaughtered innocents and their distraught mother, so the Nuntius remarks, ought to purge the most obdurate Romans (and Englishmen) of hardness of heart by exciting pity.

Nothing un-Aristotelian appears in Jonson's juxtaposition of fortune's wheel and the stirring of the tragic emotions; Dryden, in the passage just quoted, makes the same juxtaposition; Sidney, in his much celebrated allusion to tragic catharsis in his *Apologie*, recalls earlier Continental interpreters, especially Minturno:

> So that the right use of Comedy will (I think) by nobody be blamed, and much less of the high and excellent Tragedy, that . . . with stirring the affects of admiration and commiseration, teacheth the uncertainty of this world, and upon how weak foundations gilden roofs are builded; . . . . But how much it can move, *Plutarch* yieldeth a notable testimony of the abominable Tyrant *Alexander Pheraeus*; from whose eyes a Tragedy, well made represented, drew abundance of tears, who, without all pity had murdred infinite numbers and some of his own blood; so as he, that was not ashamed to make matters for Tragedies, yet could not resist the sweet violence of a Tragedy. And if it wrought no further good in him, it was that he, despite of himself, withdrew himself from harkening to that which might mollify his hardened heart.[36]

Sidney suggests the usual disjunction between pity and fear, commiseration and admiration. The close association between the presentation of the operation of fortune's wheel and the stirring of tragic emotions is automatic in Sidney, Jonson, and Dryden. Indeed, Jonson's unheard-of claims for the emotive function of comedy probably derive from his respect rather than his contempt for Aristotle, for the tragic emotions are rigidly limited to two by Aristotelian tradition, while the comic emotions (deriving probably from the conflation of poetics and rhetoric) could include "all perturbations in common life."

36. "An Apologie for Poetrie," in *Elizabethan Critical Essays*, I, 177–178. Sidney would be hard put to reconcile his villain protagonist Alexander Pheraeus with a simultaneous stirring of admiration and commiseration.

TRAGEDY: CHARACTER AND FABLE

Jonson, as late as 1603 and even 1611, centered his tragedies on blatantly evil protagonists. He clearly ignores the Aristotelian dictum that the downfall of an utter villain should not be displayed in tragedy, since though one might find poetic justice satisfied, one would not pity merited misfortune or fear for a rascal with whom one had nothing in common. Aristotle does say that a villain's fall—his poetic justicing—"would doubtless satisfy the moral sense." And here quite obviously is the reason for Jonson's choice of tragic protagonists and fables. All art is to teach joyfully, to satisfy the moral sense. Tragedy had to be made to serve as best it could. Thus Jonson's disjoining of what seems to be in Aristotle a single, if complex, tragic function. Within this frame, the primary end of tragedy as poetry, delightful teaching, may, indeed, best be served by an exhibiting of the downfall of the utter villain, though in the process the end of tragedy as a special genre is fragmented. We no longer have tragic fables of good men flawed and brought down, men whose downfalls simultaneously raise and purge pity and fear. We have fables of villains whose downfalls, in so far as they affect only themselves, reveal the fate of evil under providential justice so as to raise fear and purge pride. The downfalls, in so far as they affect the innocent, stir right commiseration and purge hardness of heart.

Jonson is no more interested in psychological subtleties in tragedy than he is interested in them in comedy; in moral subtleties, even less so, if that is possible. Truth to tell, Swinburne's characterization of Jonson's tragedies as tragedies of humours is not so wide of the mark as might be supposed. Whatever Swinburne meant by "humours," Jonson meant that evil moral condition that occurs when man's carnal appetite gains ascendency over his reason. Jonson himself suggests, or seems to, that his humours are not limited to the comedies (p. 124). The characterizations found in Jonsonian tragedy do exhibit difference in degree from the characterizations in his comedy. His austere statement in *Discoveries* might well be a description of his tragic heroes: "Natures that are hardened to evil, you shall sooner break, than make straight; they are like poles that are crooked, and dry: there is no attempting them" (p. 3). Natures *hardened* to evil are, for Jonson, per se the best subjects for tragedy. His tragedies have more in common with Seneca's *Thyestes* than with the great tragedies of the Greeks (or of Shakespeare); his conception of the tragic fable is closer to that of Scaliger or Puttenham than it is to that of Aristotle. Jonson remarks in *Discoveries*: "He puts off man, and goes into beast, that is cruel." Yet he seems to have been interested not so much in the psychological and ethical process of the putting off of the man by man as in the fall and punishment of the beast in him—all done, of course, with perfect decorum, art, correctness, and proper form. The effect is quite strange—like medieval grotesques carved in a Roman temple.

Jonson's primitive conception of tragic character and fable have been precisely the conceptions that have most disappointed modern critics of Jonsonian tragedy. One recalls Dryden's rather different appraisal:

> In his works you find little to retrench or alter. Wit, and language, and humour also in some measure, we had before him; but something of art was wanting to the Drama, till he came. . . . In *Sejanus* and *Catiline* . . . he so represents old Rome to us, in its rites, ceremonies, and customs, that if one of their poets had written either of his tragedies, we had seen less of it than in him. . . . If I would compare him with Shakespeare, I must acknowledge him the more correct poet, but Shakespeare the greater wit. . . . I admire him, but I love Shakespeare.[37]

Art, correctness, truth of argument, verisimilitude, imitation, correctness of language, freedom from romantic excesses—these are the elements that Dryden finds to admire in Jonsonian tragedy. Jonson had found English tragedy a sort of wild thing and had tried to impose upon it some measure of civilized restraint, to teach his age the "offices of a *Tragic* writer." Or so he thought; and Dryden seems to have taken him more or less at his own estimate. There is no more curious episode in the history of English literary criticism, surely— Jonson and Dryden professing their love for the man who wrote *King Lear*, and demonstrating so egregiously how blind such love can be. Shakespearean tragedy? Between them, Jonson and Dryden brought their brand of classical theory to England and fired tragedies thence like foxes.

37. "An Essay of Dramatic Poetry," in *Essays*, I, 81–82.

THE MASQUE

That Jonson himself conceived of the masque as a legitimate and noble literary form there can be no doubt. That he saw the end of the masque to be the same as the end of comedy and tragedy he makes explicit in his introduction to *Love's Triumph*. He was so far from conceiving of masques as "glittering bubbles," that he calls them "mirrors of man's life" which "ought always to carry a mixture of profit, with them, no less than delight."[38] There is no reason to believe that he was trying to fool either his audience or himself, and in a well-known but often badly interpreted passage in *Hymenaei*, he likens the invention in a masque to its *soul*, the spectacle to its *body*:

> It is a noble and just advantage, that the things subjected to *understanding* have of those which are objected to the *sense*, that the one sort are but momentary, and merely taking; the other impressing, and lasting: Else the glory of all these *solemnities* had perish'd like a blaze, and gone out, in the beholders' eyes. So short-liv'd are the *bodies* of all things, in comparison of their *souls*. And, though *bodies* oft-times have the ill luck to be sensually preferr'd, they find afterwards, the good fortune (when *souls* live) to be utterly forgotten. This it is hath made the most royal *Princes*, and greatest *persons* (who are commonly the *personaters* of these *actions*) not only studious of riches, and magnificence in the outward celebration, or show; (which rightly becomes them) but curious after the most high, and hearty *inventions*, to furnish the inward parts: (and those grounded upon *antiquity*, and solid *learnings*) which, though their voice be taught to sound to present occasions, their *sense*, or doth, or should always lay hold on more remov'd *mysteries*.   [p. 143]

This is no attack on spectacle in the masque; the royal princes and noble persons who produce, act, and view the masques are studious

38. I am indebted to the following studies of Jonson's masques: D. J. Gordon, "Poet and Architect," *JWCI*, XII (1949), 152–178; W. Todd Furniss, "Jonson's Anti-masques," *Renaissance News* (Spring 1958), 21–22; Dolora Cunningham, "The Jonsonian Masque as a Literary Form," *ELH*, XXII (June 1955), 108–124; and John Meagher, *Method and Meaning in Jonson's Masques* (South Bend, Ind., University of Notre Dame Press, 1966), a comprehensive and valuable study. The Herford and Simpson discussion of the Jonsonian masque (a good introduction) ought to be supplemented by the Cunningham study at least: C. H. Herford and Percy and Evelyn Simpson, eds., *Ben Jonson* (11 vols.; Oxford: Clarendon Press, 1925–1952), II, 249–334.

of a "magnificence" which rightly becomes them. But the masque is not all spectacle, as Daniel had said in *Tethys' Festival*. Daniel's is the "glittering bubble" theory of the masque. Jonson did his best to destroy it.

For Jonson, spectacle is delightful, and all concerned with the masques are rightly studious of spectacle. But it is invention which furnishes "the inward parts." The *voice* of invention sounds to present occasions, and the *sense* (the symbolic sense) of invention must "lay hold on more remov'd *mysteries*." D. J. Gordon has pointed out that "invention" was a widely used term in discussions of the masque and that it meant the whole dramatic fable carrying out the given argument or theme. Ostensibly the fable and theme have to do with some contemporary occasion; more profoundly, fable and theme are so handled by the poet's invention that they symbolize the "more remov'd mysteries."

And fable and theme are the soul of the masque. Jonson demands only that the body not be preferred to them. The soul is the "form" of the body, the body being "formed" by it; and (in the masque) poetry, costume, architecture, music, and dance constitute the body which the soul must form, the whole consort dancing together in harmony. As Jonson says earlier, in *King's Entertainment* (p. 143), each part is at once symbolically expressive in its own right and "so connected, and disposed" as to contribute harmoniously to the greater meaning of the whole invention. The "hierarchical" structure, as Mrs. Cunningham aptly calls it, of the Jonsonian masque is composed of an orderly succession of independent parts. Through the invention of the poet, the masque achieves its unity, a unity in diversity.

The Jonsonian masque is also a "studie of magnificence." And Jonson recognizes the importance of spectacle to such a study: the pomp and splendor alone, he says of *Hymenaei*, were "of power to surprise with delight, and steal away the *spectators* from themselves." The magnificence reflects the royal patron; it also provokes admiration; it serves the moral end of the form, since through the means of admiration the poet "doth reign in men's affections; . . . invade, and break in upon them; and makes their minds like the thing he writes" (p. 12).

And now we can see why Jonson quarreled with his great architect friend and master of the art of masque spectacle, Inigo Jones. Insofar as the argument is theoretical and not personal, it centers on Jonson's sense of the hierarchical structure of the masque. In his hierarchy, the poet's invention is the unifying element whose expression all of the masque's "distinct members" in harmony serve. In his view, Inigo Jones destroys the hierarchy, making a part to do the work of the whole; as he complains in "An Expostulation" (p. 151), without the poet's invention, the masque disintegrates into chaos and obscurantism, becomes a riot of colors, scenes, music, and costume "as no thought can teach / Sense what they are!" It is only as they move in harmonious subordination to the forming fable of the poet that these "distinct members" contribute to "the illustration of the whole."

Jonson sometimes satirizes those who would allow the antimasque to disrupt the symbolic unity of the whole masque form, his conception of the ideal antimasque being clearly set forth in *The Masque of Queens* (p. 147): the antimasque should be strictly subordinate to the main, its function threefold—to provide variety and contrast and to contribute to the symbolic unity of the whole. In *Hymenaei*, he warns readers of his masques that he can give them only the literary portion of the masque with any accuracy and that his attempts at describing the whole will leave behind only a shadow of what it really was; the spirit of the whole "cannot by imagination, much less description be recovered." Most of Jonson's criticism of the antimasque warns against its becoming a disunifying and merely spectacular element. In *The Masque of Augurs*, he ridicules the inartistic antimasques of certain of his contemporaries by causing the masque-making poet-aster Van-goose to defend them. When Van-goose describes a typically irrelevant "Gally-mawfrey" of an inartistic antimasque, the Groom of the Revels asks, not unreasonably, "What has all this to do with our Masque?" Van-goose responds, not unpredictably (p. 149):

O Sir, all de better, vor an Antick-maske, de more absurd it be, and vrom de purpose, it be ever all de better. If it go from de Nature of de ting, it is de more *Art*: for dear is *Art*, and dear is *Nature*; you shall see. *Hochos-pochos, Paucos Palabors.*

To imply that Jonson's main masques are a sort of formal, and unfortunate, epilogue to his antimasques is to accuse Jonson of a Vangoose ignorance. Such an implication is wrong. If Jonson allowed the antimasque and its comic "strangenesse" to disrupt the unity of the whole masque form, he did so in absolute contradiction of his own clear critical precepts.

Note on the Text

I have arranged Jonson's criticism under eight headings: General Treatises, The Function of a Poet and Critic, Comical Satire, Comedy, Tragedy, Masque, Contemporary Poets and Playwrights, and Contemporary Actors and Audiences. Where a passage deals with several subjects, which is often the case, I have simply placed it under the heading that seems most nearly central.

I have pretty thoroughly modernized (though I have not tried to Americanize) Jonson's spelling throughout. That is, I have changed *occupie* to *occupy*, *hee* to *he*, *Tragedie* to *Tragedy*, *mone* to *moan*, *hurles* to *hurls*, *Mens faces* to *Men's faces*, *aeternitie* to *eternity*, *selfe-louing* to *self-loving*, *vnless* to *unless*, *child-hood* to *childhood*, etc. I have not changed *requir'd* to *required*: when Jonson writes *required*, he means the word to have three syllables. By the same token, I have not altered *Nor made he'his play* to *Nor made he his play*; Jonson is here indicating that *he'his* must be pronounced as one syllable.

I have not altered the punctuation except in the passages from Drummond on the *Conversations*. Jonson's punctuation is dramatic as well as grammatical, and to change it is necessarily to distort. In a few passages where the punctuation seems simply perverse, I have appended a textual note.

Except where Jonson himself translates a Latin or Greek passage in the body of his text, I have placed English translations in brackets in the text, quoting the original in a footnote. In some of the prose passages I have incorporated Jonson's marginal notes into the text, and I have once or twice altered the paragraphing.

Because they are so numerous and integral, Latin words and phrases in the selections from *Discoveries* are left in the text. Translations in brackets follow immediately, except where Jonson himself has provided a close translation. Three asterisks (* * *) have been used to indicate editorial omissions.

Unless otherwise noted, the quoted text is based on the authoritative folio, quarto, or holograph, though I have not hesitated to adopt the Herford and Simpson version where the original text obviously suggests a printing house corruption.

JAMES D. REDWINE, JR.

Bowdoin College

I
THE ART OF CRITICISM:
GENERAL TREATISES

Timber, or Discoveries: Made upon Men and Matter as They Have Flowed Out of His Daily Readings or Had Their Reflux to His Peculiar Notion of the Times

Discoveries *is, as the title suggests, a collection of notes on art and life. Most of the notes are translations or adaptations from other writers, ancient and modern. What Jonson himself would have made from these notes had he used them in a publication, no one knows. They come to us as a posthumous collection of fragments merely. But it seems clear enough that many of these fragments constitute what Jonson conceived to be the best available statements of his own most cherished critical precepts. Perhaps Jonson answers those critics of* Discoveries *who express disappointment that there is little that is truly original in the collection when he writes in one fragment, "Among diverse opinions of an Art, and most of them contrary in themselves, it is hard to make election; and therefore, though a man cannot invent new things after so many, he may do a welcome work yet to help posterity to judge rightly of the old."*

The following selections are from the 1640 folio.

Ingenia [Natures]. Natures that are hardened to *evil*, you shall sooner break, than make straight; they are like poles that are crooked, and dry: there is no attempting them. (ll. 36–38.)

Opinio. Opinion is a light, vain, crude, and imperfect thing, settled in the Imagination, but never arriving at the understanding, there to obtain the tincture of *Reason*. We labour with it more than Truth. There is much more holds us, than presseth us. An ill fact is one thing,

3

an ill fortune is another: Yet both oftentimes sway us alike, by the error of our thinking. (ll. 43–49.)

Jactura vitae [Waste of life]. What a deal of cold business doth a man mis-spend the better part of life in! in scattering *compliments*, tendering *visits*, gathering and venting *news*, following *Feasts* and *Plays*, making a little winter-love in a dark corner. (ll. 56–59.)

Mutua auxilia [Mutual aid]. Learning needs rest: Sovereignty gives it. Sovereignty needs counsel: Learning affords it. There is such a Consociation of offices, between the *Prince*, and whom his favour breeds, that they may help to sustain his power, as he their knowledge. It is the greatest part of his Liberality, his Favour: And from whom doth he hear discipline more willingly, or the Arts discours'd more gladly, than from those, whom his own bounty, and benefits have made able and faithful? (ll. 65–73.)

Perspicuitas, Elegantia [Clarity, Elegance]. A man should so deliver himself to the nature of the subject, whereof he speaks, that his hearer may take knowledge of his discipline with some delight: and so apparel fair, and good matter, that the studious of elegancy be not defrauded; redeem Arts from their rough, and braky seats, where they lay hid, and overgrown with thorns, to a pure, open, and flowery light: where they may take the eye, and be taken by the hand. (ll. 116–123.)

Non nimium credendum antiquitati [Not too much reliance on the Ancients]. I know *Nothing* can conduce more to letters, than to examine the writings of the *Ancients*, and not to rest in their sole Authority, or take all upon trust from them, provided the plagues of *Judging*, and *Pronouncing* against them be away; such as are *envy*, *bitterness*, *precipitation*, *impudence*, and *scurrile scoffing*. For to all the observations of the *Ancients*, we have our own experience: which, if we will use, and apply, we have better means to pronounce. It is true they open'd the gates, and made the way, that went before us; but as Guides, not Commanders: *Non Domini nostri, sed Duces fuêre.* Truth lies open to all: it is no man's *several. Patet omnibus veritas; nondum est occupata. Multum ex illa, etiam futuris relictum est.* [Much arises from the Ancients, yet much has been left to posterity.]

Dissentire licet [It is lawful to disagree]. If in some things I dissent from others, whose *Wit, Industry, Diligence,* and *Judgement* I look up at, and admire: let me not therefore hear presently of Ingratitude, and Rashness. For I thank those, that have taught me, and will ever: but yet dare not think the *scope* of their labour, and enquiry, was to envy their posterity, what they also could add, and find out. *Sed cum ratione* [But with reason].

Non mihi cedendum, Sed veritati [Not because it is mine, but because it is Truth's]. If I err, pardon me: *Nulla ars simul & inventa est, & absoluta* [No art is perfect the day it is born.]. I do not desire to be equal to those that went before; but to have my reason examin'd with theirs, and so much faith to be given them, or me, as those shall evict. I am neither *Author,* or *Fautor* of any sect. I will have no man addict himself to me; but if I have anything right, defend it as Truth's, not mine (save as it conduceth to a common good.) It profits not me to have any man fence, or fight for me, to flourish, or take a side. Stand for *Truth,* and 'tis enough. (ll. 129–159.)

Honesta Ambitio [Virtuous Ambition]. If divers men seek *Fame,* or *Honour,* by divers ways; so both be honest, neither is to be blam'd: But they that seek *Immortality,* are not only worthy of leave, but of praise. (ll. 175–178.)

Calumniae fructus [The reward of calumny]. I am beholden to *Calumny,* that she hath so endeavor'd, and taken pains to belie me. It shall make me set a surer Guard on myself, and keep a better watch upon my *Actions.* (ll. 206–209.)

Non nova res livor. Envy is no new thing, nor was it born only in our times. The Ages past have brought it forth, and the coming Ages will. So long as there are men fit for it, *quorum odium virtute relicta placent* [for whom ill-will is pleasing since virtue is abandoned], it will never be wanting. It is a barbarous envy, to take from those men's virtues, which because thou canst not arrive at, thou impotently despairest to imitate. Is it a crime in me that I know that, which others had not yet known, but from me? or that I am the Author of many things, which never would have come in thy thought, but that I taught them? It is a new, but a foolish way you have found out,

that whom you cannot equal, or come near in doing, you would destroy, or ruin with evil speaking: As if you had bound both your wits,
and natures prentices to slander, and then came forth the best
Artificers, when you could form the foulest calumnies.

Nil gratius protervo libro [Nothing more pleasing than a brash work].
Indeed, nothing is of more credit, or request now, than a petulant
paper, or scoffing verses; and it is but convenient to the times and
manners we live with, to have then the worst writings, and studies
flourish, when the best begin to be despis'd. *Ill Arts* begin, where good
end.

Iam litterae sordent [Now the Art of letters has become squalid]. The
time was, when men would learn, and study good things; not envy
those that had them. Then men were had in price for learning: now,
letters only make men vile. He is upbraidingly call'd a *Poet*, as if it
were a most contemptible *Nick-name*. But the *Professors* (indeed) have
made the learning cheap. Railing, and tinkling *Rhymers*, whose Writings the vulgar more greedily read; as being taken with the scurrility,
and petulancy, of such wits. He shall not have a Reader now, unless
he jeer and lie. It is the food of men's natures: the diet of the times!
Gallants cannot sleep else. The Writer must lie, and the gentle Reader
rests happy, to hear the worthiest works misinterpreted; the clearest
actions obscured; the innocentest life traduc'd; And in such a licence
of lying, a field so fruitful of slanders, how can there be matter wanting to his laughter? Hence comes the *Epidemical* Infection. For how
can they escape the contagion of the Writings, whom the virulency
of the calumnies hath not stav'd off from reading?

Sed seculi morbus [But it is the sickness of the times]. *Nothing* doth
more invite a greedy Reader, than an unlook'd-for *subject*. And what
more unlook'd-for, than to see a person of an unblam'd life, made
ridiculous, or odious, by the Artifice of lying? But it is the disease of
the Age: and no wonder if the world, growing old, begin to be infirm:
Old age it self is a disease. It is long since the sick world began to
dote, and talk idly: Would she had but doted still; but her dotage is
now broke forth into a madness, and become a mere frenzy.

Alastoris malitia [Alastor's malice]. This *Alastor*, who hath left nothing unsearch'd, or unassail'd, by his impudent, and licentious lying
in his anguish writings (for he was in his cold quaking fit all the

while:) what hath he done more, than a troublesome base cur? bark'd, and made a noise afar off: had a fool, or two to spit in his mouth, and cherish him with a musty bone? But they are rather enemies of my fame, than me, these Barkers.

Mali choragi fuere [They were bad property-men]. It is an Art to have so much judgement, as to apparel a Lie well, to give it a good dressing; that though the nakedness would show deform'd and odious, the suiting of it might draw their Readers. Some love any Strumpet (be she never so shop-like, or meritorious[1]) in good clothes. But these, nature could not have form'd them better, to destroy their own testimony; and over-throw their calumny. (ll. 258–320.)

Of the two (if either were to be wish'd) I would rather have a plain down-right wisdom, than a foolish and affected eloquence. For what is so furious, and *Bethl'em*-like,[2] as a vain sound of chosen and excellent words, without any subject of *sentence*, or *science* mix'd? (ll. 343–347.)

Vulgi expectatio. Expectation of the *Vulgar* is more drawn, and held with newness, than goodness; we see it in *Fencers*, in *Players*, in *Poets*, in *Preachers*, in all, where *Fame* promiseth anything; so it be new, though never so naught, and depraved, they run to it, and are taken. Which shows, that the only decay, or hurt of the best men's *reputation* with the people, is, their wits have outliv'd the people's palates. They have been too much, or too long a feast. (ll. 405–412.)

De Vere Argutis [Of the truly witty]. I do hear them say often: Some men are not witty; because they are not everywhere witty; than which nothing is more foolish. If an eye or a nose be an excellent part in the face, therefore be all eye or nose? I think the eyebrow, the forehead, the cheek, chin, lip, or any part else, are as necessary, and natural in the place. But now nothing is good that is natural: Right and natural language seems to have least of the wit in it; that which is writh'd and tortur'd, is counted the more exquisite. Cloth of Bodkin, or Tissue, must be embroidered; as if no face were fair, that were not powdered, or painted? No beauty to be had, but in wresting, and

---

1. Latin, *meritorius*: making money by prostitution.
2. The hospital of St. Mary of Bethlehem, an insane asylum.

writhing our own tongue? Nothing is fashionable, till it be deform'd;
and this is to write like a *Gentleman*. All must be as affected, and preposterous as our Gallants' clothes, sweet bags, and night-dressings:
in which you would think our men lay in, like *Ladies*: it is so curious.
(ll. 570–586.)

Censura de Poetis [Concerning the judging of poets]. *Nothing* in our
Age, I have observ'd, is more preposterous, than the *running judgements* upon *Poetry* and *Poets*; when we shall hear those things commended, and cried up for the best writings, which a man would
scarce vouchsafe, to wrap any wholesome drug in; he would never
light his *Tobacco* with them. And those men almost nam'd for *Miracles*, who yet are so vile, that if a man should go about, to examine,
and correct them, he must make all they have done, but one blot.
Their good is so entangled with their bad, as forcibly one must draw
on the other's death with it. A Sponge dipped in Ink will do all:
Comitetur punica librum/Spongia. [Let a Punic sponge accompany the
book.]

Et paulo post, *Non possunt . . . multae una litura potest.* [No number of
erasures will amend it; only a general wiping-out.][3]

Yet their vices have not hurt them: Nay, a great many they have
profited; for they have been lov'd for nothing else. And this false
opinion grows strong against the best men: if once it take root with
the *Ignorant*. *Cestius*,[4] in his time, was preferr'd to *Cicero*; so far, as the
Ignorant durst: They learn'd him without book, and had him often
in their mouths. But a man cannot imagine that thing so foolish, or
rude, but will find, and enjoy an Admirer; at least, a Reader, or
Spectator. The Puppets are seen now in despite of the Players: *Heath's
Epigrams*, and the *Skuller's Poems* have their applause.[5] (ll. 587–612.)

Poetry, in this latter Age, hath prov'd but a mean *Mistress*, to such
as have wholly addicted themselves to her, or given their names up
to her family. They who have but saluted her on the by, and now and
then tendered their visits, she hath done much for, and advanced in

3. Marital *Epigrams* IV.x.
4. The rhetorician, an opponent of Cicero.
5. John Heath's undistinguished *Epigrams* was published in 1610. John Taylor,
a Thames waterman, published a collection of his doggerel in 1630.

the way of their own professions (both the *Law*, and the *Gospel*) beyond all they could have hoped, or done for themselves, without her
favour. Wherein she doth emulate the judicious, but preposterous
bounty of the time's *Grandees*: who accumulate all they can upon the
Parasite, or *Freshman* in their friendship; but think an old Client, or
honest servant, bound by his place to write, and starve.

Indeed, the multitude commend Writers, as they do Fencers, or
Wrestlers; who if they come in robustiously, and put for it, with a
deal of violence, are received for the *braver fellows*: when many times
their own rudeness is a cause of their disgrace; and a slight touch of
their Adversary, gives all that boisterous force the foil. But in these
things, the unskillful are naturally deceiv'd, and judging wholly by
the bulk, think rude things greater than polish'd; and scatter'd more
numerous, than compos'd: Nor think this only to be true in the sordid
multitude, but the neater sort of our *Gallants*: for all are the
multitude; only they differ in clothes, not in judgement or understanding.

I remember, the Players have often mentioned it as an honour to
Shakespeare, that in his writing, (whatsoever he penn'd) he never
blotted out line. My answer hath been, would he had blotted a
thousand. Which they thought a malevolent speech. I had not told
posterity this, but for their ignorance, who choose that circumstance
to commend their friend by, wherein he most faulted. And to justify
mine own candor, (for I lov'd the man, and do honour his memory
(on this side Idolatry) as much as any.) He was (indeed) honest, and
of an open, and free nature: had an excellent *Phantasy*; brave notions,
and gentle expressions: wherein he flow'd with that facility, that
sometime it was necessary he should be stopp'd: *Sufflaminandus erat*
[He needed his brakes]; as *Augustus* said of *Haterius*.[6] His wit was in
his own power; would the rule of it had been so too. Many times he
fell into those things, could not escape laughter: As when he said in
the person of *Cæsar*, one speaking to him; *Cæsar, thou dost me wrong*.
He replied: *Cæsar did never wrong, but with just cause*: and such like;
which were ridiculous. But he redeemed his vices, with his virtues.
There was ever more in him to be praised, than to be pardoned. (ll.
622–668.)

6. *Controversiae* IV. 7–11. Haterius, a senator and orator, died in 26 A.D.

Ingeniorum discrimina. In the difference of wits, I have observ'd; there are many notes: And it is a little *Mastery* to know them: to discern, what every nature, every disposition will bear: For, before we sow our land, we should plough it. There are no fewer forms of minds, than of bodies amongst us. The variety is incredible; and therefore we must search. Some are fit to make *Divines,* some *Poets,* some *Lawyers,* some *Physicians;* some to be sent to the plough, and trades.

There is no doctrine will do good, where nature is wanting. Some wits are swelling, and high; others low and still: Some hot and fiery; others cold and dull: One must have a bridle, the other a spur.

There be some that are forward, and bold; and these will do every little thing easily: I mean, that is hard by, and next them: which they will utter, unretarded, without any shamefastness. These never perform much, but quickly. They are, what they are on the sudden; they show presently, like *Grain,* that, scatter'd on the top of the ground, shoots up, but takes no root; has a yellow blade, but the ear empty. They are wits of good promise at first, but there is an **Ingenistitium:*[7] They stand still at sixteen, they get no higher.

You have others, that labour only to ostentation; and are ever more busy about the colors, and surface of a work, than in the matter, and foundation: For that is hid, the other is seen.

Others, that in composition are nothing, but what is rough and broken: *Quae per salebras, alteo, saxa cadunt.* [Which fall over rough crags and high rocks.] And if it would come gently, they trouble it of purpose. They would not have it run without rubs, as if that style were more strong and manly, that stroke the ear with a kind of unevenness. These men err not by chance, but knowingly, and willingly; they are like men that affect a fashion by themselves, have some singularity in a Ruff, Cloak, or Hat-band; or their beards, specially cut to provoke beholders, and set a mark upon themselves. They would be reprehended, while they are look'd on. And this vice, one that is in authority with the rest, loving, delivers over to them to be imitated: so that oft-times the faults which he fell into, the others seek for: This is the danger, when vice becomes a *Precedent.*

Others there are, that have no composition at all; but a kind of tuning, and rhyming fall, in what they write. It runs and slides, and

7. Jonson's marginal note: "a wit-stand."

only makes a sound. Women's-*Poets* they are call'd: as you have
women's-*Tailors*.

> *They write a verse, as smooth, as soft, as cream;*
> *In which there is no torrent, nor scarce stream.*

You may sound these wits, and find the depth of them, with your
middle finger. They are *Cream-bowl*, or but puddle deep.

Some, that turn over all books, and are equally searching in all
papers, that write out of what they presently find or meet, without
choice; by which means it happens, that what they have discredited,
and impugned in one work, they have before, or after, extolled the
same in another. Such are all the *Essayists*, even their Master *Montaigne*. These, in all they write, confess still what books they have read
last; and therein their own folly, so much, that they bring it to the
Stake raw, and undigested: not that the place did need it neither;
but that they thought themselves furnished, and would vent it.

Some again, who (after they have got authority, or, which is less,
opinion, by their writings, to have read much) dare presently to
feign whole books, and Authors, and lie safely. For what never was,
will not easily be found; not by the most *curious*.

And some, by a cunning protestation against all reading, and false
vindication of their own *naturals*, think to divert the *sagacity* of their
Readers from themselves, and cool the scent of their own *fox-like*
thefts; when yet they are so rank, as a man may find whole pages together usurp'd from one Author, their necessities compelling them to
read for present use, which could not be in many books; and so come
forth more ridiculously, and palpably guilty, than those, who, because they cannot trace, they yet would slander their industry.

But the Wretcheder are the obstinate contemners of all helps, and
Arts: such as presuming on their own *Naturals* (which perhaps are
excellent) dare deride all diligence, and seem to mock at the terms,
when they understand not the things; thinking that way to get off
wittily, with their Ignorance. These are imitated often by such, as
are their Peers in negligence, though they cannot be in nature: And
they utter all they can think, with a kind of violence, and *indisposition*;
unexamin'd, without relation, either to person, place, or any fitness

else; and the more willful, and stubborn, they are in it, the more learned they are esteem'd of the *multitude*, through their excellent vice of Judgement: who think those things the stronger, that have no Art: as if to break, were better than to open; or to rent asunder, gentler than to loose.

It cannot but come to pass, that these men, who commonly seek to do more than enough, may sometimes happen on something that is good, and great; but very seldom: And when it comes, it doth not recompence the rest of their ill. For their jests, and their sentences (which they only, and ambitiously seek for) stick out, and are more eminent; because all is sordid, and vile about them; as lights are more discern'd in a thick darkness, than a faint shadow. Now because they speak all they can (however unfitly) they are thought to have the greater copy; Where the learned use ever election, and a mean; they look back to what they intended at first, and make all an even, and proportion'd body. The true Artificer will not run away from nature, as he were afraid of her; or depart from life, and the likeness of Truth; but speak to the capacity of his hearers. And though his language differ from the vulgar somewhat; it shall not fly from all humanity, with the *Tamerlanes*, and *Tamer-Chams* of the late Age, which had nothing in them but the *scenical* strutting, and furious vociferation, to warrant them to the ignorant gapers. He knows it is his only Art, so to carry it, as none but Artificers perceive it. In the meantime perhaps he is call'd barren, dull, lean, a poor Writer (or by what contumelious word can come in their cheeks) by these men, who without labour, judgement, knowledge, or almost sense, are received, or preferr'd before him. He gratulates them, and their fortune. Another Age, or juster men, will acknowledge the virtues of his studies: his wisdom, in dividing: his subtlety, in arguing: with what strength he doth inspire his Readers; with what sweetness he strokes them: in inveighing, what sharpness; in Jest, what urbanity he uses. How he doth reign in men's affection; how invade, and break in upon them; and makes their minds like the thing he writes. Then in his Elocution to behold, what word is proper: which hath ornament: which height: what is beautifully translated: where figures are fit: which gentle, which strong to show the composition *Manly*. And how he hath avoided faint, obscure, obscene, sordid, humble, improper, or effeminate *Phrase*; which is not only prais'd of the most, but commended, (which is worse) especially for that it is naught.

* * *

Cicero is said to be the only wit, that the people of *Rome* had equalled to their *Empire*. *Ingenium par imperio* [genius is power]. We have had many, and in their several Ages, (to take in but the former Seculum). Sir Thomas More, the elder Wyatt, Henry, Earl of Surrey; Sir Thomas Chaloner, Sir Thomas Smith, Sir Thomas Elyot, Bishop Gardiner, were for their times admirable: and the more, because they began Eloquence with us. Sir Nicholas Bacon, was singular, and almost alone, in the beginning of Queen Elizabeth's times. Sir Philip Sidney, and Mr. Hooker (in different matter) grew great Masters of wit, and language; and in whom all vigor of Invention, and strength of judgement met. The Earl of Essex, noble and high; and Sir Walter Raleigh, not to be contemn'd, either for judgement, or style. Sir Henry Saville grave, and truly letter'd; Sir Edwin Sandys, excellent in both: Lord Egerton, the Chancellor, a grave, and great Orator; and best, when he was provok'd. But his learned, and able (though unfortunate) *Successor*[8] is he, who hath fill'd up all numbers; and perform'd that in our tongue, which may be compar'd, or preferr'd, either to insolent *Greece*, or haughty *Rome*. In short, within his view, and about his times, were all the wits born, that could honor a language, or help study. Now things daily fall: wits grow downward, and *Eloquence* grows backward: So that he may be nam'd, and stand as the *mark*, and ἀκμὴ [*Acme*] of our language. (ll. 669–800, 899–923.)

De corruptela morum [Of the corruption of manners]. *There* cannot be one color of the mind; another of the wit. If the mind be staid, grave, and compos'd, the wit is so; that vitiated, the other is blown, and deflowr'd. Do we not see, if the mind languish, the members are dull? Look upon an effeminate person: his very gate confesseth him. If a man be fiery, his motion is so: if angry, 'tis troubled, and violent. So that we may conclude: Wheresoever, manners, and fashions are corrupted, Language is. It imitates the public riot. The excess of

8. Sir Francis Bacon.

Feasts, and apparel, are the notes of a sick State; and the wantonness of language, of a sick mind. (ll. 948–958.)

De malignitate studentium [Of the corruption of learning]. *There* be some men are born only to suck out the poison of books: *Habant venenum pro victu; imo, pro deliciis.* [They have poison for their food, even their *dainties*]. And such are they that only relish the obscene, and foul things in *Poets*: Which makes the profession taxed. But by whom? men, that watch for it, and (had they not had this hint) are so unjust valuers of Letters; as they think no Learning good, but what brings in gain. It shows they themselves would never have been of the professions they are; but for the profits and fees. But, if another Learning, well used, can instruct to good life, inform manners; no less persuade, and lead men, than they threaten, and compel; and have no reward: is it therefore the worse study? I could never think the study of *Wisdom* confin'd only to the Philosopher: or of [*Piety*][9] to the *Divine*: or of *State* to the *Politic*. But that he which can feign a *Common-wealth* (which is the *Poet*) can govern it with *Counsels*, strengthen it with *Laws*, correct it with *judgements*, inform it with *Religion*, and *Morals*; is all these. We do not require in him mere *Elocution*; or an excellent faculty in verse; but the exact knowledge of all virtues, and their Contraries; with ability to render the one lov'd, the other hated, by his proper embattling them. The Philosophers did insolently, to challenge only to themselves that which the greatest *Generals*, and gravest *Counsellors* never durst. For such had rather do, than promise the best things. (ll. 1020–1045.)

De vita humana [Concerning human life]. *De piis & probis* [Of the good and the proper]. *I have* considered, our whole life is like a *Play*: wherein every man, forgetful of himself, is in travail with expression of another. Nay, we so insist in imitating others, as we cannot (when it is necessary) return to our selves: like Children, that imitate the vices of *Stammerers* so long, till at last they become such; and make the habit to another nature, as it is never forgotten.

Good men are the Stars, the Planets of the Ages wherein they live, and illustrate the times. *God* did never let them be wanting to the

9. The folio reads: "Poetry."

world: As *Abel*, for an example, of Innocency; *Enoch* of Purity, *Noah* of Trust in God's mercies, *Abraham* of Faith, and so of the rest. These, sensual men thought mad, because they would not be partakers, or practisers of their madness. But they, plac'd high on the top of all virtue, look'd down on the Stage of the world, and contemned the Play of *Fortune*. For though the most be Players, some must be *Spectators*. (ll. 1093–1109.)

Poesis, et Pictura. Poetry, and *Picture,* are Arts of a like nature; and both are busy about imitation. It was excellently said of *Plutarch, Poetry* was a speaking Picture, and *Picture* a mute Poesy. For they both invent, feign, and devise many things, and accommodate all they invent to the use, and services of nature. Yet of the two, the Pen is more noble, than the Pencil. For that can speak to the Understanding; the other, but to the Sense. They both behold pleasure, and profit, as their common Object; but should abstain from all base pleasures, lest they should err from their end; and while they seek to better men's minds, destroy their manners. They both are born *Artificers,* not made. Nature is more powerful in them than study.

Whosoever loves not *Picture,* is injurious to Truth: and all the wisdom of *Poetry.* Picture is the invention of Heaven: the most ancient, and most akin to Nature. It is itself a silent work: and always of one and the same habit: Yet it doth so enter, and penetrate the inmost affection (being done by an excellent Artificer) as sometimes it o'ercomes the power of speech, and oratory. There are diverse graces in it; so are there in the Artificers. One excels in care, another in reason, a third in easiness, a fourth in nature and grace. Some have diligence, and comeliness: but they want Majesty. They can express a human form in all the graces, sweetness, and elegancy; but they miss the Authority. They can hit nothing but smooth cheeks; they cannot express roughness, or gravity. Others aspire to Truth so much, as they are rather Lovers of likeness, than beauty. *Zeuxis,* and *Parrhasius,* are said to be contemporaries:[10] The first, found out the reason of lights, and shadows in Picture: the other, more subtly examined the lines.

10. Both Zeuxis and Parrhasius were fifth-century B.C. Greek artists.

In Picture, light is requir'd no less than shadow: so in style, height, as well as humbleness. But beware they be not too humble; as *Pliny* pronounc'd of *Regulus'*[11] writings: You would think them written, not on a child, but by a child. Many, out of their own obscene Apprehensions, refuse proper and fit words; as *occupy, nature,* and the like: So the curious industry in some of having all alike good, hath come nearer a vice, than a virtue.

Picture took her feigning from *Poetry*: from *Geometry* her rule, compass, lines, proportion, and the whole *Symmetry*. *Parrhasius* was the first won reputation, by adding *Symmetry* to Picture: he added subtlety to the countenance, elegancy to the hair, loveliness to the face; and, by the public voice of all Artificers, deserved honour in the outer lines. *Eupompus*[12] gave it splendor by numbers, and other elegancies. From the *Optics* it drew reasons; by which it considered, how things plac'd at distance, and afar off, should appear less: how above, or beneath the head, should deceive the eye, &c. So from thence it took shadows, recessor,[13] light, and height'nings. From moral *Philosophy* it took the soul, the expression of Senses, Perturbations, Manners, when they would paint an angry person, a proud, an inconstant, an ambitious, a brave, a magnanimous, a just, a merciful, a compassionate, an humble, a dejected, a base, and the like. They made all height'nings bright, all shadows dark, all swellings from a plane; all solids from breaking. See (*Vitruv.* li. 6. & 7.)[14] where he complains of their painting *Chimeras*, by the vulgar unaptly called *Grotesque*: Saying, that men who were born truly to study, and emulate nature, did nothing but make monsters against nature; which *Horace* so laugh'd at. The Art *Plastic* was molding in clay, or potter's earth anciently. This is the Parent of *Statuary*: *Sculpture, Graving* and *Picture*, cutting in brass, and marble, all serve under her. *Socrates* taught *Parrhasius*, and *Clito* (two noble Statuaries) first to express manners by their looks in Imagery. *Polygnotus*, and *Aglaophon* were ancienter.[15]

11. See Pliny *Epistles* IV.vii.7.

12. A fourth-century B.C. Greek painter, founder of the Sicyonic school.

13. Recession?

14. The note should read: *De Architectura* VIII.73.

15. Polygnotus lived in the fifteenth century B.C.; Aglaophon was his father and teacher. Socrates' influence on Clito is mentioned by Xenophon in *Memorabilia* XII.x.

After them *Zeuxis*, who was the Law-giver to all Painters, after *Parrhasius*. They were contemporaries, and liv'd both about *Philip's* time, the Father of *Alexander* the Great.

There liv'd in this latter Age six famous Painters in *Italy*: who were excellent, and emulous of the Ancients: *Raphael de Urbino*, *Michel Angelo Buonarota, Titian, Antonio of Correggio, Sebastian of Venice*, *Julio Romano*, and *Andrea Sertorio*. (ll. 1509–1585.)

De Stylo, et optimo scribendi genere [Of style, and the best way of writing]. *For* a man to write well, there are required three Necessaries. To read the best Authors, observe the best Speakers: and much exercise of his own style. In style to consider, what ought to be written; and after what manner; He must first think, and excogitate his matter; then choose his words, and examine the weight of either. Then take care in placing, and ranking both matter, and words, that the composition be comely; and to do this with diligence, and often. No matter how slow the style be at first, so it be labour'd, and accurate: seek the best, and be not glad of the forward conceits, or first words, that offer themselves to us, but judge of what we invent; and order what we approve. Repeat often, what we have formerly written; which beside, that it helps the consequence, and makes the juncture better, it quickens the heats of imagination, that often cools in the time of setting down, and gives it new strength, as if it grew lustier, by the going back. As we see in the contention of leaping, they jump farthest, that fetch their race largest: or, as in throwing a Dart, or Javelin, we force back our arms, to make our loose the stronger. Yet, if we have a fair gale of wind, I forbid not the steering out of our sail, so the favour of the gale deceive us not. For all that we invent doth please us in the conception, or birth; else we would never set it down. But the safest is to return to our Judgement, and handle over again those things, the easiness of which might make them justly suspected. So did the best Writers in their beginnings; they impos'd upon themselves care, and industry. They did nothing rashly. They obtain'd first to write well, and then custom made it easy, and a habit. By little and little, their matter show'd itself to 'hem more plentifully; their words answer'd, their composition followed; and all, as in a well-order'd family, presented itself in the place. So that the sum of

all is: Ready writing makes not good writing; but good writing brings
on ready writing: Yet when we think we have got the faculty, it is
even then good to resist it: as to give a Horse a check sometimes with
[a] bit, which doth not so much stop his course, as stir his mettle.
Again, whether a man's *Genius* is best able to reach, thither it should
more and more contend, lift and dilate itself, as men of low stature,
raise themselves on their toes; and so oft-times, get even if not eminent. Besides, as it is fit for grown and able writers to stand of themselves, and work with their own strength, to trust and endeavour by
their own faculties: so it is fit for the beginner, and learner, to study
others, and the best. For the mind, and memory are more sharply
exercis'd in comprehending another man's things, than our own; and
such as accustom themselves, and are familiar with the best Authors,
shall ever and anon find somewhat of them in themselves, and in the
expression of their minds, even when they feel it not, be able to utter
something like theirs, which hath an Authority above their own.
Nay, sometimes it is the reward of a man's study, the praise of quoting
another man fitly: And though a man be more prone, and able for
one kind of writing, than another, yet he must exercise all. For as
in an Instrument, so in style, there must be a Harmony, and consent
of parts. (ll. 1697–1754.)

Praecipiendi modi [Teaching the rules]. I take this labour in teaching others, that they should not be always to be taught; and I would
bring my Precepts into practise. For rules are ever of less force, and
value, than experiments. Yet with this purpose, rather to show the
right way to those that come after, than to detect any that have
slipp'd before by error, and I hope it will be more profitable. For
men do more willingly listen, and with more favour, to precept, than
reprehension. Among diverse opinions of an Art, and most of them
contrary in themselves, it is hard to make election; and therefore,
though a man cannot invent new things after so many, he may do a
welcome work yet to help posterity to judge rightly of the old. But
Arts and Precepts avail nothing, except nature be beneficial, and
aiding. And therefore these things are no more written to a dull
disposition, than rules of husbandry to a barren Soil. No precepts
will profit a Fool; no more than beauty will the blind, or music the

deaf. As we should take care, that our style in writing, be neither dry, nor empty: we should look again it be not winding, or wanton with farfetch'd descriptions; Either is a vice. But that is worse which proceeds out of want, than that which riots out of plenty. The remedy of fruitfulness is easy, but no labour will help the contrary: I will like, and praise some things in a young Writer; which yet if he continue in, I cannot but justly hate him for the same. There is a time to be given all things for maturity; and that even your Country-husbandman can teach; who to a young plant will not put the pruning knife, because it seems to fear the iron, as not able to admit the scar. No more would I tell a green Writer all his faults, lest I should make him grieve and faint, and at last despair. For nothing doth more hurt, than to make him so afraid of all things, as he can endeavour nothing. Therefore youth ought to be instructed betimes, and in the best things: for we hold those longest, we take soonest. As the first scent of a Vessel lasts: and that tinct the wool first receives. Therefore a Master should temper his own powers, and descend to the other's infirmity. If you pour a glut of water upon a Bottle, it receives little of it; but with a Funnel, and by degrees, you shall fill many of them, and spill little of your own; to their capacity they will all receive, and be full. And as it is fit to read the best Authors to youth first, so let them be of the openest, and clearest. As *Livy* before *Sallust*, *Sidney* before *Donne*: and beware of letting them taste *Gower*, or *Chaucer* at first, lest falling too much in love with Antiquity, and not apprehending the weight, they grow rough and barren in language only. When their judgements are firm, and out of danger, let them read both, the old and the new: but no less take heed, that their new flowers, and sweetness do not as much corrupt, as the others' dryness, and squalor, if they choose not carefully. *Spenser*, in affecting the Ancients, writ no Language: Yet I would have him read for his matter; but as *Virgil* read *Ennius*. The reading of *Homer* and *Virgil* is counsell'd by *Quintilian*, as the best way of informing youth, and confirming man. For besides, that the mind is rais'd with the height, and sublimity of such a verse, it takes spirit from the greatness of the matter, and is tincted with the best things. *Tragic*, and *Lyric* Poetry is good too: and *Comic* with the best, if the manners of the Reader be once in safety. In the *Greek* Poets, as also in *Plautus*, we shall see the economy, and disposition of *Poems*, better observed than in *Terence*, and the later: who thought the sole grace, and virtue of their Fable, the sticking in of sentences, as ours do the forcing in of jests. (ll. 1755–1820.)

Praecepta Elementaria [Elementary rules]. *It* is not the passing through these Learnings that hurts us, but the dwelling and sticking about them. To descend to those extreme anxieties, and foolish cavils of *Grammarians*, is able to break a wit in pieces; being a work of manifold misery, and vainness, to be *Elementarii senes* [senile school-children]. Yet even Letters are, as it were, the Bank of words, and restore themselves to an Author, as the pawns of Language. But talking and Eloquence are not the same: to speak, and to speak well, are two things. A fool may talk, but a wise man speaks, and out of the observation, knowledge, and use of things. Many Writers perplex their Readers, and Hearers with Mere *Nonsense*. Their writings need sunshine. Pure and neat Language I love, yet plain and customary. A barbarous Phrase hath often made me out of love with a good sense; and doubtful writing hath rack'd me beyond my patience. The reason why a *Poet* is said, that he ought to have all knowledges, is that he should not be ignorant of the most, especially of those he will handle. And indeed, when the attaining of them is possible, it were a sluggish, and base thing to despair. For frequent imitation of anything, becomes a habit quickly. If a man should prosecute as much, as could be said of everything; his work would find no end. (ll. 1858–1880.)

De Orationis dignitate [Of the dignity of speech]. *Speech* is the only benefit man hath to express his excellency of mind above other creatures. It is the Instrument of *Society*. Therefore *Mercury*, who is the President of Language, is called *Deorum hominumque interpres* [the interpreter of gods and men]. In all speech, words and sense, are as the body, and the soul. The sense is as the life and soul of Language, without which all words are dead. Sense is wrought out of experience, the knowledge of human life, and actions, or of the liberal Arts, which the *Greeks* call'd *Ε'γκυκλοπαιδειατ*. Words are the People's; yet there is a choice of them to be made. For *Verborum delectus, origo est eloquentiae* [Delight in words is the beginning of eloquence]. They are to be chose according to the persons we make speak, or the things we speak of. Some are of the Camp, some of the Councilboard, some of the Shop, some of the Sheepcote, some of the Pulpit, some of the Bar, &c. And herein is seen their Elegance, and Propriety, when we use them fitly, and draw them forth to their just strength and nature, by way of Translation, or *Metaphor*. But in this Translation we must only serve necessity (*Nam temere nihil transfertur a prudenti* [A wise man does not use metaphor rashly]) or commodity, which is a kind of necessity; that is, when we either absolutely want a word to express by, and that is necessity; or when we have not so fit a word, and that is commodity. As when we avoid loss by it, and escape obsceneness, and gain in the grace and property, which helps significance. *Metaphors* farfetch'd hinder to be understood, and affected, lose their grace. Or when the person fetcheth his translations from a wrong place. As if a Privy-Counsellor should at the Table take his *Metaphor* from a Dicing house, or Ordinary, or a Vintner's Vault; or a Justice of Peace draw his similitudes from the *Mathematics*; or a *Divine* from a Bawdy house, or Taverns; or a Gentleman of *Northamptonshire*, *Warwickshire*, or the *Midland*, should fetch all his Illustrations to his country neighbours from shipping, and tell them of the main *sheet*, and the Bowline. *Metaphors* are thus many times deform'd, as in him that said, *Castratam morte Aphracani Rempublicam* [The state was castrated by the death of Africanus]. And another, . . . *stercus curiae Glauciam* [Glaucia, the dung of the Senate]. And *Cana nive conspuit Alpes* [It spit upon the Alps with white snow]. All attempts that are new in this kind, are dangerous, and somewhat hard, before they be softened with use. A man coins not a new word without some peril, and less fruit; for if it happen to be received, the praise is but moderate; if refus'd, the scorn is assur'd. Yet we must adventure, for things, at first hard and rough, are by use made tender and gentle. It is an honest error that is committed, following great *Chiefs*.

Custom is the most certain Mistress of Language, as the public stamp makes the current money. But we must not be too frequent with the mint, every day coining. Nor fetch words from the extreme and utmost ages; since the chief virtue of a style is perspicuity, and nothing so vicious in it, as to need an Interpreter. Words borrow'd of Antiquity, do lend a kind of Majesty to style, and are not without their delight sometimes. For they have the Authority of years, and out of their intermission do win to themselves a kind of grace like newness. But the eldest of the present, and newest of the past Language is the best. For what was the ancient Language, which some men so dote upon, but the ancient Custom? Yet when I name Custom, I understand not the vulgar Custom: For that were a precept no less dangerous to Language, than life, if we should speak or live after the manners of the vulgar: But that I call Custom of speech, which is the consent of the Learned; as Custom of life, which is the consent of the good. *Virgil* was most loving of Antiquity; yet how rarely doth he insert *aquai*, and *pictai*! *Lucretius* is scabrous and rough in these; he seeks 'hem: As some do *Chaucerisms* with us, which were better expung'd and banish'd. Some words are to be cull'd out for ornament and colour, as we gather flowers to straw houses, or make Garlands; but they are better when they grow to our style; as in a Meadow, where though the mere grass and greenness delights, yet the variety of flowers doth heighten and beautify. Marry, we must not play, or riot too much with them, as in *Paronomasies*: Nor use too swelling, or ill-sounding words; *Quae per salebras, altaque saxa cadunt* [which fall over rough crags and high rocks]. It is true, there is no sound but shall find some Lovers, as the bitter'st confections are grateful to some palates. Our composition must be more accurate in the beginning and end, than in the midst; and in the end more, than in the beginning; for through the midst the stream bears us. And this is attain'd by Custom more than care, or diligence. We must express readily, and fully, not profusely. There is difference between a liberal, and a prodigal hand. As it is a great point of Art, when our matter requires it, to enlarge, and veer out all sail; so to take it in, and contract it, is of no less praise when the Argument doth ask it. Either of them hath their fitness in the place. A good man always profits by his endeavour, by his help; yea, when he is absent; nay, when he is dead, by his example and memory. So good Authors in their style: A strict and succinct style is that, where you can take away nothing without loss, and that loss to be manifest (Tacitus).[16]

16. Jonson is here adapting from Vives *De Ratione Dicendi* I.93–101 (*Opera*, 1555). He substitutes Tacitus for Vives' Lycius as the best example of the "strict and succinct" style. The note on the unintelligible or "abrupt" style is presumably an error: Seneca is Vives' authority for the obscurity of Fabianus' style. The note should probably read: "(Seneca on Fabianus)."

The brief style is that which expresseth much in little (*The Laconic*). The concise style, which expresseth not enough, but leaves somewhat to be understood (Suetonius). The abrupt style, which hath many breaches, and doth not seem to end, but fall (Seneca & Fabianus). The congruent, and harmonious fitting of parts in a sentence, hath almost the fastening, and force of knitting, and connexion: As in stones well squar'd, which will rise strong a great way without mortar.

Periods are beautiful when they are not too long; for so they have their strength too, as in a Pike or Javelin. As we must take the care that our words and sense be clear; so, if the obscurity happen through the Hearer's, or Reader's want of understanding, I am not to answer for them; no more than for their not listening or marking; I must neither find them ears, nor mind. But a man cannot put a word so in sense, but some thing about it will illustrate it, if the Writer understand himself. For Order helps much to Perspicuity, as Confusion hurts. *Rectitude lucem adfert; obliquitas et circumductio offuscat* [Straightness sheds light; indirection obscures]. We should therefore speak what we can, the nearest way, so as we keep our gate, not leap; for too short may as well be not let into the memory, as too long not kept in. Whatsoever loseth the grace, and clearness, converts into a Riddle; the obscurity is mark'd, but not the value. That perisheth, and is pass'd by, like the Pearl in the Fable. Our style should be like a skein of silk, to be carried, and found by the right thread, not ravel'd, and perplex'd; then all is a knot, a heap. There are words, that do as much raise a style, as others can depress it. Superlation, and overmuchness amplifies. It may be above faith, but never above a mean. It was ridiculous in *Cestius*, when he said of *Alexander*: *Fremit Oceanus, quasi indignetur, quod Terras relinquas*. [The ocean roars as if indignant that you quit the land.][17] But propitiously from *Virgil*:— *Credas innare revulsa / Cycladas*. [You would believe the uprooted Cyclades were swimming in the sea.][18]

He doth not say it was so, but seem'd to be so. Although it be somewhat incredible, that is excus'd before it be spoken. But there are *Hyperboles*, which will become one Language, that will by no

17. Quoted by Marcus Seneca *Suasoriae* I.ii.12.
18. *Aeneid* VIII. 691–692.

means admit another. As *Eos esse Populi Romani exercitus, qui coelum possint perrumpere* [To be those armies of the people of Rome that might break through the heavens]:[19] who would say this with us, but a mad man? Therefore we must consider in every tongue what is us'd, what receiv'd. *Quintilian* warns us, that in no kind of Translation, or *Metaphor*, or *Allegory*, we make a turn from what we began; As if we fetch the original of our *Metaphor* from sea, and billows; we end not in flames and ashes; It is a most foul inconsequence. Neither must we draw out our *Allegory* too long, lest either we make ourselves obscure, or fall into affectation, which is childish. But why do men depart at all from the right, and natural ways of speaking? Sometimes for necessity, when we are driven, or think it fitter to speak that in obscure words, or by circumstance, which utter'd plainly would offend the hearers. Or to avoid obsceneness, or sometimes for pleasure, and variety; as Travelers turn out of the highway, drawn, either by the commodity of a foot-path, or the delicacy, or freshness of the fields. And all this is call'd εσχηματισμενγ, or figur'd Language. (ll. 1881–2030.)

Oratio imago animi [Speech the image of the soul]. *Language* most shows a man: speak that I may see thee. It springs out of the most retired, and inmost parts of us, and is the Image of the Parent of it, the mind. No glass renders a man's form, or likeness, so true as his speech. Nay, it is likened to a man; and as we consider feature, and composition in a man; so words in Language: in the greatness, aptness, sound, structure, and harmony of it. Some men are tall, and big, so some Language is high and great. Then the words are chosen, their sound ample, the composition full, the absolution plenteous, and pour'd out, all grave, sinewy and strong. Some are little, and Dwarfs: so of speech it is humble, and low, the words poor and flat; the members and *Periods*, thin and weak, without knitting, or number. The middle are of a just stature. There the Language is plain, and pleasing: even without stopping, round without swelling; all well-turn'd, compos'd, elegant, and accurate. The vicious Language is vast, and gaping, swelling, and irregular; when it contends to be

19. Vives attributes this quotation to Caesar.

high, full of Rock, Mountain, and pointedness: as it affects to be low, it is abject, and creeps, full of bogs, and holes. And according to their Subject, these styles vary, and lose their names: For that which is high and lofty, declaring excellent matter, becomes vast and tumorous, speaking of petty and inferior things: so that which was even, and apt in a mean and plain subject, will appear most poor and humble in a high Argument. Would you not laugh, to meet a great Counsellor of state in a flat cap, with his trunk hose, and a hobby-horse Cloak, his Gloves under his girdle, and yond Haberdasher in a velvet Gown, furr'd with sables? There is a certain latitude in these things, by which we find the degrees. The next thing to the stature, is the figure and feature in Language: that is, whether it be round, and straight, which consists of short and succinct *Periods*, numerous, and polish'd; or square and firm, which is to have equal and strong parts, every where answerable, and weighed. The third is the skin, and coat, which rests in the well-joining, cementing, and coagmentation of words; when as it is smooth, gentle, and sweet; like a Table, upon which you may run your finger without rubs, and your nail cannot find a joint; not horrid, rough, wrinkled, gaping, or chapp'd. After these the flesh, blood, and bones come in question. We say it is a fleshy style, when there is much *Periphrasis*, and circuit of words; and when with more than enough, it grows fat and corpulent; *Arvina orationis* [the fat of speech], full of suet and tallow. It hath blood, and juice, when the words are proper and apt, their sound sweet, and the *Phrase* neat and pick'd. *Oratio uncta, & bene pasta* [sleek and well-fed speech]. But where there is Redundancy, both the blood and juice are faulty, and vicious. *Redundat sanguine, quae multo plus dicit, quam necesse est.* [That style oozes blood that says more than is necessary.] Juice in Language is somewhat less than blood; for if the words be but becoming, and signifying, and the sense gentle, there is Juice: but where that wanteth, the Language is thin, flagging, poor, starv'd, scarce covering the bone; and shows like stones in a sack. Some men, to avoid Redundancy, run into that; and while they strive to have no ill blood, or Juice, they lose their good. There be some styles, again, that have not less blood, but less flesh, and corpulence. These are bony, and sinewy: *Ossa habent, et nervos* [They have bones and sinews].

It was well noted by the late L. St. *Alban*,[20] that the study of words is the first distemper of Learning: Vain matter the second: And a third distemper is deceit, or the likeness of truth; Imposture held up by credulity. All these are the Cobwebs of Learning, and to let them grow in us, is either sluttish or foolish. Nothing is more ridiculous, than to make an Author a *Dictator*, as the schools have done *Aristotle*. The damage is infinite, knowledge receives by it. For to many things a man should owe but a temporary belief, and a suspension of his own Judgement, not an absolute resignation of himself, or a perpetual captivity. Let *Aristotle*, and others have their dues; but if we can make farther Discoveries of truth and fitness than they, why are we envied? Let us beware while we strive to add, we do not diminish, or deface; we may improve, but not augment. By discrediting falsehood, Truth grows in request. We must not go about like men anguish'd, and perplex'd, for vicious affectation of praise: but calmly study the separation of opinions, find the errors have intervened, awake Antiquity, call former times into question; but make no parties with the present, nor follow any fierce undertakers, mingle no matter of doubtful credit, with the simplicity of truth, but gently stir the mold about the root of the Question, and avoid all digladiations, facility of credit, or superstitious simplicity; seek the consonancy, and concatenation of Truth; stoop only to point of necessity, and what leads to convenience. Then make exact animadversion where style hath degenerated, where flourish'd, and thriv'd in choiceness of Phrase, round and clean composition of sentence, sweet falling of the clause, varying an illustration by tropes and figures, weight of Matter, worth of Subject, soundness of Argument, life of Invention, and depth of Judgement. This is *Monte potiri*, to get the hill. For no perfect Discovery can be made upon a flat or a level. (ll. 2031–2124.)

De Poetica

We have spoken sufficiently of Oratory; let us now make a diversion to *Poetry*. *Poetry*, in the Primogeniture, had many peccant humours, and is made to have more now, through the Levity, and inconstancy of men's Judgements. Whereas, indeed, it is the most prevailing Eloquence, and of the most exalted *Carat*. Now the discredits and

20. Sir Francis Bacon.

disgraces are many it hath receiv'd, through men's study of Depravation or Calumny: their practise being to give it diminution of Credit, by lessening the Professors' estimation, and making the Age afraid of their Liberty: And the Age is grown so tender of her fame, as she calls all writings *Aspersions*. That is the State-word, the Phrase of Court, (*Placentia College*) which some call *Parasites' Place*, the Inn of *Ignorance*.

Whilst I name no persons, but deride follies; why should any man confess, or betray himself? why doth not that of *St. Jerome* come into their mind; *Ubi generalis est de vitiis disputatio, ibi nullius esse personae injuriam* [When the discussion of faults is general, no one receives any injury].[21] Is it such an inexpiable crime in *Poets*, to tax vices generally; and no offence in them who, by their exception, confess they have committed them particularly? Are we fallen into those times that we must not *Auriculuas teneras mordaci rodere vero* [gnaw tender little ears with biting truth].[22]

Remedii votum semper verius erat, quam spes. [The desire for remedy was always truer than the hope.]. If men may by no means write freely, or speak truth, but when it offends not; why do *Physicians* cure with sharp medicines, or corrosives? Is not the same equally lawful in the cure of the mind, that is in the cure of the body? Some vices, (you will say) are so foul, that it is better they should be done, than spoken. But they that take offence where no Name, Character, or Signature doth blazon them, seem to me like affected as women; who, if they hear anything ill spoken of the ill of their Sex, are presently mov'd, as if the contumely respected their particular: and, on the contrary, when they hear good of good women, conclude, that it belongs to them all. If I see anything that toucheth me, shall I come forth a betrayer of myself, presently? No; if I be wise, I'll dissemble it; if honest, I'll avoid it: lest I publish that on my own forehead, which I saw there noted without a title. A man, that is on the mending hand, will either ingenuously confess, or wisely dissemble his disease. And, the wise, and virtuous, will never think any thing belongs to themselves that is written, but rejoice that the good are warn'd not to be such; and the ill to leave to be such. The Person

21. Quoted by Erasmus in *Epistola Apologetica*.
22. Persius *Satires* I.107–108.

offended hath no reason to be offended with the writer, but with himself; and so to declare that properly to belong to him, which was so spoken of all men, as it could be no man's several, but his that would willfully and desperately claim it. It sufficeth I know, what kind of persons I displease, men bred in the declining, and decay of virtue, betroth'd to their own vices; that have abandoned, or prostituted their good names; hungry and ambitious of infamy, invested in all deformity, enthrall'd to ignorance and malice, of a hidden and conceal'd malignity, and that hold a concomitancy with all evil.

What is a Poet?

A Poet is that, which by the Greeks is call'd κατ' ἐξοχὴν, ὁ ποιητὴς, a Maker, or a feigner: His Art, an Art of imitation, or feigning; expressing the life of man in fit measure, numbers, and harmony, according to Aristotle: From the word ποιεῖν, which signifies to make, or feign. Hence, he is call'd a Poet, not he which writeth in measure only; but that feigneth and formeth a fable, and writes things like the Truth. For, the Fable and Fiction is (as it were) the form and Soul of any Poetical work, or Poem.

What mean you by a Poem?

A Poem is not alone any work, or composition of the Poet's in many, or few verses; but even one alone verse sometimes makes a perfect Poem. As, when Aeneas hangs up, and consecrates the Arms of Abas, with this Inscription: Aeneas haec de Danais victoribus arma [Aeneas consecrates these arms won from the conquering Greeks].[23] And calls it a Poem, or Carmen. Such are those in Martial. Omnia, Castor, emis: sic fiet, ut omnia vendas [Now you buy everything, Castor; in Time, you will sell everything].[24] And, Pauper videri cinna vult, et est pauper [Cinna wishes to seem a pauper, and is a pauper].[25]

So were Horace his Odes call'd, Carmina; his Lyric Songs. And Lucretius designates a whole book, in his sixth: Quod in primo quoque carmine claret [Which is set forth in the first part of my carmen].[26] And

23. Aeneid III.288.
24. Martial Epigrams VII.xcviii.
25. Ibid. VII.xix.
26. Lucretius De rerum naturae VI.937.

anciently, all the Oracles were call'd, *Carmina*; or, whatever Sentence
was express'd, were it much, or little, it was call'd, an *Epic, Dramatic,
Lyric, Elegiac,* or *Epigrammatic Poem.*

But, how differs a Poem from what we call Poesy?

A Poem, as I have told you, is the work of the Poet; the end, and
fruit of his labour, and study. Poesy is his skill, or Craft of making:
the very Fiction itself, the reason, or form of the work. And these
three voices differ, as the thing done, the doing, and the doer; the
thing feign'd, the feigning, and the feigner: so the *Poem,* the *Poesy,*
and the *Poet.* Now, the *Poesy* is the habit, or the Art: nay, rather the
Queen of Arts which had her Original from heaven, received thence
from the *Hebrews,* and had in prime estimation with the *Greeks,* trans-
mitted to the *Latins,* and all Nations, that profess'd Civility. The
Study of it (if we will trust *Aristotle*) offers to mankind a certain rule,
and Pattern of living well, and happily; disposing us to all Civil
offices of Society. If we will believe Tully, it nourisheth, and instruc-
teth our Youth; delights our Age; adorns our Prosperity; comforts
our Adversity; entertains us at home; keeps us company abroad,
travels with us; watches; divides the times of our earnest, and sports;
shares in our Country recesses, and recreations; insomuch as the
wisest and best learned have thought her the absolute Mistress of
manners, and nearest of kin to virtue. And, whereas they entitle
Philosophy to be a rigid, and austere *Poesy*: they have (on the contrary)
styled *Poesy,* a dulcet, and gentle *Philosophy,* which leads on, and
guides us by the hand to Action, with a ravishing delight, and incredible Sweetness. But, before we handle the kinds of *Poems,* with their
special differences; or make court to the Art itself, as a Mistress, I
would lead you to the knowledge of our *Poet,* by a perfect informa-
tion, what he is, or should be by nature, by exercise, by imitation,
by Study; and so bring him down through the disciplines of *Grammar,
Logic, Rhetoric,* and the *Ethics,* adding somewhat, out of all, peculiar
to himself, and worthy of your Admittance, or reception.

1. *Ingenium* [Genius]. First, we require in our *Poet,* or maker, (for
that Title our Language affords him, elegantly, with the *Greek*) a
goodness of natural wit. For, whereas all other Arts consist of Doctrine, and Precepts: the *Poet* must be able by nature, and instinct, to

pour out the Treasure of his mind; and, as *Seneca* saith, *Aliquando secundum Anacreontem insanire, jucundum esse* [It is pleasant sometimes to be out of one's mind, according to Anacreon]:[27] by which he understands, the *Poetical Rapture*. And according to that of *Plato*; *Frustra Poeticas fores sui compos pulsavit* [A man in his right mind knocks in vain at poetry's door]: And of *Aristotle*: *Nullum magnum ingenium sine mixtura elementiae fuit. Nec potest grande aliquid, & supra caeteros loqui, nisi mota mens* [There was never a great genius without a mixture of insanity. Nor can the mind do or speak magnificently unless the mind is swayed by emotion].[28] Then it riseth higher, as by a divine Instinct, when it contemns common, and known conceptions. It utters somewhat above a mortal mouth. Then it gets aloft, and flies away with his Rider, whether, before, it was doubtful to ascend. This the *Poets* understood by their *Helicon, Pegasus,* or *Parnassus*; and this made *Ovid* to boast:

> *Est, Deus in nobis; agitante calescimus illo:*
> *Sedibus aethereis spiritus ille venit.*

> [There is a god within us; when he is stirred, we grow warm.
> That spirit comes from heavenly regions.][29]

And *Lipsius*, to affirm; *Scio, Poetam neminem praestantem fuisse, sine parte quadam uberiore divinae aurae* [I know there has never been an excellent poet without a greater share than normal of divine inspiration].[30] And, hence it is, that the coming up of good Poets, (for I mind not *mediocres*, or *imos*) is so thin and rare among us; Every beggarly Corporation affords the State a *Mayor*, or two *Bailiffs*, yearly: but, *Solus Rex, aut Poeta, non quotannis nascitur* [Only a king, or a poet, is not born every year].[31]

2. *Exercitatio* [Hard work]. To this perfection of Nature in our *Poet*, we require Exercise of those parts, and frequent. If his wit will not arrive suddenly at the dignity of the Ancients, let him not yet fall out with it, quarrel, or be overhastily Angry: offer, to turn it away from

27. Seneca *De Tranquillitate Animi* XVII.10–11.
28. *Problems* XXX.1.
29. *Fasti* VI, 5–6; *Ars Amatoria* III.549–550.
30. *Electra* II.xvii. Lipsius, 1547–1606, was a famous editor of Latin literature.
31. Adapted from lines by Florus.

Study, in a humor; but come to it again upon better cogitation; try an other time, with labour. If then it succeed not, cast not away the Quills, yet: nor scratch the Wainscot, beat not the poor Desk; but bring all to the forge, and file, again; turn it anew. There is no Statute *Law* of the Kingdom bids you be a Poet, against your will; or the first Quarter. If it come, in a year, or two, it is well. The common Rhymers pour forth Verses, such as they are, (*ex tempore*) but there never comes from them one Sense, worth the life of a Day. A Rhymer, and a *Poet*, are two things. It is said of the incomparable *Virgil*, that he brought forth his verses like a Bear, and after form'd them with licking. *Scaliger*, the Father,[32] writes it of him, that he made a quantity of verses in the morning, which afore night he reduced to a less number. But, that which *Valerius Maximus*[33] hath left recorded of *Euripides*, the *tragic Poet*, his answer to *Alcestis*, another *Poet*, is as memorable, as modest: who, when it was told to *Alcestis*, that *Euripides* had in three days brought forth but three verses, and those with some difficulty, and throes; *Alcestis*, glorying he could with ease have sent forth a hundred in the space; *Euripides* roundly replied, Like enough. But, here is the difference; thy verses will not last those three days; mine will to all time. Which was, as to tell him, he could not write a verse. I have met many of these Rattles, that made a noise, and buzz'd. They had their hum; and, no more. Indeed, things, wrote with labour, deserve to be so read, and will last their Age.

3. *Imitatio* [Imitation]. The third requisite in our *Poet*, or Maker, is *Imitation*, to be able to convert the substance, or Riches of another *Poet*, to his own use. To make choice of one excellent man above the rest, and so to follow him, till he grow very *He*: or, so like him, as the Copy may be mistaken for the Principal. Not, as a Creature, that swallows, what it takes in, crude, raw, or undigested; but, that feeds with an Appetite, and hath a Stomach to concoct, divide, and turn all into nourishment. Not, to imitate servilely, as *Horace* saith, and catch at vices, for virtue: but, to draw forth out of the best, and choicest flowers, with the Bee, and turn all into Honey, work it into

32. Julius Caesar Scaliger, father of Joseph J.
33. Roman author, d. first century A.D.; his book of anecdotes became a popular source book for writers.

one relish, and savour: make our *Imitation* sweet: observe, how the best writers have imitated, and follow them. How *Virgil*, and *Statius*[34] have imitated *Homer*; how *Horace, Archilochus*; how *Alcæus*, and the other *Lyrics*: and so of the rest.

4. *Lectio* [Reading]. But, that, which we especially require in him is an exactness of Study, and multiplicity of reading, which maketh a full man, not alone enabling him to know the *History*, or Argument of a *Poem*, and to report it: but so to master the matter, and Style, as to show, he knows, how to handle, place, or dispose of either, with *elegancy*, when need shall be. And not think, he can leap forth suddenly a *Poet*, by dreaming he hath been in *Parnassus*, or, having wash'd his lips (as they say) in *Helicon*. There goes more to his making, than so.

Ars corona [Art is the crown]. For to Nature, Exercise, Imitation, and Study, *Art* must be added, to make all these perfect. And, though these challenge to themselves much, in the making up of our Maker, it is Art only can lead him to perfection, and leave him there in possession, as planted by her hand. It is the assertion of *Tully*, If to an excellent nature, there happen an accession, or conformation of Learning, and Discipline, there will then remain somewhat noble, and singular. For, as *Simylus* saith in *Stobæus*:

οὔτε φύοις ικανή γινεται τεχνης ατερ,
οὔτε πάντεχνη μὴ φυοιν κεκτημενη.[35]

without Art, Nature can never be perfect; &, without Nature, Art can claim no being. But, our Poet must beware, that his Study be not only to learn of himself; for, he that shall affect to do that, confesseth his ever having a Fool to his master. He must read many; but, ever the best, and choicest: those, that can teach him anything, he must ever account his masters, and reverence: among whom *Horace*, and (he that taught him) *Aristotle*, deserve to be the first in estimation.

34. Statius, a first-century A.D. Latin writer of such epics as the *Thebaid*. Archilochus, an eighth-century B.C. Greek lyric poet. Alcaeus, a sixth-century B.C. Greek poet of Lesbos.

35. Quoted by Stobaeus *Florilequium* II. 352. Jonson's translation follows immediately in the text. Stobaeus, the fifth-century A.D. Greek anthologist, was famous for preserving fragments of early Greek writers such as Simylus, fourth century B.C.

Aristotle was the first accurate *Critic*, and truest Judge; nay, the greatest *Philosopher*, the world ever had: for, he noted the vices of all knowledges, in all creatures, and out of many men's perfections in a Science, he formed still one Art. So he taught us two Offices together, how we ought to judge rightly of others, and what we ought to imitate specially in ourselves. But all this in vain, without a natural wit, and a Poetical nature in chief. For, no man, so soon as he knows this, or reads it, shall be able to write the better; but as he is adapted to it by Nature, he shall grow the perfecter Writer. He must have *Civil prudence*, and *Eloquence*, & that whole; not taken up by snatches, or pieces, in Sentences, or remnants, when he will handle business, or carry Councils, as if he came then out of the Declamor's gallery, or Shadows, but furnish'd out of the body of the State, which commonly is the School of men. The *Poet* is the nearest Borderer upon the Orator, and expresseth all his virtues, though he be tied more to numbers; is his equal in ornament, and above him in his strengths. And, (of the kind) the *Comic* comes nearest: Because, in moving the minds of men, and stirring of affections (in which Oratory shows, and especially approves her eminence) he chiefly excells. What figure of a Body was *Lysippus*[36] ever able to form with his Graver, or *Apelles*[37] to paint with his Pencil, as the Comedy to life expresseth so many, and various affections of the mind? There shall the Spectator see some, insulting with Joy; other, fretting with Melancholy; raging with Anger; mad with Love; boiling with Avarice; undone with Riot; tortur'd with expectation; consum'd with fear: no perturbation in common life, but the Orator finds an example of it in the Scene. And then, for the Elegancy of Language, read but this Inscription on the *Grave* of a *Comic Poet*:

> *Immortales mortales, si fas esset, flere,*
> *Flerent divae Camoenae Naevium Poetam;*
> *Itaque postquam est Orcino traditus thesauro,*
> *Obliti sunt Romae, lingua loqui Latina.*

36. Greek sculptor whose work became the basis for the Hellenistic style; fourth century B.C.

37. The most famous Greek painter of antiquity, known only through descriptions of his work; fourth century B.C.

[If it were right for the immortal ones to weep,
The Muses would be weeping for Nevius the Poet;
For after he was handed down to Hades,
They forgot in Rome to speak the Latin tongue.][38]

Or, that modester Testimony given by *Lucius Aelius Stilo*[39] upon *Plautus*; who affirmed, *Musas, si latine loqui voluissent, Plautino sermone fuisse loquuturas* [The Muses, if they had wished to speak in Latin, would have used Plautus' style]. And that illustrious judgement by the most learned *M. Varro*[40] of him; who pronounced him the *Prince* of *Letters*, and *Elegancy*, in the *Roman* Language.

I am not of that opinion to conclude a *Poet's* liberty within the narrow limits of laws, which either the *Grammarians*, or *Philosophers* prescribe. For, before they found out those Laws, there were many excellent Poets, that fulfill'd them. Amongst whom none more perfect than *Sophocles*, who liv'd a little before *Aristotle*. Which of the *Greeklings* durst ever give precepts to *Demosthenes*? or to *Pericles*, (whom the Age surnam'd *heavenly*) because he seem'd to thunder, and lighten, with his Language? or to *Alcibiades*, who had rather Nature for his guide, than Art for his master?

But, whatsoever Nature at any time dictated to the most happy, or long exercise to the most laborious; that the wisdom, and Learning of *Aristotle*, hath brought into an Art: because, he understood the Causes of things: and what other men did by chance or custom, he doth by reason; and not only found out the way not to err, but the short way we should take, not to err.

Many things in *Euripides* hath *Aristophanes* wittily reprehended;[41] not out of Art, but out of Truth. For, *Euripides* is sometimes peccant, as he is most times perfect. But, Judgement when it is greatest, if reason doth not accompany it, is not ever absolute.

To judge of Poets is only the faculty of Poets; and not of all Poets, but the best. *Nemo infaelicius de Poetis judicavit, quam qui de Poetis scripsit*

38. This epitaph for Gnaeus Naevius, third century B.C., who wrote the first Roman epic and drama, is preserved in the *Noctes Atticae* of Aulus Gellius.

39. Lucius Aelius Stilo, an early Roman grammarian and instructor of Varro and Cicero.

40. Marcus Terentius Varro, first century B.C., one of the most erudite and prolific Roman men of letters.

41. In *The Frogs*.

[No one has judged more unhappily of Poets than the Critics].[42] But, some will say, *Critics* are a kind of Tinkers; that make more faults, than they mend ordinarily. See their diseases, and those of *Grammarians*. It is true, many bodies are the worse for the meddling with: And the multitude of *Physicians* hath destroyed many sound patients, with their wrong practise. But the office of a true *Critic*, or *Censor*, is, not to throw by a letter anywhere, or damn an innocent Syllable, but lay the words together, and amend them; judge sincerely of the Author, and his matter, which is the sign of solid, and perfect learning in a man. Such was *Horace*, an Author of much Civility; and (if any one among the heathen can be) the best master, both of virtue, and wisdom; an excellent, and true judge upon cause, and reason; not because he thought so; but because he knew so, out of use and experience.

Cato, the *Grammarian*, a defender of *Lucilius*.

> *Cato Grammaticus, Latina Syren,*
> *Qui solus legit, & facit Poetas.*
> [Cato the Grammarian, Latin Syren,
> Who alone reads and makes poets.][43]

Quintilian of the same heresy, but rejected.[44]

Horace his judgement of *Chaerillus*, defended against *Joseph Scaliger*. And of *Laberius*, against *Julius*.

But chiefly his opinion of *Plautus*, vindicated[45] against many, that are offended, and say, it is a hard Censure upon the parent of all conceit, and sharpness. And, they wish it had not fallen from so great a master, and Censor in the Art: whose bondmen knew better how to judge of *Plautus*, than any that dare patronize the family of learning in this Age; who could not be ignorant of the judgement of the times, in which he liv'd, when *Poetry*, and the *Latin* Language were

42. J. J. Scaliger, *Confutatio Fabulae Burdonum.*

43. Quoted by Suetonius *De Grammaticis* II. Lucilius was the first great Roman satirist; see p. 99 and footnote.

44. In this passage, Jonson is jotting down notes on his reading of Heinsius: Heinsius accepts Cato's defense of Lucilius, but rejects Quintilian's; he also defends Horace against the objections raised by Joseph and Julius Scaliger. Chaerillus, fifth century B.C., wrote Athenian tragedy. Laberius, first-century B.C. Roman writer attacked by Horace.

45. Horace's opinion, vindicated by Heinsius.

at the height: especially, being a man so conversant, and inwardly familiar with the censures of great men, that did discourse of these things daily amongst themselves. Again, a man so gracious, and in high favour with the Emperor, as *Augustus* often called him his witty *Manling*, (for the littleness of his stature;) and (if we may trust Antiquity) had design'd him for a Secretary of Estate; and invited him to the Palace, which he modestly pray'd off, and refus'd.

Horace did so highly esteem *Terence* his Comedies, as he ascribes the Art in Comedy to him alone, among the *Latins*, and joins him with *Menander*.

Now, let us see what may be said for either, to defend *Horace* his judgement to posterity; and not wholly to condemn *Plautus*.

The parts of a Comedy are the same with a *Tragedy*, and the end is partly the same. For, they both delight, and teach: the *Comics* are called διδάσκαλοι [Teachers], of the *Greeks*; no less than the *Tragics*.

Nor, is the moving of laughter always the end of *Comedy*, that is rather a fouling for the people's delight, or their fooling. For, as *Aristotle* says rightly, the moving of laughter is a fault in Comedy, a kind of turpitude, that depraves some part of a man's nature without a disease. As a wry face without pain moves laughter, or a deformed vizard, or a rude Clown, dress'd in a Lady's habit, and using her actions, we dislike, and scorn such representations; which made the ancient Philosophers ever think laughter unfitting in a wise man. And this induc'd *Plato* to esteem of *Homer*, as a sacrilegious Person; because he presented the *Gods* sometimes laughing. As, also, it is divinely said of *Aristotle*, that to seem ridiculous is a part of dishonesty, and foolish.

The wit of the old Comedy. So that, what either in the words, or Sense of an Author, or in the language, or Actions of men, is awry, or depraved, doth strangely stir mean affections, and provoke for the most part to laughter. And therefore it was clear that all insolent, and obscene speeches; jests upon the best men; injuries to particular persons; perverse, and sinister Sayings (and the rather unexpected) in the old Comedy, did move laughter; especially, where it did imitate any dishonesty; and scurrility came forth in the place of wit: which who understands the nature and *Genius* of laughter, cannot but perfectly know.

Of which *Aristophanes* affords an ample harvest, having not only outgone *Plautus*, or any other in that kind; but express'd all the moods, and figures, of what is ridiculous, oddly. In short, as Vinegar is not accounted good, until the wine be corrupted: so jests that are true and natural, seldom raise laughter, with the beast, the multitude. They love nothing, that is right, and proper. The farther it runs from reason, or possibility with them, the better it is. What could have made them laugh, like to see *Socrates* presented, that Example of all good life, honesty, and virtue, to have him hoisted up with a Pulley, and there play the Philosopher, in a basket? Measure, how many foot a Flea could skip *Geometrically*, by a just Scale, and edify the people from the engine? This was *Theatrical* wit, right Stage-jesting, and relishing a Playhouse, invented for scorn, and laughter; whereas, if it had savour'd of equity, truth, perspicuity, and Candor, to have tasted a wise, or a learned Palate, spit it out presently; this is bitter and profitable, this instructs, and would inform us: what need we know anything, that are nobly born, more than a Horserace, or a hunting match, our day to break with Citizens, and such innate mysteries? This is truly leaping from the Stage to the Tumbrel again, reducing all wit to the original Dungcart. (ll. 2290–2677.)

Of the magnitude, and compass of any
Fable, Epic, or Dramatic.
What the measure of a Fable is. The Fable, or Plot of a Poem, defin'd. To the resolving of this *Question*, we must first agree in the definition of the Fable. The Fable is call'd the *Imitation* of one entire, and perfect Action; whose parts are so joined, and knit together, as nothing in the structure can be chang'd, or taken away, without impairing, or troubling the whole; of which there is a proportionable magnitude in the members. As for example; if a man would build a house, he would first appoint a place to build it in, which he would define within certain bounds: So in the Constitution of a *Poem*, the Action is aim'd at by the *Poet*, which answers Place in a building; and that Action hath his largeness, compass, and proportion. But, as a Court, or Kings Palace, requires other dimensions than a private house: So the *Epic* asks a magnitude, from other Poems. Since, what is Place in the one, is Action in the other, the difference is in space. So that by

this definition we conclude the fable, to be the *imitation* of one perfect, and entire Action; as one perfect, and entire place is requir'd to a building. By perfect, we understand that, to which nothing is wanting; as Place to the building, that is rais'd, and Action to the fable, that is form'd. It is perfect, perhaps, not for a Court, or King's Palace, which requires a greater ground; but for the structure we would raise. So the space of the Action, may not prove large enough for the *Epic Fable*, yet be perfect for the *Dramatic*, and whole.

What we understand by Whole. Whole, we call that, and perfect, which hath a *beginning*, a *midst*, and an *end*. So the place of any building may be whole, and entire, for that work; though too little for a palace. As, to a *Tragedy* or a *Comedy*, the Action may be convenient, and perfect, that would not fit an *Epic Poem* in Magnitude. So a Lion is a perfect creature in himself, though it be less, than that of a *Buffalo*, or a *Rhinoceros*. They differ; but *in specie*: either in the kind is absolute. Both have their parts, and either the whole. Therefore, as in every body; so in every Action, which is the subject of a just work, there is requir'd a certain proportionable greatness, neither too vast, nor too minute. For that which happens to the Eyes, when we behold a body, the same happens to the Memory, when we contemplate an action. I look upon a monstrous Giant, as *Tityus*, whose body cover'd nine Acres of Land, and mine eye sticks upon every part; the whole that consists of those parts, will never be taken in at one entire view. So in a *Fable*, if the Action be too great, we can never comprehend the whole together in our Imagination. Again, if it be too little, there ariseth no pleasure out of the object, it affords the view no stay: it is beheld and vanisheth at once. As if we should look upon an Ant or Pismire, the parts fly the sight, and the whole considered is almost nothing. The same happens in Action, which is the object of Memory, as the body is of sight. Too vast oppresseth the Eyes, and exceeds the Memory: too little scarce admits either.

What the utmost bound of a fable. Now, in every Action it behooves the *Poet* to know which is his utmost bound, how far with fitness, and a necessary proportion, he may produce, and determine it. That is, till either good fortune change into the worse, or the worse into the better. For, as a body without proportion cannot be goodly, no more can the Action, either in *Comedy* or *Tragedy*, without his fit bounds.

And every bound, for the nature of the Subject, is esteem'd the best that is largest, till it can increase no more: so it behooves the Action in *Tragedy*, or *Comedy*, to be let grow, till the necessity ask a Conclusion: wherein two things are to be considered; First, that it exceed not the compass of one Day: Next, that there be place left for digression, and Art. For the *Episodes*, and digressions in a Fable, are the same that household stuff, and other furniture are in a house. And so far for the measure, and extent of a *Fable Dramatic*.

What by one, and entire. Now, that it should be one, and entire. One is considerable two ways: either, as it is only separate, and by itself: or as being compos'd of many parts, it begins to be one, as those parts grow, or are wrought together. That it should be one the first way alone, and by itself, no man that hath tasted letters ever would say, especially having required before a just Magnitude, and equal Proportion of the parts in themselves. Neither of which can possibly be, if the Action be single and separate, not compos'd of parts, which laid together in themselves, with an equal and fitting proportion, tend to the same end; which thing out of Antiquity itself, hath deceiv'd many; and more this Day it doth deceive.

So many there be of old, that have thought the Action of one man to be one: As of *Hercules, Theseus, Achilles, Ulysses*, and other *Heroes*; which is both foolish and false; since by one and the same person many things may be severally done, which cannot fitly be referred, or joined to the same end: which not only the excellent *Tragic Poets*, but the best Masters of the *Epic, Homer*, and *Virgil* saw. For, though the Argument of an *Epic Poem* be far more diffus'd, & pour'd out, than that of *Tragedy*; yet *Virgil*, writing of *Aeneas*, hath pretermitted many things. He neither tells how he was born, how brought up; how he fought with *Achilles*; how he was snatch'd out of the battle by *Venus*; but that one thing, how *he came into Italy*, he prosecutes in twelve books. The rest of his journey, his error by Sea, the Sack of *Troy*, are put not as the Argument of the work, but *Episodes* of the Argument. So *Homer* laid by many things of *Ulysses* and handled no more, than he saw tended to one and the same end.

Contrary to which and foolishly those *Poets* did, whom the *Philosopher* taxeth; Of whom one gather'd all the Actions of *Theseus*; another put all the Labours of *Hercules* in one work. So did he, whom

Juvenal mentions in the beginning, *hoarse Codrus*,[46] that recited a volume compil'd, which he call'd his *Theseide*, not yet finish'd, to the great trouble both of his hearers and himself: Amongst which there were many parts had no coherence, nor kindred one with other, so far they were from being one Action, one *Fable*. For as a house, consisting of diverse materials, becomes one structure, and one dwelling; so an Action, compos'd of diverse parts, may become one *Fable Epic*, or *Dramatic*. For *example*, in a *Tragedy*, look upon *Sophocles* his *Ajax*: *Ajax* depriv'd of *Achilles's* Armour, which he hop'd from the suffrage of the *Greeks*, disdains; and, growing impatient of the Injury, rageth, and turns mad. In that humour he doth many senseless things; and at last falls upon the *Grecian* flock, and kills a great Ram for *Ulysses*: Returning to his Sense, he grows asham'd of the scorn, and kills himself; and is by the *Chiefs* of the *Greeks* forbidden burial. These things agree, and hang together, not as they were done; but as seeming to be done; which made the Action whole, entire, and absolute.

The conclusion concerning the Whole, and the Parts. For the *whole*, as it consisteth of parts; so without all the parts it is not the whole; and to make it absolute, is requir'd, not only the parts, but such parts as are true. For a part of the whole was true; which if you take away, you either change the whole, or it is not the whole. For, if it be such a part, as being present or absent, nothing concerns the whole, it cannot be call'd a part of the whole: and such are the *Episodes*, of which hereafter. For the present, here is one example; The single Combat of *Ajax* with *Hector*, as it is at large describ'd in *Homer*, nothing belongs to this *Ajax* of *Sophocles*. (ll. 2678–2815.)

46. Juvenal refers to himself as "hoarse as Cordus" (*sic*) in *Satires* I.2. Nothing is known of Cordus.

Horace His Art of Poetry

Drummond tells us that Jonson read him a preface to this translation of the Ars Poetica, *a dialogue in which he discussed poetry with John Donne. The preface perished in the fire of 1623, and only the translation remains. Most students of Jonson wish it had been the other way around. His rather literal translation is often graceless, and Latin scholars point out that some of the translations are actually blunders. But since the influence of the Ars* Poetica *on Jonson is pervasive and profound, it is helpful to be able to check, at any given point, what Jonson interpreted Horace as saying. Occasionally, at least, Jonson's translation of a Horatian text throws light on the way Jonson reconciles his own critical precepts with the great classical tradition. The most interesting of these is, perhaps, his translation of lines 309–322, where Horace's famous assertion that an otherwise weak play may be well received if it has enough moral passages and moral characters is translated as saying that such a play will "more strongly take the people" if it is "humoured right."*

The structure of Jonson's translation is more or less as follows: On Poetry in General—the poem as a unified whole (1–52); The Form of the Poem— decorum, diction, meters (53–120); The Art of the Drama (121–410); The Poet—genius and training, (411–642).

This selection is from the revised version in the 1640 folio.

If to a Woman's head a Painter would
Set a Horseneck, and divers feathers fold
On every limb, ta'en from a several creature,
Presenting upwards, a fair female feature,
Which in some swarthy fish uncomely ends:
Admitted to the sight, although his friends,
Could you contain your laughter? Credit me,

This piece, my *Pisos*,[1] and that book agree,
Whose shapes, like sick men's dreams, are feign'd so vain,
As neither head, nor foot, one form retain.   10
But equal power, to Painter, and to Poet,
Of daring all, hath still been given; we know it:
And both do crave, and give again, this leave.
Yet, not as therefore wild, and tame should cleave
Together: not that we should Serpents see
With Doves; or Lambs, with Tigers coupled be.
    In grave beginnings, and great things profest,
Ye have ofttimes, that may o'ershine the rest,
A Scarlet piece, or two, stitch'd in: when or[2]
Diana's Grove, or Altar, with bor-   20
D'ring Circles of swift waters that entwine
The pleasant grounds, or when the River *Rhine*,
Or Rainbow is describ'd. But here was now
No place for these. And, Painter, hap'ly, thou
Know'st only well to paint a Cypress tree.
What's this? if he whose money hireth thee
To paint him, hath by swimming, hopeless, scap'd,
The whole fleet wreck'd? A great jar to be shap'd,
Was meant at first. Why, forcing still about
Thy labouring wheel, comes scarce a Pitcher out?   30
In short; I bid, Let what thou work'st upon,
Be simple quite throughout, and wholly one.
    Most Writers, noble Sire, and either Son,
Are, with the likeness of the truth, undone.
My self for shortness labour; and I grow
Obscure. This, striving to run smooth, and flow,
Hath neither soul, nor sinews. Lofty he
Professing greatness, swells: That, low by lee
Creeps on the ground; too safe, too afraid of storm.
This, seeking, in a various kind, to form   40
One thing prodigiously, paints in the woods
A Dolphin, and a Boar amid' the floods.
So, shunning faults, to greater fault doth lead,
When in a wrong, and artless way we tread.

1. Horace's *Ars Poetica* is in the form of an epistle to the distinguished Roman family Piso.
2. I.e., when either.

The worst of Statuaries, here about
Th'*Æmilian* School,[3] in brass can fashion out
The nails, and every curled hair disclose;
But in the main work hapless: since he knows
Not to design the whole. Should I aspire
To form a work, I would no more desire 50
To be that Smith; than live, mark'd one of those,
With fair black eyes, and hair; and a wry nose.
    Take, therefore, you that write, still, matter fit
Unto your strength, and long examine it,
Upon your shoulders. Prove what they will bear,
And what they will not. Him, whose choice doth rear
His matter to his power, in all he makes,
Nor language, nor clear order e'er forsakes.
The virtue of which order, and true grace,
Or I am much deceiv'd, shall be to place 60
Invention. Now, to speak; and then defer
Much, that might now be spoke: omitted here
Till fitter season.[4] Now, to like of this,
Lay that aside, the *Epic's* office is.
    In using also of new words, to be
Right spare, and wary: then thou speak'st to me
Most worthy praise, when words that common grew,
Are, by the cunning placing, made mere new.
Yet, if by chance, in utt'ring things abstruse,
Thou need new terms; thou mayst, without excuse, 70
Feign words, unheard of to the well-truss'd race
Of the *Cethegi*;[5] And all men will grace,
And give, being taken modestly, this leave,
And those thy new, and late-coin'd words receive,
So they gall gently from the *Grecian* spring,
And come not too much wrested. What's that thing,
A Roman to *Cæcilius*[6] will allow,
Or *Plautus*, and in *Virgil* disavow,
Or *Varius*?[7] Why am I now envi'd so,

3. A gladiatorial school near the Forum.
4. I.e., do not try to do everything at once; the artist must discipline himself to know when to stop.
5. A patrician family, ancestors of the conspirator in Jonson's *Catiline*.
6. A writer of comedies, second century B.C.
7. A writer and friend of Virgil, author of tragic poem *Thyestes*.

If I can give some small increase? when, lo,　　　　80
Cato's and *Ennius'*[8] tongues have lent much worth,
And wealth unto our language; and brought forth
New names of things. It hath been ever free,
And ever will, to utter terms that be
Stamp'd to the time. As woods whose change appears
Still in their leaves, throughout the sliding years,
The firstborn dying; so the aged state
Of words decay, and phrases born but late
Like tender buds shoot up, and freshly grow.
Our selves, and all that's ours, to death we owe:　　　90
Whether the Sea receiv'd into the shore,
That from the North, the Navy safe doth store,
A Kingly work; or that long barren fen
Once rowable, but now doth nourish men
In neighbour-towns, and feels the weighty plough;
Or the wild river, who hath changed now
His course so hurtful both to grain, and seeds,
Being taught a better way. All mortal deeds
Shall perish: so far off it is, the state,
Or grace of speech, should hope a lasting date.　　　100
Much phrase that now is dead, shall be reviv'd;
And much shall die, that now is nobly liv'd,
If Custom please; at whose disposing will
The power, and rule of speaking resteth still.

* * *

The Comic matter will not be express'd
In tragic Verse; no less *Thyestes'* feast[9]
Abhors low numbers, and the private strain
Fit for the sock: Each subject should retain
The place allotted it, with decent thews.
If now the turns, the colours, and right hues
Of Poems here describ'd, I can, nor use,
Nor know to observe: why (i'the Muses' name)
Am I call'd Poet? wherefore with wrong shame,
Perversely modest, had I rather owe　　　130
To ignorance still, than either learn, or know?

8. Cato the Censor, famous as the earliest writer of good Latin prose, second century B.C. Ennius wrote the first Roman epic.
9. In Seneca's *Thyestes*, Thyestes is served the flesh of his sons.

Yet, sometime, doth the Comedy excite
Her voice, and angry *Chremes*[10] chafes out-right
With swelling throat: and, oft, the tragic wight
Complains in humble phrase. Both *Telephus*,
And *Peleus*,[11] if they seek to heart-strike us
That are Spectators, with their misery,
When they are poor, and banish'd, must throw by
Their bombard phrase, and foot-and-half-foot words.
'Tis not enough, th'elaborate Muse affords   140
Her Poem's beauty, but a sweet delight
To work the hearers' minds, still, to their plight.
Men's faces, still, with such as laugh, are prone
To laughter; so they grieve with those that moan.
If thou would'st have me weep, be thou first drown'd
Thy self in tears, then me thy loss will wound,
Peleus, or *Telephus*. If you speak vile
And ill-penn'd things, I shall, or sleep, or smile.
Sad language fits sad looks; stuff'd menacings,
The angry brow; the sportive, wanton things;   150
And the severe, speech ever serious.
For nature, first, within doth fashion us
To every state of fortune; she helps on,
Or urgeth us to anger; and anon
With weighty sorrow hurls us all along,
And tortures us: and, after, by the tongue
Her truchman, she reports the mind's each throw.
If now the phrase of him that speaks, shall flow,
In sound, quite from his fortune; both the rout,
And Roman Gentry, jeering, will laugh out.   160
It much will differ, if a God speak, then,
Or an *Hero*; if a ripe old man,
Or some hot youth, yet in his flourishing course;
Where[12] some great Lady, or her diligent Nurse;
A vent'ring Merchant, or the Farmer free
Of some small thankful land: whether he be
Of *Colchis* born; or in *Assyria* bred;

10. A character in a comedy, perhaps the old man in Terence's *The Self-Punisher*.
11. Telephus, son of Hercules, and Peleus, father of Achilles, are typical subjects for tearful treatment.
12. I.e., whether. Below, barbaric Colchis is contrasted to effete Assyria: decorum demands that a character's language reflect the region from which he comes.

Or, with the milk of *Thebes*; or *Argus*, fed.
Or follow fame, thou that dost write, or feign
Things in themselves agreeing: If again   170
Honour'd *Achilles* chance by thee be seiz'd,
Keep him still active, angry, unappeas'd;
Sharp, and condemning laws, at him should aim;
Be nought so'above him but his sword let claim.
Medea make brave with impetuous scorn;
Ino bewail'd; *Ixion* false, forsworn;
Poor *Iö* wandring; wild *Orestes* mad:
If something strange, that never yet was had
Unto the *Scene* thou bringst, and dar'st create
A mere new person, look he keep his state   180
Unto the last, as when he first went forth,
Still to be like himself, and hold his worth.

* * *

[*The poet is a creator, not a reporter. Consequently, he can avoid whatever
is not appropriate to his genius or his artistic purpose. He does well to avoid
promising more in the opening than he can perform, and*]

He ever hastens to the end, and so
(As if he knew it) raps his hearer to
The middle of his matter: letting go
What he despairs, being handled, might not show.
And so well feigns, so mixeth cunningly
Falsehood with truth, as no man can espy
Where the midst differs from the first: or where
The last doth from the midst disjoin'd appear.
Hear, what it is the People, and I desire:
If such a one's applause thou dost require,   220
That tarries till the hangings be ta'en down,
And sits, till th'*Epilogue* says *Clap*, or *Crown*:
The customs of each age thou must observe,
And give their years, and natures, as they swerve,
Fit rites. The Child, that now knows how to say,
And can tread firm, longs with like lads to play;
Soon angry, and soon pleas'd, is sweet, or sour,
He knows not why, and changeth every hour.

Th'unbearded Youth, his Guardian once being gone,
Loves Dogs, and Horses; and is ever one   230
I'the open field; is Wax like to be wrought
To every vice, as hardly to be brought
To endure counsel: a Provider slow
For his own good, a careless letter-go
Of money, haughty, to desire soon mov'd,
And then as swift to leave what he hath lov'd.
    These studies alter now, in one, grown man;
His better'd mind seeks wealth, and friendship: then
Looks after honours, and bewares to act
What straightway he must labour to retract.   240
    The old man many evils do girt round;
Either because he seeks, and, having found,
Doth wretchedly the use of things forbear,
Or do's all business coldly, and with fear;
A great deferrer, long in hope, grown numb
With sloth, yet greedy still of what's to come:
Froward, complaining, a commender glad
Of the times past, when he was a young lad;
And still correcting youth, and censuring.
    Man's coming years much good with them do bring: 250
And his departing take much thence: lest, then,
The parts of age to youth be given; or men
To children; we must always dwell, and stay
In fitting proper adjuncts to each day.
    The business either on the Stage is done,
Or acted told. But, ever, things that run
In at the ear, do stir the mind more slow
Than those the faithful eyes take in by show,
And the beholder to himself doth render.
Yet, to the Stage, at all thou mays't not tender   260
Things worthy to be done within, but take
Much from the sight, which fair report will make
Present anon:[13] *Medea* must not kill
Her Sons before the people; nor the ill-

13. The mythical horrors of Medea and Atreus, the mythical metamorphoses of Procne and Cadmus, may be reported but they cannot be presented on stage without destroying the audience's willing suspension of disbelief. Jonson takes this advice to heart in his tragedies.

Natur'd, and wicked *Atreus* cook, to th'eye,
His Nephews entrails; nor must *Progne* fly
Into a Swallow there; Nor *Cadmus* take,
Upon the Stage, the figure of a Snake.
What so is shown, I not believe, and hate.

Nor must the Fable, that would hope the Fate,   270
Once seen, to be again call'd for, and play'd,
Have more or less than just five Acts: nor laid,
To have a God come in; except a knot
Worth his untying happen there: And not
Any fourth man, to speak at all, aspire.

An Actor's parts, and Office, too, the Choir[14]
Must maintain mainly; not be heard to sing,
Between the Acts, a quite clean other thing
Than to the purpose leads, and fitly 'grees.
It still must favour good men, and to these   280
Be won a friend; it must both sway, and bend
The angry, and love those that fear to offend.
Praise the spare diet, wholesome justice, laws,
Peace, and the open ports, that peace doth cause.
Hide faults, pray to the Gods, and wish aloud
Fortune would love the poor, and leave the proud.

* * *

For Tragedy is fair,
And far unworthy to blurt out light rhymes;
But, as a Matron drawn at solemn times
To Dance, so she should, shamefac'd, differ far
From what th'obscene, and petulant Satires[15] are.   340

Nor I, when I write Satires, will so love
Plain phrase, my *Pisos*, as alone, to approve
Mere reigning words: nor will I labour so
Quite from all face of Tragedy to go,
As not make difference, whether *Davus*[16] speak,
And the bold *Pythias*, having cheated weak

14. The chorus.

15. The satires being discussed here are Greek satyr plays. They were thought
to have given birth to Old Comedy and to nondramatic satire.

16. Davus, Pythias, Simo, and Silenus: typical or literary names for the slave,
the girl, the grave old man, and the ribald old man. No matter what the mode,
decorum demands that different character types speak differently.

Simo; and, of a talent wip'd his purse;
Or old *Silenus, Bacchus'* guard, and Nurse.
    I can out of known gear, a fable frame,
And so, as every man may hope the same;   350
Yet he that offers at it, may sweat much,
And toil in vain: the excellence is such
Of Order, and Connexion; so much grace
There comes sometimes to things of meanest place.
But, let the *Fauns*, drawn from their Groves, beware,
Be I their Judge, they do at no time dare
Like men streetborn, and near the Hall,[17] rehearse
Their youthful tricks in overwanton verse:
Or crack out bawdy speeches, and unclean.
The Roman Gentry, men of birth, and mean   360
Will take offence, at this: Nor, though it strike
Him that buys a chiches blanch't,[18] or chance to like
The nutcrackers throughout, will they therefore
Receive, or give it an applause, the more.
    To these succeeded the old Comedy,
And not without much praise; till liberty
Fell into fault so far, as now they saw
Her licence fit to be restrain'd by law:
Which law receiv'd, the *Chorus* held his peace,
His power of foully hurting made to cease.   370

* * *

    Our Ancestors did *Plautus'* numbers praise,[19]
And jests; and both to admiration raise   400
Too patiently, that I not fondly say;
If either you, or I, know the right way
To part scurrility from wit: or can
A lawful Verse, by th'ear, or finger scan.
    Our Poets, too, left nought unproved here;
Nor did they merit the less Crown to wear,
In daring to forsake the *Grecian* tracts,
And celebrating our own homeborn facts;

17. Westminster Hall, near the center of city life. Horace speaks of men who dwell almost in the Forum. "Fauns," whether satyrs or rustics, should not speak the language of the city.
    18. Blanched peas, food for the poor.
    19. The subject switches here from Old Comedy to New Comedy.

Whether the guarded *Tragedy* they wrought,
Or 'twere the gowned *Comedy* they taught.   410
    Nor had our Italy more glorious been
In virtue, and renown of arms, than in
Her language, if the Stay, and Care t'have mended,
Had not our every Poet like offended.
But you, *Pompilius'* offspring,[20] spare you not
To tax that Verse, which many a day, and blot
Have not kept in; and (lest perfection fail)
Not, ten times o'er, corrected to the nail.
Because *Democritus*[21] believes a wit
Happier than wretched art, and doth, by it,   420
Exclude all sober Poets, from their share
In *Helicon*; a great sort will not pare
Their nails, nor shave their beards, but to bypaths
Retire themselves, avoid the public baths;
For so, they shall not only gain the worth,
But fame of Poets, they think, if they come forth,
And from the Barber *Licinus* conceal
Their heads, which three *Anticyras*[22] cannot heal.
O I left-witted,[23] that purge every spring
For choler! If I did not, who could bring   430
Out better Poems? But I cannot buy
My title, at their rate, I had rather, I,
Be like a Whetstone, that an edge can put
On steel, though 't self be dull, and cannot cut.
I, writing nought my self, will teach them yet
Their Charge, and Office, whence their wealth to fet,[24]
What nourisheth, what formed, what begot
The Poet, what becometh, and what not:
Whither truth may, and whether error bring.

20. The Pisos, to whom the poem is addressed. "Many a day and blot" must "keep in" and "correct to the nail" lasting art.

21. Cicero *De Divinatione* I.xxxvii says that Democritus thought great poets must be mad men. Horace (and Jonson) probably oversimplify the problem of the poets' "madness." The objection here is to Democritus' preferring "wit" (madness) to "art" (discipline).

22. Anticyra, a city located on the Corinthian Gulf, was famous for its hellebore, a remedy for madness.

23. Jonson's coinage: foolish; wrong-witted.

24. Fetch.

The very root of writing well, and spring   440
Is to be wise; thy matter first to know;
Which the *Socratic* writings best can show:
And, where the matter is provided still,
There words will follow, not against their will.
He, that hath studied well the debt, and knows
What to his Country, what his friends he owes,
What height of love, a Parent will fit best,
What brethren, what a stranger, and his guest,
Can tell a Statesman's duty, what the arts
And office of a Judge are, what the parts   450
Of a brave Chief sent to the wars: He can,
Indeed, give fitting dues to every man.
And I still bid the learned Maker look
On life, and manners, and make those his book,
Thence draw forth true expressions. For, sometimes,
A Poem, of no grace, weight, art, in rhymes,
With specious places, and being humour'd right,
More strongly takes the people with delight,
And better stays them there, than all fine noise
Of verse mere-matterless, and tinkling toys.   460
  The Muse not only gave the *Greeks* a wit,
But a well-compass'd mouth to utter it;
Being men were covetous of nought, but praise.
Our Roman Youths they learn the subtle ways
How to divide, into a hundred parts,
A pound, or piece, by their long compting arts:

* * *

  O, when once the canker'd rust,
And care of getting, thus, our minds hath stain'd,
Think we, or hope, there can be Verses feign'd
In juice of *Cedar* worthy to be steep'd,
And in smooth *Cypress* boxes to be keep'd?
Poets would either profit, or delight,
Or mixing sweet, and fit, teach life the right.

* * *

  Let what thou feign'st for pleasure's sake, be near
The truth; nor let thy Fable think, what e'er
It would, must be: lest it alive would draw

The Child, when *Lamia*'[25] has din'd, out of her maw.   510
The *Poems* void of profit, our grave men
Cast out by voices; want they pleasure, then
Our Gallants give them none, but pass them by:
But he hath every suffrage, can apply
Sweet mix'd with sour, to his Reader, so
As doctrine, and delight together go.
   This book will get the *Sosii*[26] money; This
Will pass the Seas, and long as nature is,
With honour make the far-known Author live.

* * *

   As Painting, so is Poesy. Some man's hand
Will take you more, the nearer that you stand;   540
As some the farther off: This loves the dark;
This, fearing not the subtlest Judge's mark,
Will in the light be view'd: This, once, the sight
Doth please; this, ten times over, will delight.

* * *

   'Tis now inquir'd, which makes the nobler Verse,
Nature or Art. My Judgement will not pierce
Into the Profits, what a mere rude brain
Can; or all toil, without a wealthy vein:
So doth the one, the other's help require,
And friendly should unto one end conspire.

* * *

   If to *Quintilius*,[27] you recited ought:
He'd say, Mend this, good friend, and this; 'tis naught.
If you denied, you had not better strain,
And twice, or thrice had 'ssayd it, still in vain:
He'd bid, blot all: and to the anvil bring
Those ill-turn'd Verses, to new hammering.
Then: If your fault you rather had defend
Than change; no word, or work, more would he spend   630
In vain, but you, and yours, you should love still
Alone, without a rival, by his will.

25. A mythical ogress who destroyed children to revenge the loss of her own.
26. Horace's bookseller.
27. Quintilius Varus, friend of Virgil and Horace.

A wise, and honest man will cry out shame
On artless Verse; the hard ones he will blame;
Blot out the careless, with his turned pen;
Cut off superfluous ornaments; and when
They're dark, bid clear this: all that's doubtful wrote
Reprove; and, what is to be changed, note:
Become an *Aristarchus*.[28] And, not say,
Why should I grieve my friend, this trifling way?   640
These trifles into serious mischiefs lead
The man once mock'd, and suffer'd wrong to tread.

* * *

28. A type of the true critic for Jonson and for Horace. Among other things, he
established the text of Homer.

II

THE FUNCTIONS OF A POET AND A CRITIC

Poetry and Study

From 1601 quarto of Every Man in His Humour, *I.i.16–21. Lorenzo Senior states the materialistic objection to poetry as the fruit of study.*

> My self was once a *student*, and indeed
> Fed with the self-same humour he is now,
> Dreaming on nought but idle *Poetry*:
> But since, Experience hath awaked my spirits,
> And reason taught them, how to comprehend
> The soverign use of study.

On the Dignity of Poetry

*Lorenzo Junior answers his father's attack on poetry (as being ranked abjectly in general opinion) with a fervid defense. Doctor Clement agrees, but distinguishes between poetry and the derivative doggerel of contemporary poetasters. (*Ibid., V.iii.309–334.)

LO. *ju.* Opinion, O God let gross opinion
> Sink & be damned as deep as *Barathrum*.[1]
> If it may stand with your most wish'd content,
> I can refell opinion, and approve
> The state of poesy, such as it is,
> Blessed, eternal, and most true divine:
> Indeed if you will look on Poesy,
> As she appears in many, poor and lame,
> Patch'd up in remnants and old worn rags,
> Half starv'd for want of her peculiar food,
> Sacred invention, then I must confirm,
> Both your conceit and censure of her merit.
> But view her in her glorious ornaments,
> Attired in the majesty of art,
> Set high in spirit with the precious taste
> Of sweet philosophy, and which is most,
> Crown'd with the rich traditions of a soul,
> That hates to have her dignity profan'd,
> With any relish of an earthly thought:
> Oh then how proud a presence doth she bear.

1. Hell.

Then is she like herself, fit to be seen
Of none but grave and consecrated eyes:
Nor is it any blemish to her fame,
That such lean, ignorant, and blasted wits,
Such brainless gulls, should utter their stolen wares
With such applauses in our vulgar ears:
Or that their slubberd lines have current pass,
From the fat judgements of the multitude,
But that this barren and infected age,
Should set no difference twixt these empty spirits,
And a true Poet: than which reverend name,
Nothing can more adorn humanity.

CLEM. Aye, *Lorenzo*, but election is now governed altogether by the influence
of humour,[2] which instead of those holy flames that should direct and light
the soul to eternity, hurls forth nothing but smoke and congested vapours,
that stifle her up, & bereave her of all sight & motion. But she must have
store of *Ellebore*[3] given her to purge these gross obstructions: oh that's well
said, give me thy torch, come lay this stuff together. So, give fire? there
see, see, how our Poet's glory shines brighter,[4] and brighter, still, still it
increaseth, oh now its at the highest, and now it declines as fast: you may
see gallants, *Sic transit gloria mundi.*

THE COURT AS FOUNTAIN OF MANNERS AND ARTISTIC EIDOLON
TO THE LAND

From the 1616 folio of Cynthia's Revels, or The Fountain of Self-
love, *the dedication.*

TO THE SPECIAL FOUNTAIN OF MANNERS: The Court

Thou art a bountiful, and brave spring: and waterest all the noble plants
of this *Island*. In thee, the whole Kingdom dresseth itself, and is ambitious
to use thee as her glass. Beware, then, thou render men's figures truly, and
teach them no less to hate their deformities, than to love their forms: For, to
grace, there should come reverence; and no man can call that lovely, which
is not also venerable. It is not powd'ring, perfuming, and every day smelling

2. I.e., a man's election to be a poet is governed these days by the influence of
humour instead of divine inspiration.
3. Hellebore was supposed to be a remedy for mental disease.
4. The doggerel of a poetaster is being burned on stage.

of the tailor, that converteth to a beautiful object: but a mind, shining through any sun, which needs no false light either of riches, or honors to help it. Such shalt thou find some here, even in the reign of *Cynthia* (a *Crites*, and an *Arete*.)[5] Now, under thy *Phœbus*,[6] it will be thy province to make more: Except thou desirest to have thy source mix with the *Spring* of *self-Love*, and so wilt draw upon thee as welcome a discovery of thy days, as was then made of her nights.

Thy servant, but not slave,

BEN JONSON.

THE TRUE CRITIC AND POET

Mercury describes Crites, a type of the perfect poet-critic. (Ibid., *II.iii.123–145.*)

MER. *Crites.* A creature of a most perfect and divine temper. One, in whom the humours and elements are peaceably met, without emulation of precedence: he is neither too phantastically melancholy, too slowly phlegmatic, too lightly sanguine, or too rashly choleric, but in all, so compos'd & order'd, as it is clear, *Nature* went about some full work, she did more than make a man, when she made him. His discourse is like his behaviour, uncommon, but not unpleasing; he is prodigal of neither. He strives rather to be that which men call judicious, than to be thought so: and is so truly learned, that he affects not to show it. He will think, and speak his thought, both freely: but as distant from depraving another man's merit, as proclaiming his own. For his valour, 'tis such, that he dares as little to offer an injury, as receive one. In sum, he hath a most ingenuous and sweet spirit, a sharp and season'd wit, a straight judgment, and a strong mind. *Fortune* could never break him, nor make him less. He counts it his pleasure, to despise pleasures, and is more delighted with good deeds, than goods. It is a competence to him that he can be virtuous. He doth neither covet, nor fear; he hath too much reason to do either: and that commends all things to him.

5. Crites and Arete are characters in *Cynthia's Revels*. Crites, Jonson's alter ego and spokesman, is a type of the perfect poet; Arete is his wise friend.
6. *Cynthia's Revels* discovers the folly of self-love among some of Cynthia's (Queen Elizabeth's) courtiers, just as it praises the moral virtue of a Crites or an Arete. Phoebus' (King James') courtiers are warned to emulate Crites and Arete, not the court fools.

THE TRUE CRITIC AND POET: A SUMMARY

*Crites is described again, this time by the honest Arete. (*Ibid., *V.viii.18–28.)*

ARE.　　　Lo, here the man, celestial *Delia*,
　　　　　Who (like a circle bounded in itself)
　　　　　Contains as much, as man in fullness may.
　　　　　Lo, here the man, who not of usual earth,
　　　　　But of that nobler, and more precious mold,
　　　　　Which *Phœbus'* self doth temper, is compos'd;
　　　　　And, who (though all were wanting to reward)
　　　　　Yet, to himself he would not wanting be:
　　　　　Thy favour's gain is his ambition's most,
　　　　　And labour's best; who (humble in his height)
　　　　　Stands fixed silent in thy glorious sight.

ON THE DIGNITY OF POETRY

From the 1616 folio of Poetaster, *I.ii.225–256. The young Ovid has been warned by his father to forget poetry, a vulgar pastime at best, and to resume his study of the law. After his father has departed, Ovid soliloquizes on poetry.*

OVID *ju.*　I'll give attendance on you, to your horse, sir, please you—
OVID *se.*　No: keep your chamber, and fall to your studies; do so: the gods
　　of *Rome* bless thee.
OVID *ju.*　And give me stomach to digest this *law*,
　　　　　That should have follow'd sure, had I been he.
　　　　　O sacred *poesy*, thou spirit of arts,
　　　　　The soul of science, and the queen of souls,
　　　　　What profane violence, almost sacrilege,
　　　　　Hath here been offered thy divinities!
　　　　　That thine own guiltless poverty should arm
　　　　　Prodigious ignorance to wound thee thus!
　　　　　For thence, is all their force of argument
　　　　　Drawn forth against thee; or from the abuse
　　　　　Of thy great powers in adultrate brains:
　　　　　When, would men learn but to distinguish spirits,
　　　　　And set true difference twixt those jaded wits
　　　　　That run a broken pace for common hire,

And the high raptures of a happy *Muse*,
Borne on the wings of her immortal thought,
That kicks at earth with a disdainful heel,
And beats at heaven gates with her bright hooves;
They would not then with such distorted faces,
And desp'rate censures stab at *poesy*.
They would admire bright knowledge, and their minds
Should ne'er descend on so unworthy objects,
As gold, or titles: they would dread far more,
To be thought ignorant, than be known poor.
"The time was once, when wit drown'd wealth: but now,
"Your only barbarism is t'have wit, and want.
"No matter now in virtue who excels,
"He, that hath coin, hath all perfection else.

POETRY'S MEMORIALIZING FUNCTION

Augustus Caesar and Maecenas, types of true patrons of poetry, discuss poetry as an eternizing art. (Ibid., V.i.17–37.)

* * *

CAESAR.
Sweet *poesy's* sacred garlands crown your gentry:
Which is, of all the faculties on earth,
The most abstract, and perfect; if she be
True born, and nurs'd with all the sciences.
She can so mold *Rome*, and her monuments,
Within the liquid marble of her lines,
That they shall stand fresh, and miraculous,
Even, when they mix with innovating dust;
In her sweet streams shall our brave *Roman* spirits
Chase, and swim after death, with their choice deeds
Shining on their white shoulders; and therein
Shall *Tiber*, and our famous rivers fall
With such attraction, that th'ambitious line
Of the round world shall to her center shrink,
To hear their music: And, for these high parts,
Caesar shall reverence the *Pierian* arts.
MAEC.   Your Majesty's high grace to *poesy*,
Shall stand 'gainst all the dull detractions

Of leaden souls; who (for the vain assumings
Of some, quite worthless of her sovereign wreaths)
Contain her worthiest *prophets*[7] in contempt.

THE PATRON, THE POET, AND POVERTY: VIRGIL AND HORACE

*As Caesar, Maecenas, Gallus, Tibullus, and Horace discuss Virgil as the ideal poet, Jonson's conception of poetry as the expression of the beautiful, the true, and the good emerges. The poet is the best artist, best philosopher, and best moralist. (*Ibid., *V.i.75–141.)*

* * *

CAES.
    What think you three, of *Virgil*, gentlemen,
    (That are of his profession, though rank'd higher)
    Or *Horace*, what sayest thou, that art the poorest,
    And likeliest to envy, or to detract?
HORA. *Caesar* speaks after common men, in this,
    To make a difference of me, for my poorness:
    As if the filth of poverty sunk as deep
    Into a knowing spirit, as the bane
    Of riches doth, into an ignorant soul.
    No, *Caesar*, they be pathless, moorish minds,
    That being once made rotten with the dung
    Of damned riches, ever after sink
    Beneath the steps of any villain.
    But knowledge is the *nectar*, that keeps sweet
    A perfect soul, even in this grave of sin;
    And for my soul, it is as free, as *Caesar's*:
    For, what I know is due, I'll give to all.
    "He that detracts, or envies virtuous merit,
    "Is still the covetous, and the ignorant spirit."
CAES. Thanks, *Horace*, for thy free, and wholesome sharpness:
    Which pleaseth *Caesar* more, than servile fawns.
    "A flatter'd prince soon turns the prince of fools."
    And for thy sake, we'll put no difference more
    Between the great, and good, for being poor.
    Say then, lov'd *Horace*, thy true thought of *Virgil*.

7. The ancient notion of the poet as prophet became a Renaissance commonplace.

HORA. I judge him of a rectified spirit,
By many resolutions of discourse
(In his bright reason's influence) refin'd
From all the tartarous moods of common men;
Bearing the nature, and similitude
Of a right heavenly body: most severe
In fashion, and collection of himself,
And then as clear, and confident as *Jove*.

GALL. And yet so chaste, and tender is his ear,
In suffering any syllable to pass,
That, he thinks, may become the honour'd name
Of issue to his so examin'd self;
That all the lasting fruits of his full merit
In his own *poems*, he doth still distaste:[8]
As if his mind's peace, which he strove to paint,
Could not with fleshly pencils have her right.

TIBU. But, to approve his works of sovereign worth,
This observation (me thinks) more than serves:
And is not vulgar. That, which he hath writ,
Is with such judgement, labour'd, and distill'd
Through all the needful uses of our lives,
That could a man remember but his lines,
He should not touch at any serious point,
But he might breathe his spirit out of him.

CAES. You mean, he might repeat part of his works,
As fit for any conference, he can use?[9]

TIBU. True, royal *Caesar*.   CAES. Worthily observ'd:
And a most worthy virtue in his works.
What thinks material *Horace*, of his learning?

HORA. His learning labours not the school-like gloss,[10]
That most consists in *echoing* words, and terms,
And soonest wins a man an empty name:
Nor any long, or far-fetch circumstance,
Wrapp'd in the curious generalities of arts:
But a direct, and *analytic* sum

8. Perhaps Jonson recalls that Virgil is reputed to have ordered from his death bed that the *Aeneid* be destroyed.

9. The sense seems clear if the last three words of the sentence are omitted.

10. Grammatical glosses, which depended primarily on philological trivia. The poet's learning is not the learning of the pedant.

Of all the worth and first effects of arts.
And for his *poesy*, 'tis so ramm'd with life,
That it shall gather strength of life, with being,
And live hereafter, more admir'd, than now.

CAES.   This one consent, in all your dooms of him,
And mutual loves of all your several merits,
Argues a truth of merit in you all.

THE GREAT TRADITION: THE TRAINING OF A POET

*The poetaster Crispinus—Jonson's satirical version of Marston—is given
a pill to purge him of his inartistic excesses. He is then given the following
lecture by Virgil, the gist of whose advice is "fair abstinence"—moderation.
(Ibid., V.iii.531–561.)*

VIRG.   These pills can but restore him for a time;
Not cure him quite of such a malady,
Caught by so many surfeits; which have fill'd
His blood, and brain, thus full of crudities:
'Tis necessary, therefore, he observe
A strict and wholesome diet. Look, you take
Each morning, of old *Cato's* principles[11]
A good draught, next your heart; that walk upon,
Till it be well digested: Then come home,
And taste a piece of *Terence*, suck his phrase
In stead of licorice; and, at any hand,
Shun *Plautus*, and old *Ennius*, they are meats
Too harsh for a weak stomach. Use to read
(But not without a *tutor*) the best *Greeks*:
As *Orpheus, Musaeus, Pindarus,*
Hesiod, Callimachus, and *Theocrite,*
High *Homer*, but beware of *Lycophron*:[12]
He is too dark, and dangerous a dish.
You must not hunt for wild, outlandish terms,
To stuff out a peculiar *dialect*;
But let your *matter* run before your *words*:

11. Dionysius Cato, a silver-age Latin writer studied in Elizabethan schools.
12. Callimachus, third-century B.C. Hellenistic poet. Lycophron, Alexandrian poet and grammarian, a student of the occult, third century B.C.

And if, at any time, you chance to meet
Some *Gallo-belgick* phrase, you shall not straight
Rack your poor verse to give it entertainment;
But let it pass: and do not think yourself
Much damnified, if you do leave it out;
When, nor[13] your understanding, nor the sense
Could well receive it. This fair abstinence,
In time, will render you more sound, and clear;
And this have I prescrib'd to you, in place
Of a strict sentence * * *

KNOWLEDGE AND CRITICISM

From the preface of the 1616 folio of Catiline.

TO THE READER IN ORDINARY

The Muses forbid, that I should restrain your meddling, whom I see already busy with the Title, and tricking over the leaves: It is your own. I departed with my right, when I let it first abroad. And, now, so secure an Interpreter I am of my chance, that neither praise, nor dispraise from you can affect me. Though you commend the two first Acts, with the people, because they are the worst; and dislike the Oration of *Cicero*, in regard you read some pieces of it, at School, and understand them not yet; I shall find the way to forgive you. Be anything you will be, at your own charge. Would I had deserv'd but half so well of it in translation, as that ought to deserve of you in judgment, if you have any. I know you will pretend (whosoever you are) to have that, and more. But all pretenses are not just claims. The commendation of good things may fall within a many, their approbation but in a few; for the most commend out of affection, self tickling, an easiness, or imitation: but men judge only out of knowledge. That is the trying faculty. And, to those works that will bear a judge, nothing is more dangerous than a foolish praise. You will say I shall not have yours, therefore; but rather the contrary, all vexation of Censure. If I were not above such molestations now, I had great cause to think unworthily of my studies, or they had so of me. But I leave you to your exercise. Begin.

To the Reader extraordinary.

You I would understand to be the better Man, though Places in Court go otherwise:
to you I submit my self, and work. Farewell.

13. Neither.

THE OFFICE OF A POET: THE POET AS COOK

From the 1623–1624 quarto of Neptune's Triumph for the Return of Albion, *lines 28–116, 212–233, 321–331, 504–513.*

POET.   You are not his Majesty's *Confectioner?* Are you?

COOK.   No, but one that has as good title to the room, his *Master-Cook.* What are you, Sir?

POET.   The most unprofitable of his servants, I, Sir, the *Poet.* A kind of a *Christmas* engine; one, that is used, at least once a year, for a trifling instrument, of wit, or so.

COOK.   Were you ever a *Cook?*

POET.   A *Cook?* no surely.

COOK.   Then you can be no good *Poet:* for a good *Poet* differs nothing at all from a *Master Cook.* Either's Art is the wisdom of the Mind.

POET.   As how, Sir?

COOK.   I am by my place, to know how to please the palates of the guests; so, you, are to know the palate of the times: study the several tastes, what every Nation, the *Spaniard*, the *Dutch*, the *French*, the *Walloon*, the *Neapolitan*, the *Brittan*, the *Sicilian*, can expect from you.

POET.   That were a heavy and hard task, to satisfy *Expectation*, who is so severe an exactress of duties; ever a tyrannous mistress: and most times a pressing enemy.

COOK.   She is a powerful great Lady, Sir, at all times, and must be satisfied: So must her sister, Madam *Curiosity*, who hath as dainty a palate as she, and these will expect.

POET.   But, what if they expect more than they understand?

COOK.   That's all one, Mr. *Poet*, you are bound to satisfy them. For, there is a palate of the understanding, as well as of the Senses. The Taste is taken with good relishes, the Sight with fair objects, the Hearing with delicate sounds, the Smelling with pure scents, the Feeling with soft and plump bodies, but the understanding with all these: for all which you must begin at the Kitchen. There, the *Art* of *Poetry* was learned and found out, or nowhere: and the same day, with the *Art* of *Cookery*.

POET.   I should have giv'n it rather to the Cellar, if my suffrage had been asked.

COOK.   O, you are for the *Oracle* of the *Bottle*,[14] I see; Hogshead *Trismegistus*:[15]

14. Jonson's marginal note advises the reader to consult Rabelais, *Pantagruel*, V, where the Temple of the Holy Bottle is approached by way of a vineyard and through a portal inscribed "In wine is truth."

15. Rabelais' La Bouteille Trimegiste, the Thrice-Great Bottle. The pun is,

He is your *Pegasus*. Thence flows the spring of your *Muses*, from that *hoof*.
    Seduced *Poet*, I do say to thee,—
    A Boiler, Range, and Dresser were the fountains
    Of all the knowledge, in the *Universe*,
    And that's the Kitchen. Where, a *Master Cook*—
    Thou do'st not know the man! nor canst thou know him!
    Til thou hast serv'd some years in that deep school,
    That's both the Nurse, and Mother of the *Arts*,
    And hear'st him read, interpret, and demonstrate.
    A *Master Cook*! why, he is the man of men,
    For a Professor! He designs, he draws,
    He paints, he carves, he builds, he fortifies,
    Makes *Citadels* of curious fowl, and fish,
    Some he dry-ditches, some moats round with broths;
    Mounts marrowbones; cuts fifty-angled custards;
    Rears bulwark pies; and, for his outer works,
    He raiseth ramparts of immortal crust;
    And teacheth all the *tactics* at one dinner:
    What ranks, what files, to put his dishes in;
    The whole *Art Military*! Then he knows
    The influence of the stars, upon his meats;
    And all their seasons, tempers, qualities,
    And so, to fit his relishes, and sauces!
    He'has *Nature* in a pot! 'bove all the Chemists,
    Or bare-breech'd brethren of the *Rosy Cross*!
    He is an *Architect*, an *Engineer*,
    A *Soldier*, a *Physician*, a *Philosopher*,
    A general *Mathematician*!
POET.   It is granted
COOK.   And, that you may not doubt him for a *Poet*,
POET.   This Fury shows, if there were nothing else. And 'tis divine!
COOK.   Then, Brother *Poet*.
POET.   Brother.

* * *

COOK.   But where's your *Antimasque* now, all this while? I hearken after
them.
POET.   Faith, we have none.

---

of course, on Hermes Trismegistus, the supposed author of the Hermetic books.
The cook chooses to think that the poet's way to the occult is the bottle, not the
works of Hermes.

COOK.　None?

POET.　　　　None, I assure you, neither do I think them
　　　　　A worthy part of presentation,
　　　　　Being things so *heterogene*, to all devise,
　　　　　Mere *Byworks*, and at best *Outlandish* nothings.

COOK.　　　O, you are all the heaven awry, Sir!
　　　　　For blood of *Poetry*, running in your veins,
　　　　　Make not your self so ignorantly simple.
　　　　　Because, Sir, you shall see I am a *Poet*,
　　　　　No less than *Cook*, and that I find you want
　　　　　A special service, here, an *Antimasque*,
　　　　　I'll fit you with a dish out of the Kitchen,
　　　　　Such, as I think, will take the present palates,
　　　　　A *metaphorical* dish!

[*Here follows a description of the cook's "Gally-mawfrey."*]

* * *

COOK.　　The fruit looks so.
　　　　　Good child, go pour 'hem out, show their concoction.
　　　　　They must be rotten boil'd, the broth's the best on't,
　　　　　And that's the Dance. The stage here is the Charger.
　　　　　And, Brother *Poet*, though the serious part
　　　　　Be yours, yet, envy not the *Cook* his art.

POET.　Not I. [For the most stately procession loves festivity.][16]

　　The Antimasque is danc'd by the persons describ'd, coming
　　　　　　　　　　out of the pot.

* * *

The Revels follow.
Which ended, the Fleet is discovered, while the three
Cornets play.

THE OFFICE OF A POET

From the 1631 folio of The Staple of News.

THE PROLOGUE FOR THE STAGE

For your own sakes, not his, he bad me say,
Would you were come to hear, not see a Play.
Though we his *Actors* must provide for those,
Who are our guests, here, in the way of shows,

16. *Nam lusus ipse Triumphus amat.* (Martial *Epigrams* VII.viii.10.)

The maker hath not so; he'ld have you wise,
Much rather by your ears, than by your eyes:
And prays you'll not prejudge his Play for ill,
Because you mark it not, and sit not still;
But have a longing to salute, or talk
With such a female, and from her to walk
With your discourse, to what is done, and where,
How, and by whom, in all the town; but here.
Alas! what is it to his Scene, to know
How many Coaches in *Hyde Park* did show
Last spring, what fare today at *Medley's* was,
If *Dunstan*, or the *Phœnix* best wine has?
They are things—But yet, the Stage might stand as well,
If it did neither hear these things, nor tell.
Great noble wits, be good unto your selves,
And make a difference 'twixt Poetic elves,
And Poets: All that dabble in the ink,
And defile quills, are not those few, can think,
Conceive, express, and steers the souls of men,
As with a rudder, round thus, with their pen.
He must be one that can instruct your youth,
And keep your *Acme* in the state of truth,
Must enterprise this work; mark but his ways,
What flight he makes, how new; And then he says,
If that not like you, that he sends tonight,
'Tis you have left to judge, not he to write.

THE FUNCTIONS OF THE CRITIC: THE KINDS

From the prologue of the 1640 folio of The Sad Shepherd, or A Tale of
Robin Hood. *Jonson defends "mongrel tragi-comedy" as he defines his own
peculiar version of the pastoral drama. His emphasis on the "mere English"
nature of his subject and on the appropriateness of "rustic" laughter and variety
of style suggest that even the never-never land of pastoral tragi-comedy seemed
to Jonson susceptible of more realistic treatment.*

THE PROLOGUE

He that hath feasted you these forty years,
And fitted *Fables*, for you finer ears,
Although at first, he scarce could hit the bore;

Yet you, with patience hark'ning more and more,
At length have grown up to him, and made known,
The Working of his *Pen* is now your own:
He prays you would vouchsafe, for your own sake,
To hear him this once more, but, sit awake.
And though he now present you with such wool,
As from mere *English* Flocks his *Muse* can pull,
He hopes when it is made up into Cloth;
Not the most curious head here will be loath
To wear a Hood of it; it being a Fleece,
To match, or those of *Sicily*, or *Greece*.
His *Scene* is *Sherwood*: And his *Play* a *Tale*
Of *Robinhood's* inviting from the Vale
Of *Belvoir*, all the *Shepherds* to a Feast:
Where, by the casual absence of one Guest,
The Mirth is troubled much, and in one Man
As much of sadness shown, as Passion can.
The sad young *Shepherd*, whom we here present,[17]
Like his woe's Figure, dark and discontent,
For his lost Love; who in the *Trent* is said
To have miscarried; 'las! what knows the head
Of a calm River, whom the feet have drown'd?
Hear what his sorrows are; and, if they wound
Your gentle breasts, so that the *End* crown all,
Which in the Scope of one day's chance may fall:
Old *Trent* will send you more such *Tales* as these,
And shall grow young again, as one doth please.[18]
But here's an Heresy of late let fall;
That Mirth by no means fits a *Pastoral*;
Such say so, who can make none, he presumes:
Else, there's no *Scene*, more properly assumes
The Sock. For whence can sport in kind arise,
But from the Rural Routs and Families?
Safe on this ground then, we not fear today,
To tempt your laughter by our rustic *Play*.
Wherein if we distaste, or be cry'd down,
We think we therefore shall not leave the Town;

17. Jonson's note: "The sad shepherd passeth silently over the stage."
18. Jonson's note: "Here the Prologue thinking to end, returns upon a new purpose, and speaks on."

Nor that the Fore-wits, that would draw the rest
Unto their liking, always like the best.
The wise, and knowing *Critic* will not say,
This worst, or better is, before he weigh,
Where[19] every piece be perfect in the kind:
And then, though in themselves he difference find,
Yet if the place require it where they stood,
The equal fitting makes them equal good.
You shall have Love and Hate, and Jealousy,
As well as Mirth, and Rage, and Melancholy:
Or whatsoever else may either move,
Or stir affections, and your likings prove.
But that no style for *Pastoral* should go
Current, but what is stamp'd with *Ah*, and *O*;
Who judgeth so, may singularly err;
As if all *Poesy* had one Character:
In which what were not written, were not right,
Or that the man who made such one poor flight,
In his whole life, had with his winged skill
Advanc'd him upmost on the *Muses*' hill.
When he like *Poet* yet remains, as those
Are *Painters* who can only make a *Rose*.
From such your wits redeem you, or your chance,
Lest to a greater height you do advance
Of Folly, to contemn those that are known
Artificers, and trust such as are none.

19. Whether.

III
COMICAL SATIRE

THE CHARACTER OF A PERFECT SATIRIST

From the 1616 folio of Every Man Out of His Humour, *a description of the character Asper, a type of the perfect comic satirist.*

ASPER his Character.

He is of an ingenious and free spirit, eager and constant in reproof, without fear controlling the world's abuses. One, whom no servile hope of gain, or frosty apprehension of danger, can make to be a Parasite, either to time, place, or opinion.

THE POET AS CENSOR AND SATIRIST: THE HUMOURS METAPHOR AND OLD COMEDY

In the opening chorus, Asper serves as Jonson's spokesman as Jonson lectures the audience on the nature of comical satire and humours. Cordatus is "a friend of the author" whose function is to comment on and defend the artistry of the play. Mitis' function is to ask the right questions. (Ibid., *chorus before Act I.)*

CORDATUS, ASPER, MITIS

Nay, my dear Asper, stay your mind:
ASP. Away.
Who is so patient of this impious world,
That he can check his spirit, or rein his tongue?
Or who hath such a dead unfeeling sense,
That heaven's horrid thunders cannot wake?
To see the earth, crack'd with the weight of sin,
Hell gaping under us, and o'er our heads
Black rav'nous ruin, with her sail-stretch'd wings,
Ready to sink us down, and cover us.
Who can behold such prodigies as these,
And have his lips sealed up? not I: my language
Was never ground into such oily colours,
To flatter vice and daub iniquity:
But (with an armed, and resolved hand)
I'll strip the ragged follies of the time,
Naked, as at their birth: COR. (Be not too bold.
ASP.   You trouble me) and with a whip of steel,
Print wounding lashes in their iron ribs.
I fear no mood stamp'd in a private brow,

75

When I am pleas'd t'unmask a public vice.
I fear no strumpet's drugs, nor ruffian's stab,
Should I detect their hateful luxuries:
No broker's, usurer's, or lawyer's gripe,
Were I dispos'd to say, they're all corrupt.
I fear no courtier's frown, should I applaud
The easy flexure of his supple hams.
Tut, these are so innate, and popular,
That drunken custom would not shame to laugh
(In scorn) at him, that should but dare to tax 'hem.
And yet, not one of these but knows his[1] works,
Knows what damnation is, the devil, and hell,
Yet, hourly they persist, grow rank in sin,
Puffing their souls away in perj'rous air,
To cherish their extortion, pride, or lusts.
MIT.   Forbear, good *Asper*, be not like your name.[2]
ASP.   O, but to such, whose faces are all zeal,
And (with the words of *Hercules*) invade
Such crimes as these! that will not smell of sin,
But seem as they were made of sanctity:
Religion in their garments, and their hair
Cut shorter then their eyebrows! when the conscience
Is vaster than the ocean, and devours
More wretches than the *Counters*.[3]   MIT.   Gentle *Asper*,
Contain your spirit in more stricter bounds,
And be not thus transported with the violence
Of your strong thoughts.   COR.   Unless your breath had power
To melt the world, and mold it new again,
It is in vain, to spend it in these moods.
ASP.   I not observ'd this thronged round till now.
Gracious, and kind spectators, you are welcome,
Apollo, and the *Muses* feast your eyes
With graceful objects, and may our *Minerva*
Answer your hopes, unto their largest strain.
Yet here, mistake me not, judicious friends.
I do not this, to beg your patience,

1. His own.
2. Like an asp? "Rough," as in the Latin meaning of *asper*?
3. In this passage, Jonson's contempt for Puritans ("Hypocrites") is the theme.
Counters are city jails.

Or servilely to fawn on your applause,
Like some dry brain, despairing in his merit:
Let me be censur'd, by th'austerest brow,
Where I want art, or judgement, tax me freely:
Let envious censors, with their broadest eyes,
Look through and through me, I pursue no favour,
Only vouchsafe me your attentions,
And I will give you music worth your ears.
O, how I hate the monstrousness of time,
Where every servile imitating spirit,
(Plagu'd with an itching leprosy of wit)
In a mere halting fury, strives to fling
His ulc'rous body in the *Thespian* spring,[4]
And straight leaps forth a Poet! but as lame
As *Vulcan*, or the founder of *Cripplegate*.[5]

MIT. In faith, this Humour will come ill to some,
You will be thought to be too peremptory.

ASP. This Humour? good; and why this Humour, *Mitis*?
Nay, do not turn, but answer. MIT. Answer? what?

ASP. I will not stir your patience, pardon me,[6]
I urg'd it for some reasons, and the rather
To give these ignorant well-spoken days,
Some taste of their abuse of this word Humour.

COR. O, do not let your purpose fall, good *Asper*,
It cannot but arrive most acceptable,
Chiefly to such, as have the happiness,
Daily to see how the poor innocent word
Is rack'd, and tortur'd. MIT. I, I pray you proceed.

ASP. Ha? what? what is't? COR. For the abuse of Humour.

ASP. O, I crave pardon, I had lost my thoughts.
Why, Humour (as 'tis *ens*)[7] we thus define it
To be a quality of air or water,
And in itself holds these two properties,
Moisture, and fluxure: As, for demonstration,
Pour water on this floor, 'twill wet and run:

4. Does Jonson here join the classical spring of poetic inspiration and the archetypal Christian spring of cleansing? At any rate, no spring will help the poetasters, who are seen as inwardly corrupt.

5. St. Giles, said to have chosen to remain cripple to mortify the flesh.

6. Mitis is angered by Asper's peremptory attack.

7. As it is in its essence.

Likewise the air (forc'd through a horn, or trumpet)
Flows instantly away, and leaves behind
A kind of dew; and hence we do conclude,
That whatsoe'er hath fluxure, and humidity,
As wanting power to contain itself,
Is Humour. So in every human body
The choler, melancholy, phlegm, and blood,
By reason that they flow continually
In some one part, and are not continent,
Receive the name of Humours. Now thus far
It may, by *Metaphor*, apply itself
Unto the general disposition:
As when some one peculiar quality
Doth so possess a man, that it doth draw
All his affects,[8] his spirits, and his powers,
In their confluctions, all to run one way,
This may be truly said to be a Humour.
But that a rook, in wearing a pied feather,
The cable hat-band, or the three piled ruff,
A yard of shoetie, or the *Switzer's* knot
On his *French* garters,[9] should affect a Humour!
O, 'tis more than most ridiculous.

cor.   He speaks pure truth now, if an Idiot
Have but an apish, or phantastic strain,
It is his Humour.   asp.   Well I will scourge those apes;
And to these courteous eyes[10] oppose a mirror,
As large as is the stage, whereon we act:
Where they shall see the time's deformity
Anatomiz'd in every nerve, and sinew,
With constant courage, and contempt of fear.

mit.   *Asper*, (I urge it as your friend) take heed,
The days are dangerous, full of exception,
And men are grown impatient of reproof.   asp.   Ha, ha:
You might as well have told me, yond' is heaven,
This earth, these men; and all had mov'd alike.
Do not I know the time's condition?

---

8. Passions.

9. The feather, hat-band, ruff, shoestrings, and garters were all foppish and faddish innovations among the gallants of the day.

10. The audience.

Yes, *Mitis*, and their souls, and who they be,
That either will, or can except against me.
None, but a sort of fools, so sick in taste,
That they condemn all physic of the mind,
And, like gall'd camels, kick at every touch.
Good men, and virtuous spirits, that loathe their vices,
Will cherish my free labours, love my lines,
And with the fervour of their shining grace,
Make my brain fruitful to bring forth more objects,
Worthy their serious, and intentive eyes.
But why enforce I this? as fainting? No.
If any, here, chance to behold himself,
Let him not dare to challenge me of wrong,
For, if he shame to have his follies known,
First he should shame to act them: my strict hand
Was made to seize on vice, and with a grip
Squeeze out the humour of such spongy natures,
As lick up every idle vanity.

COR. Why this is right *Furor Poeticus*!
Kind gentlemen, we hope your patience
Will yet conceive the best or entertain
This supposition, that a madman speaks.

ASP. What? are you ready there? *Mitis* sit down:
And my *Cordatus*. Sound hough,[11] and begin.
I leave you two, as censors, to sit here:
Observe what I present, and liberally
Speak your opinions, upon every *Scene*,
As it shall pass the view of these spectators.
Nay, now, y'are tedious Sirs, for shame begin.
And *Mitis*, note me, if in all this front,
You can espy a gallant of this mark,
Who (to be thought one of the judicious)
Sits with his arms thus wreath'd, his hat pull'd here,
Cries meow, and nods, then shakes his empty head,
Will show more several motions in his face,
Than the new *London, Rome*, or *Nineveh*,[12]
And (now and then) breaks a dry biscuit jest,

11. To the actors: sound the trumpet to announce that the first act is beginning.
12. Motions were puppet plays. *London, Rome*, and *Nineveh* are presumably titles of such shows.

Which that it may more easily be chew'd,
He steeps in his own laughter.   CORD. Why? will that
Make it be sooner swallow'd?   ASP. O, assure you.
Or if it did not, yet as *Horace* sings,
"*Jeiunus rarò stomachus vulgaria temnit,*"
"Mean cates are welcome still to hungry guests."
COR.   'Tis true, but why should we observe 'hem, *Asper?*
ASP.   O I would know 'hem, for in such assemblies,
Th'are more infectious than the pestilence:
And therefore I would give them pills to purge,
And make 'hem fit for fair societies.
How monstrous, and detested is't, to see
A fellow, that has neither art, nor brain,
Sit like an *Aristarchus*,[13] or stark-ass,
Taking men's lines, with a tobacco face,
In snuff, still spitting, using his wryed looks
(In nature of a vice) to wrest, and turn
The good aspect of those that shall sit near him,
From what they do behold! O, 'tis most vile.
MIT.   Nay, *Asper.*
ASP.   Peace, *Mitis,* I do know your thought.
You'll say, your guests here will except at this:
Pish, you are too timorous, and full of doubt.
Then, he, a patient, shall reject all physic,
'Cause the physician tells him, you are sick:
Or, if I say, That he is vicious,
You will not hear of virtue. Come, Y'are fond.
Shall I be so extravagant to think,
That happy judgements, and composed spirits,
Will challenge me for taxing such as these?
I am asham'd.   CORD. Nay, but good pardon us:
We must not bear this peremptory sail,
But use our best endeavours how to please.
ASP.   Why, therein I commend your careful thoughts,
And I will mix with you in industry
To please, but whom? attentive auditors,
Such as will join their profit with their pleasure,
And come to feed their understanding parts:
For these, I'll prodigally spend my self,

13. The pun was a popular one apparently. The attack is not on Aristarchus, presumably, but rather on would-be critics.

And speak away my spirit into air;
For these, I'll melt my brain into invention,
Coin new conceits, and hang my richest words
As polished jewels in their bounteous ears.
But stay, I lose my self, and wrong their patience;
If I dwell here, they'll not begin, I see:
Friends sit you still, and entertain this troupe
With some familiar, and by-conference,
I'll haste them sound. Now gentlemen, I go
To turn an actor, and a Humorist,
Where (ere I do resume my present person)
We hope to make the circles of your eyes
Flow with distilled laughter: if we fail,
We must impute it to this only chance,
"*Art* hath an enemy call'd *Ignorance*."

COR. How do you like his spirit, *Mitis*?

MIT. I should like it much better, if he were less confident.

COR. Why, do you suspect his merit?

MIT. No, but I fear this will procure him much envy.

COR. O, that sets the stronger seal on his desert, if he had no enemies, I should esteem his fortunes most wretched at this instant.

MIT. You have seen his play, *Cordatus*? pray you, how is't?

COR. Faith sir, I must refrain to judge, only this I can say of it, 'tis strange, and of a particular kind by itself, somewhat like *Vetus Comœdia*:[14] a work that hath bounteously pleased me, how it will answer the general expectation, I know not.

MIT. Does he observe all the laws of *Comedy* in it?

COR. What laws mean you?

MIT. Why, the equal division of it into *Acts*, and *Scenes*, according to the *Terentian* manner, his true number of Actors; the furnishing of the *Scene* with *Grex*, or *Chorus*, and that the whole Argument fall within compass of a day's business.

COR. O no, these are too nice observations.

MIT. They are such as must be received, by your favour, or it cannot be authentic.

COR. Troth, I can discern no such necessity.

MIT. No?

COR. No, I assure you, *Signior*. If those laws you speak of, had been delivered us, *ab initio*, and in their present virtue and perfection, there had been some reason of obeying their powers: but 'tis extant, that that which

14. Old Comedy.

we call *Comœdia*, was at first nothing but a simple, and continued *Song*, sung by one only person, till *Susario*[15] invented a second, after him *Epicharmus* a third; *Phormus*, and *Chionides* devised to have four Actors, with a *Prologue* and *Chorus*; to which *Cratinus* (long after) added a fifth and sixth, *Eupolis* more; *Aristophanes* more than they: every man in the dignity of his spirit and judgement, supplied something. And (though that in him this kind of *Poem* appeared absolute, and fully perfected) yet how is the face of it changed since, in *Menander, Philemon, Cecilius, Plautus*, and the rest; who have utterly excluded the *Chorus*, altered the property of the persons, their names, and natures, and augmented it with all liberty, according to the elegance and disposition of those times, wherein they wrote? I see not then, but we should enjoy the same licence, or free power, to illustrate and heighten our invention as they did; and not be tied to those strict and regular forms, which the niceness of a few (who are nothing but form) would thrust upon us.

MIT.   Well, we will not dispute of this now: but what's his *Scene*?

COR.   Marry, *Insula Fortunata*, Sir.

MIT.   O, the fortunate Island? Mass, he has bound himself to a strict law there.

COR.   Why so?

MIT.   He cannot lightly alter the *Scene*, without crossing the seas.

COR.   He needs not, having a whole island to run through, I think.

MIT.   No? how comes it then, that in some one Play we see so many seas, countries, and kingdoms, pass'd over with such admirable dexterity?

COR.   O, that but shows how well the Authors can travail in their vocation, and outrun the apprehension of their auditory. But leaving this, I would they would begin once: this protraction is able to sour the best-settled patience in the Theatre.

MIT.   They have answered your wish Sir: they sound.

* * *

THE HUMOURIST AS VICIOUS MAN: ENVY

*Cordatus explains to Mitis the decorum of humours characterization after Mitis objects that the envious Macilente in the scene just ended ought to have attacked the miserly Sordido's moral shortcomings. (*Ibid., *chorus after Act I.)*

15. Susario introduced comedy to Attica; Epicharmus and Phormus developed Doric comedy in Syracuse; Chionides was an Attic comedian; Cratinus is said to have introduced personal attack into Old Comedy; Eupolis was a contemporary of Aristophanes; Philemon was the first exponent of New Comedy; Caecilius Statius was a Roman writer of comedy.

GREX.

cor.   Now, Signior, how approve you this? have the Humourists express'd
themselves truly or no?

mit.   Yes (if it be well prosecuted) 'tis hitherto happy enough: but me
thinks, *Macilente* went hence too soon, he might have been made to stay,
and speak somewhat in reproof of *Sordido's* wretchedness, now at the last.

cor.   O, no, that had been extremely improper, besides, he had continued
the *Scene* too long with him, as't was, being in no more action.

mit.   You may enforce the length, as a necessary reason; but for propriety,
the *Scene* would very well have borne it, in my judgement.

cor.   O, worst of both: why, you mistake his Humour utterly then.

mit.   How? do I mistake it? is't not envy?

cor.   Yes, but you must understand, Signior, he envies him not as he is a
villain, a wolf i'the commonwealth, but as he is rich, and fortunate; for
the true condition of envy is, *Dolor alienae foelicitatis,* to have our eyes continually fix'd upon another man's prosperity, that is, his chief happiness,
and to grieve at that. * * *

The Comical Satirist's Full Stage

*Mitis objects, with more than usual acumen, that if the purpose of comical
satire is simply to parade and expose a series of humourous characters, it might
be more economically done one character at a time. Cordatus counters with an
appeal not to action, but to variety. (*Ibid., *chorus after Act II, Scene iii.)*

GREX.

mit.   Me think's, *Cordatus,* he dwelt somewhat too long on this *Scene*; it hung
i' the hand.

cor.   I see not where he could have insisted less, and t'have made the
humours perspicuous enough.

mit.   True, as his subject lies: but he might have altered the shape of his
argument, and explicated them better in single *Scenes.*

cor.   That had been single indeed: why? be they not the same persons in
this, as they would have been in those? and is it not an object of more
state, to behold the *Scene* full, and relieved with variety of speakers to the
end, than to see a vast empty stage, and the actors come in (one by one)
as if they were dropp'd down with a feather,[16] into the eye of the spectators?

16. I.e., dropped into the eyes of the spectators one by one, as a drop of ink
(or paint, or medicine) from a quill?

MIT. Nay, you are better traded with these things than I and therefore I'll subscribe to your judgement; marry, you shall give me leave to make objections.

COR. O, what else? it's the special intent of the author, you should do so: for thereby others (that are present) may as well be satisfied, who happily would object the same you do.

THE SATIRIST'S OBJECTS AND THE APPLICATION OF SATIRE

*Mitis worries that Jonson's attack on a satiric character such as Fastidious Brisk, a fool who affects the outward graces of a courtier, will be interpreted as an attack upon all courtiers. Cordatus objects, not on the New Comedy grounds that vices rather than persons are being attacked, but on the grounds that one individual character is being satirized, not a whole class of men. (*Ibid., *Chorus after Act II.)*

GREX.

MIT. Well, I doubt, this last *Scene* will endure some grievous torture.

COR. How? you fear 'twill be rack'd, by some hard construction?

MIT. Do not you?

COR. No, in good faith: unless mine eyes could light me beyond sense. I see no reason, why this should be more liable to the rack, than the rest: you'll say, perhaps, the city will not take it well, that the merchant is made here to dote so perfectly upon his wife; and she again, to be so *Fastidiously* affected, as she is?

MIT. You have utter'd my thought, sir, indeed.

COR. Why (by that proportion) the court might as well take offence at him we call the courtier, and with much more pretext, by how much the place transcends, and goes before in dignity and virtue: but can you imagine that any noble, or true spirit in court (whose sinewy, and altogether un-affected graces, very worthily express him a courtier) will make any ex-ception at the opening of such an empty trunk, as this *Brisk* is! or think his own worth empeach'd, by beholding his motley inside?

MIT. No sir, I do not.

COR. No more, assure you, will any grave, wise citizen, or modest matron, take the object of this folly in *Deliro*, and his wife: but rather apply it as the foil to their own virtues. For that were to affirm, that a man, writing of *Nero*, should mean all Emperors: or speaking of *Machiavel*, comprehend all Statesmen; or in our *Sordido*, all Farmers; and so of the rest: than which, nothing can be utter'd more malicious, or absurd. Indeed, there are a sort of these narrow-eyed decipherers, I confess, that will extort strange, and abstruse meanings out of any subject, be it never so conspicuous[17] and innocently deliver'd. But to such (where e're they sit conceal'd) let them know, the author defies them, and their writing tables; and hopes, no sound or safe judgement will infect itself with their contagious comments, who (indeed) come here only to pervert, and poison the sense of what they hear, and for nought else.

THE SUPERIORITY OF COMICAL SATIRE TO NEW COMEDY

Mitis suggests that a less dangerous sort of comedy than the satirical kind he is watching would be a romantic comedy not unlike Shakespeare's Twelfth Night. *Cordatus responds with a pseudo-Ciceronian definition of comedy which suggests that comical satire is the true form of comedy. (*Ibid., *Chorus after Act III, Scene vi.)*

MIT.   I travail with another objection, signior, which I fear will be enforc'd against the author, ere I can be deliver'd of it.

COR.   What's that, sir?

MIT.   That the argument of his *Comedy* might have been of some other nature, as of a duke to be in love with a countess, and that countess to be in love with the duke's son, and the son to love the lady's waiting maid: some such cross-wooing, with a clown to their servingman, better than to be thus near, and familiarly allied to the time.

COR.   You say well, but I would fain hear one of these *autumn*-judgements define once, [What is Comedy?] if he cannot, let him content himself with Cicero's definition (till he have strength to propose to himself a better) who would have a *Comedy* to be [An imitation of life, a mirror of manners, an image of truth];[18] a thing throughout pleasant, and ridiculous, and accommodated to the correction of manners: if the maker have fail'd in any particle of this, they may worthily tax him, but if not, why—be you (that are for them) silent, as I will be for him; and give way to the actors.

THE VIOLENT AND PAINFUL IN COMEDY AND COMICAL SATIRE: THE EPITASIS

Cordatus defends the introduction of near violence into the play on the grounds of classical precedent; he also defines and locates the epitasis *of the plot structure. (*Ibid., *Chorus after Act III.)*

17. Open.

18. *Quid sit Comœdia? Imitatio vitae, Speculum consuetudinis, Imago veritatis.*

GREX.

COR.   How now, *Mitis*? what's that you consider so seriously?

MIT.   Troth, that which doth essentially please me, the warping condition
of this green, and soggy multitude: but in good faith, signior, your author
hath largely outstripp'd my expectation in this *Scene*, I will liberally confess it. For, when I saw *Sordido* so desperately intended,[19] I thought I had
had a hand of him, then.

COR.   What? you suppos'd he should have hung himself, indeed?

MIT.   I did, and had fram'd my objection to it ready, which may yet be very
fitly urg'd, and with some necessity: for though his purpos'd violence lost
th'effect, and extended not to death, yet the intent and horror of the
object, was more than the nature of a *Comedy* will in any sort admit.

COR.   I? what think you of *Plautus*, in his *Comedy*, called *Cistellaria*, there?
where he brings in *Alcesimarchus* with a drawn sword ready to kill himself,
and as he is e'en fixing his breast upon it, to be restrain'd from his resolv'd
outrage, by *Silenium*, and the bawd: is not his authority of power to give
our *Scene* approbation?

MIT.   Sir, I have this only evasion left me, to say, *I think it be so indeed, your
memory is happier than mine*: but I wonder, what engine he will use to bring
the rest out of their humours!

COR.   That will appear anon, never preoccupy your imagination withal.
Let your mind keep company with the *Scene* still, which now removes it
self from the country, to the court. Here comes *Macilente*, and signior
Brisk, freshly suited, lose not your self, for now the *Epitasis*, or busy part
of our subject is in act.

THE COMICAL-SATIRICAL STAGE PURGE

*Cordatus underscores the importance of suspense and climax in the plotting
of comical satire. (*Ibid., *Chorus after Act IV.)*

GREX.

MIT.   This *Macilente*, signior, begins to be more sociable on a sudden, methinks, than he was before: there's some portent in't, I believe.

COR.   O, he's a fellow of a strange nature. Now does he (in this calm of this
humour) plot, and store up a world of malicious thoughts in his brain,
till he is so full with 'hem, that you shall see the very torrent of his envy
break forth like a land-flood: and, against the course of all their affections

19. The avaricious Sordido has almost committed suicide after suffering
financial reverses.

oppose itself so violently, that you will almost have wonder to think, how 'tis possible the current of their dispositions shall receive so quick, and strong an alteration.

MIT. Aye, marry, sir, this is that, on which my expectation has dwelt all this while: for I must tell you, signior (though I was loath to interrupt the *Scene*) yet I made it a question in mine own private discourse, how he should properly call it, *Every man out of his Humour*, when I saw all his actors so strongly pursue, and continue their humours?

COR. Why, therein his art appears most full of lustre, and approacheth nearest the life: especially, when in the flame, and height of their humours, they are laid flat, it fills the eye better, and with more contentment. How tedious a sight were it to behold a proud exalted tree lopp'd, and cut down by degrees, when it might be felled in a moment? and so set the axe to it before it came to that pride, and fullness, were, as not to have it grow.

MIT. Well, I shall long till I see this fall, you talk of.

COR. To help your longing, signior, let your imagination be swifter then a pair of oars: and by this, suppose *Puntarvolo*, *Brisk*, *Fungoso*, and the dog arriv'd at the court gate, and going up to the great chamber. *Macilente*, and *Sogliardo*, we'll leave them on the water, till possibility and natural means may land 'hem. Here come the gallants, now prepare your expectation.

THE COMICAL-SATIRICAL CATASTROPHE:
A DEFENSE OF THE DECORUM OF A SCENE

From the 1600 quarto of Every Man Out, *preface to the original* catastrophe. *In the original version of the play, Macilente is cured of his humour by the sight of the Queen. Jonson revised the conclusion in the first printed version, but appended the following apology along with the original conclusion.*

It had another *Catastrophe* or Conclusion, at the first Playing: which ([because the Queen was characterized on stage])[20] many seem'd not to relish it; and therefore, 'twas since alter'd: yet that a right-ey'd and solid *Reader* may perceive it was not so great a part of the Heaven awry, as they would make it; we request him but to look down upon these following Reasons.

1. *There hath been* Precedent *of the like Presentation in divers Plays: and is yearly in our City.* Pageants *or shows of* Triumph.

20. *Dia to ten basilissan prosopopoesthai.*

2. *It is to be conceiv'd, that* Macilente *being so strongly possess'd with Envy, (as* the Poet *here makes him) it must be no slight or common* Object, *that should affect so sudden and strange a cure upon him, as the putting him clean* Out of his Humour.

3. *If his* Imagination *had discours'd the whole world over for an* Object, *it could not have met with a more Proper, Eminent, or worthy* Figure, *than that of her Majesty's: which his* Election[21] *(though boldly, yet respectfully) used to a* Moral *and* Mysterious *end.*[22]

4. *His greediness to catch at any* Occasion, *that might express his affection to his* Sovereign, *may worthily plead for him.*

5. *There was nothing (in his examin'd* Opinion*) that could more near or truly exemplify the power and strength of her Invaluable* Virtues, *than the working of so perfect a* Miracle *on so oppos'd a* Spirit, *who not only persisted in his* Humour, *but was now come to the* Court *with a purposed resolution (his Soul as it were new dress'd in Envy) to malign at any thing that should front him; when suddenly (against expectation, and all steel of his* Malice*) the very wonder of her* Presence *strikes him to the earth dumb, and astonish'd. From whence rising and recovering heart, his* Passion *thus utters itself.*

* * *

The Application of Satire: The "Every Man Out" Epilogue to the Audience

*Jonson's extra-dramatic spokesman, Asper, who has assumed the role of Macilente in the play proper, concludes the play with a lecture to the audience on the uses of comical satire. (*Ibid., *epilogue to the quarto version.)*

> And now with *Asper's* tongue (though not his shape)
> Kind *Patrons* of our sports (you that can judge,
> And with discerning thoughts measure the pace
> Of our strange Muse in this her *Maze* of Humour,
> You, whose true Notions do confine the forms
> And nature of sweet *Poesy*) to you
> I tender solemn and most duteous thanks,
> For your stretch'd patience and attentive grace.
> We know (and we are pleas'd to know so much)

21. *which his Election:* the selection of whom he.

22. Jonson intends more than flattery here. The "moral and mysterious" conversion of the "possessed" Macilente requires some form of divine intervention. Cf. the conversion scene in *Cynthia's Revels*, the last scene, which suggests the sacrament of penance.

The Cakes that you have tasted were not season'd
For every vulgar Palate, but prepar'd
To banquet pure and apprehensive ears:
Let then their Voices speak for our dessert;
Be their *Applause* the Trumpet to proclaim
Defiance to rebelling Ignorance,
And the green spirits of some tainted Few,
That (spite of piety) betray themselves
To Scorn and Laughter; and like guilty Children,
Publish their *infamy* before their time,
By their own fond exception. Such as these
We pawn 'hem to your *censure*, till Time, Wit,
Or Observation, set some stronger seal
Of *judgement* on their judgements; and entreat
The happier spirits in this fair-fill'd Globe,[23]
(So many as have sweet minds in their breasts,
And are too wise to think themselves are tax'd
In any general Figure, or too virtuous
To need that wisdoms imputation:)
That with their bounteous *Hands* they would confirm
This, as their pleasures' *Patent*:[24] which so sign'd,
Our lean and spent Endeavours shall renew
Their Beauties with the *Spring* to smile on you.

JONSON'S SATIRIC MUSE: THE PROFOUND, ACTIONLESS PLAY

From the 1616 folio of Cynthia's Revels, *the prologue.*

If gracious silence, sweet attention,
Quick sight, and quicker apprehension,
(The lights of judgement's throne) shine any where;
Our doubtful author hopes this is their sphere.
And therefore opens he himself to those;
To other weaker beams, his labours close:
As loath to prostitute their virgin strain,
To ev'ry vulgar, and adult'rate brain.
In this alone, his *Muse* her sweetness hath,

23. The Globe Theatre, where *Every Man Out* was first performed. Jonson's temporary quarrel with the public theaters occurred a little later.
24. The audience's applause will be as a license or patent ensuring their present and future pleasure.

She shuns the print of any beaten path;
And proves new ways to come to learned ears:
Pied ignorance she neither loves, nor fears.
Nor hunts she after popular applause,
Or foamy praise, that drops from common jaws:
The garland that she wears, their hands must twine,
Who can both censure, understand, define
What merit is: Then cast those piercing rays,[25]
Round as a crown, instead of honour'd bays,
About his *poesy*; which (he knows) affords
Words, above action: matter, above words.

SATIRIC INDIGNATION AND HUMAN RESPONSIBILITY

*Crites, here figured as the type of the true satirist, meditates on the satirist's function. (*Ibid., *I.v.24–66.)*

CRI.   * * * O vanity,
How are thy painted beauties doted on,
By light, and empty idiots! how pursu'd
With open and extended appetite!
How they do sweat, and run themselves from breath,
Rais'd on their toes, to catch thy airy forms,
Still turning giddy, till they reel like drunkards,
That buy the merry madness of one hour,
With the long irksomeness of following time!
O how despis'd and base a thing is a man,
If he not strive t'erect his grovelling thoughts
Above the strain of flesh! But how more cheap
When, even his best and understanding part,
(The crown, and strength of all his faculties)
Floats like a dead drown'd body, on the stream
Of vulgar humour, mix'd with common'st dregs?
I suffer for their guilt now, and my soul
(Like one that looks on ill-affected eyes)
Is hurt with mere intention on their follies.
Why will I view them then? my sense might ask me:
Or is't a rarity, or some new object,
That strains my strict observance to this point?

25. I.e., rays of sight and comprehension. A perceptive audience is a better reward for the poet than the traditional crown of laurel leaves.

O would it were, therein I could afford
My spirit should draw a little near to theirs,
To gaze on novelties: so vice were one.
Tut, she is stale, rank, foul, and were it not
That those (that woo her) greet her with lock'd eyes,
(In spite of all the impostures, paintings, drugs,
Which her bawd custom daubs her cheeks withal)
She would betray, her loath'd and leprous face,
And fright th'enamor'd dotards from themselves:
But such is the perverseness of our nature,
That if we once but fancy levity,
(How antic and ridiculous so e'er
It suit with us) yet will our muffled thought
Choose rather not to see it, than avoid it:
And if we can but banish our own sense,
We act our mimic tricks with that free licence,
That lust, that pleasure, that security,
As if we practic'd in a paste-board case,
And no one saw the motion, but the motion.
Well, check thy passion, lest it grow too loud:
"While fools are pitied, they wax fat, and proud."

THE COMICAL SATIRIST'S FUNCTION AND THE COURT'S RESPONSE

Mercury orders Crites to satirize the court's more foolish members, and he and Crites discuss the dangers of writing satire. (Ibid., V.i.1–43.)

MERCURY, CRITES.

It is resolv'd on, *Crites*, you must do it.

CRI.   The grace divinest *Mercury* hath done me,
In this vouchsaf'd discovery of himself,
Binds my observance in the utmost term
Of satisfaction, to his godly will:
Though I profess (without the affectation
Of an enforc'd, and form'd austerity)
I could be willing to enjoy no place
With so unequal natures.   MER.   We believe it.
But for our sake, and to inflict just pains
On their prodigious follies, aid us now:
No man is, presently,[26] made bad, with ill.

26. At once. I.e., it takes more than the portrayal of evil in a brief masque to corrupt an audience or an author.

And good men, like the sea, should still maintain
Their noble taste, in midst of all fresh humours,
That flow about them, to corrupt their streams,
Bearing no season, much less salt of goodness.
It is our purpose, *Crites*, to correct,
And punish, with our laughter, this night's sport
Which our court-*Dors*[27] so heartily intend:
And by that worthy scorn, to make them know
How far beneath the dignity of man
Their serious, and most practis'd actions are.

CRI.   I, but though *Mercury* can warrant out
His under-takings, and make all things good,
Out of the powers of his *divinity*,
Th'offence will be return'd with weight on me,
That am a creature so despis'd, and poor;
When the whole Court shall take it self abus'd
By our *ironical* confederacy.

MER.   You are deceiv'd. The better race in court
That have the true nobility, call'd virtue,
Will apprehend it, as a grateful right
Done to their separate merit: and approve
The fit rebuke of so ridiculous heads,
Who with their apish customs, and forc'd garbs,
Would bring the name of courtier in contempt,
Did it not live unblemish'd in some few,
Whom equal *Jove* hath lov'd, and *Phœbus* form'd
Of better metal, and in better mold.

CRI.   Well, since my leader on is *Mercury*,
I shall not fear to follow. If I fall,
My proper virtue shall be my relief,
That follow'd such a cause, and such a chief.

SATIRIC EXPOSURE AND THE HUMANISTIC IDEAL

Having satirized Cynthia's foolish courtiers in a satiric masque, Crites and
*Mercury discuss the effects of satiric exposure. (*Ibid., *V.iv.608–653.)*

CRI.   Now, sacred god of wit, if you can make
Those, whom our sports tax in these apish graces,

27. Court buffoons.

Kiss (like the fighting snakes) your peaceful rod;[28]
These times shall canonize you for a god.

MER. Why, *Crites*, think you any noble spirit,
Or any, worth the title of a man,
Will he incens'd, to see th'enchanted veils
Of self-conceit, and servile flattery
(Wrapp'd in so many folds, by time, and custom)
Drawn from his wronged, and bewitched eyes?
Who sees not now their shape, and nakedness,
Is blinder than the son of earth, the mole:
Crown'd with no more humanity, nor soul.

CRI. Though they may see it, yet the huge estate
Phan'sy, and form, and sensual pride have gotten,
Will make them blush for anger, not for shame;
And turn shown nakedness, to impudence.
Humour is now the test, we try things in;
All power is just: Nought that delights is sin.
And, yet the zeal of every knowing man,
(Oppress'd with hills of tyranny, cast on virtue
By the light phant'sies of fools, thus transported)
Cannot but vent the *Ætna* of his fires,
T'enflame best bosoms, with much worthier love
Than of these outward, and effeminate shades:
That, these vain joys, in which their wills consume
Such powers of wit, and soul, as are of force
To raise their beings to eternity,
May be converted on works, fitting men.
And, for the practice of a forced look,
An antique gesture, or a fustian phrase,
Study the native frame of a true heart,
An inward comeliness of bounty, knowledge,
And spirit, that may conform them, actually,
To *God's* high figures, which they have in power:
Which to neglect for a self-loving neatness,
Is sacrilege, of an unpardon'd greatness.

MER. Then let the truth of these things strengthen thee,
In thy exempt, and only man-like course:

28. The caduceus of Mercury. Mercury found the snakes fighting, parted them
with his wand, then used them coiled to the top of his wand as his emblem.

Like it the more, the less it is respected;
Though men fail, virtue is by gods protected.
See, here comes *Arete*, I'll withdraw my self.

THE SATIRIST'S SENTENCE, THE VICIOUS MAN'S SELF-PUNISHMENT, AND THE END OF SATIRE

*Crites, assigned the task of punishing the foolish courtiers he has exposed in his satiric masque, indicates that the end of satire should be positive—something like the spiritual rebirth which follows upon confession, contrition, and satisfaction. (*Ibid., *V.i.120–137.)*

CRI.   Adored *Cynthia*, and bright *Arete*,
        Another might seem fitter for this task,
        Than *Crites* far, but that you judge not so:
        For I (not to appeare vindictive,
        Or mindful of contempts, which I condemn'd
        As done of impotence) must be remiss,
        Who, as I was the author, in some sort,
        To work their knowledge into *Cynthia's* sight,
        So should be much severer to revenge
        Th'indignity, hence issuing to her name.
        But there's not one of these, who are unpain'd,
        Or by themselves unpunished: for vice
        Is like a fury to the vicious mind,
        And turns delight itself to punishment.
        But we must forward to design their doom.
        You are offenders, that must be confess'd,
        Do you confess it?   ALL.   We do.
CRI.   And, that you merit sharp correction?   ALL.   Yes.
    [*Here Crites sentences the courtiers to a ritualistic and penitential pilgrimage which is to conclude at*]
        * * * the well of knowledge, *Helicon*;
        Where purged of your present maladies,
        (Which are not few nor slender) you become
        Such as you fain would seem: and then return,
        Off'ring your service to great *Cynthia*.
        This is your sentence, if the goddess please,
        To ratify it with her high consent:
        "The scope of wise mirth unto fruit is bent."
CYN.   We do approve thy censure, belov'd *Crites*.

ENVY AND THE COMICAL SATIRIST

From the prologue to the 1616 folio of Poetaster. *The armed prologue addresses Envy, the enemy of all true poets, especially of satiric poets.*

PROLOGUE

Stay, Monster [Envy], ere thou sink, thus on thy head
Set we our bolder foot; with which we tread
Thy malice into earth: So spite should die,
Despis'd and scorn'd by noble industry.
If any muse why I salute the stage,
An armed *Prologue*; know, 'tis a dangerous age:
Wherein, who writes, had need present his *Scenes*
Forty-fold proof against the conjuring means
Of base detractors, and illiterate apes,
That fill up rooms in fair and formal shapes.
'Gainst these, have we put on this forc'd defence:
Whereof the *allegory* and hid sense
Is, that a well erected confidence
Can fright their pride, and laugh their folly hence.
Here now, put case our Author should, once more,
Swear that his play were good; he doth implore,
You would not argue him of arrogance:
How ere that common spawn of ignorance,
Our fry of writers, may beslime his fame,
And give his action that adulterate name.
Such full-blown vanity he more doth loathe,
Than base dejection: There's a mean 'twixt both.
Which with a constant firmness he pursues,
As one, that knows the strength of his own *muse*.
And this he hopes all free souls will allow;
Others, that take it with a rugged brow,
Their moods he rather pities, than envies:
His mind it is above their injuries.

THE ENEMIES OF SATIRE

The young Ovid, not yet the great Latin poet admired by Renaissance England, is surrounded by enemies of poetry generally and satire specifically. Ostensibly, the reprobate Captain Tucca and the dishonest politician Lupus are

trying to help Ovid's father convince the young man that he should become a
lawyer, not a mere poet. Actually, they appear to be attacking something like
Jonson's comical satire. Jonson's point is that with such enemies, comical satire
needs no defenders. (Ibid., *I.ii.1–19, 36–99.)*

OVID *Senior*, OVID *Junior*, LUSCUS,
TUCCA, LUPUS, PYRGUS.

Your name shall live indeed, sir; you say true: but how infamously,
how scorn'd and condemn'd in the eyes and ears of the best and gravest
Romans, that you think not on: you never so much as dream of that. Are
these the fruits of all my travail and expenses? is this the scope and aim of
thy studies? are these the hopeful courses, wherewith I have so long flat-
tered my expectation from thee? verses? *poetry*? *Ovid*, whom I thought to
see the pleader, become *Ovid* the play-maker?

OVID *ju.*   No, sir.

OVID *se.*   Yes, sir. I hear of a *tragedy* of yours coming forth for the common
players there, call'd *Medea*. By my household gods, if I come to the acting
of it, I'll add one tragic part, more than is yet expected, to it: believe me
when I promise it. What? shall I have my son a stager now? an enghle[29]
for players? a gull? a rook? a shotclog? to make suppers, and be laugh'd
at? *Publius*, I will set thee on the funeral pile, first.

OVID *ju.*   Sir, I beseech you to have patience.

* * *

LUPU.   Indeed, *Marcus Ovid*, these players are an idle generation, and do
much harm in a state, corrupt young gentry very much, I know it: I have
not been a *Tribune* thus long, and observ'd nothing: besides, they will rob
us, us, that are magistrates, of our respect, bring us upon their stages, and
make us ridiculous to the plebeians; they will play you, or me, the wisest
men they can come by still; me: only to bring us in contempt with the
vulgar, and make us cheap.

TUCC.   Th'art in the right, my venerable cropshin, they will indeed: the
tongue of the *oracle* never twang'd truer. Your courtier cannot kiss his
mistress' slippers, in quiet, for 'hem: nor your white innocent gallant pawn
his revelling suit, to make his punk a supper. An honest decayed commander, cannot skelder, cheat, nor be seen in a bawdy house, but he shall
be straight in one of their wormwood *comedies*. They are grown licentious,

29. Minion.

the rogues: libertines, flat libertines. They forget they are i' the *statute*,[30] the rascals, they are *blazon'd* there, there they are trick'd, they and their pedigrees; they need no other *heralds*, I wiss.

ovid *se.* Methinks, if nothing else, yet this alone, the very reading of the public *edicts* should fright thee from commerce with them; and give thee distaste enough of their actions. But this betrays what a student you are: this argues your proficiency in the *law*.

ovid *ju.* They wrong me, sir, and do abuse you more,

That blow your ears with these untrue reports.

I am not known unto the open stage,

Nor do I traffic in their *theaters*.

Indeed, I do acknowledge, at request

Of some near friends, and honorable *Romans*,

I have begun a *poem* of that nature.

ovid *se.* You have, sir, a *poem*? and where is't? that's the *law* you study.

ovid *ju.* *Cornelius Gallus* borrowed it to read.

ovid *se.* *Cornelius Gallus*? There's another gallant, too, hath drunk of the same poison: and *Tibullus*, and *Propertius*. But these are gentlemen of means, and revenue now. Thou art a younger brother, and hast nothing, but thy bare exhibition: which I protest shall be bare indeed, if thou forsake not these unprofitable by-courses, and that timely too. Name me a profess'd *poet*, that his *poetry* did ever afford him so much as a competency. Aye, your god of *poets* there (whom all of you admire and reverence so much) *Homer*, he whose worm-eaten statue must not be spew'd against, but with hallowed lips, and grovelling adoration, what was he? what was he?

tucc. Marry, I'll tell thee, old swaggerer; He was a poor, blind, rhyming rascal, that lived obscurely up and down in booths, and tap-houses, and scarce ever made a good meal in his sleep, the whoreson hungry beggar.

ovid *se.* He says well: Nay, I know this nettles you now, but answer me; Is't not true? you'll tell me his name shall live; and that (now being dead) his works have eternis'd him, and made him divine. But could this divinity feed him, while he liv'd? could his name feast him?

tucc. Or purchase him a *Senator's* revenue? could it?

ovid *se.* I, or give him place in the commonwealth? worship, or attendants? make him be carried in his litter?

tucc. Thou speakest sentences, old *Bias*.

lupu. All this the *law* will do, young sir, if you'll follow it.

30. According to Elizabethan statutes, actors were legally vagabonds unless sponsored by some nobleman.

THE HISTORY OF SATIRE AND THE SATIRIST'S ROLE

Through the words of Horace, Jonson intimates that harsh, personal satire is part of the great classical tradition; the appeal is to the authority of the Latin satirist Lucilius and to the historical Horace, one of whose satires Jonson is here virtually translating. (Ibid., III.v.1–140.)

HORACE, TREBATIUS.[31]

There are, to whom I seem excessive sour;
And past a *satire's* law, t'extend my power:
Others, that think whatever I have writ
Wants pith, and matter to eternise it;
And that they could, in one day's light, disclose
A thousand verses, such as I compose.
What shall I do, *Trebatius?* say.   TREB. Surcease.
HORA.   And shall my *Muse* admit no more increase?
TREB. So I advise.   HORA. An ill death let me die,
If 'twere not best; but sleep avoids mine eye:
And I use these, lest nights should tedious seem.
TREB. Rather, contend to sleep, and live like them,
That holding golden sleep in special price,
Rubb'd with sweet oils, swim silver *Tiber* thrice,
And every ev'en, with neat wine steeped be:
Or, if such love of writing ravish thee,
Then dare to sing unconquer'd *Caesar's* deeds;
Who cheers such actions, with abundant meeds.
HORA.   That, father, I desire; but when I try,
I feel defects in every faculty:
Nor is't a labour fit for every pen,
To paint the horrid troops of armed men;
The lances burst, in *Gallia's* slaughtered forces;
Or wounded *Parthians*, tumbled from their horses:
Great *Caesar's* wars cannot be fought with words.
TREB. Yet, what his virtue in his peace affords,
His fortitude, and justice thou canst show;
As wise *Lucilius*, honor'd *Scipio*.
HORA.   Of that, my powers shall suffer no neglect,
When such slight labours may aspire respect:
But, if I watch not a most chosen time,
The humble words of *Flaccus* cannot climb

31. Jonson's note points out that this scene is an adaptation of Horace *Satires* II.1.

The attentive ear of *Caesar*; nor must I
With less observance shun gross flattery:
For he, reposed safe in his own merit,
Spurns back the glosses of a fawning spirit.
TREB.   But, how much better would such accents sound,
Than, with a sad, and serious verse to wound
Pantolabus, railing in his saucy jests?
Or *Nomentanus* spent in riotous feasts?
"In *satires*, each man (though untouch'd) complains
"As he were hurt; and hates such biting strains."
HORA.   What shall I do? *Milonius* shakes his heels
In ceaseless dances, when his brain once feels
The stirring fervour of the wine ascend;
And that his eyes false number apprehend.
Castor his horse; *Pollux* loves handy fights:
[A] thousand heads, a thousand choice delights.
My pleasure is in feet, my words to close,
As, both our better, old *Lucilius*[32] does:
He, as his trusty friends, his books did trust
With all his secrets; nor, in things unjust,
Or actions lawful, ran to other men:
So, that the old man's life, describ'd was seen
As in a votive table in his lines;
And to his steps my *Genius* inclines
Lucanian, or *Apulian*, I [know] not whether;
For the *Venusian* [33] colony plows either:
Sent thither, when the *Sabines* were forc'd thence
(As old fame sings) to give the place defence
'Gainst such, as seeing it empty, might make road
Upon the empire; or there fix abode:
Whether th' *Apulian* borderer it were,
Or the *Lucanian* violence they fear.
But this my style no living man shall touch,
If first I be not forc'd by base reproach;
But, like a sheathed sword, it shall defend
My innocent life; for, why should I contend
To draw it out, when no malicious thief
Robs my good name, the treasure of my life?

32. The first great Roman satirist, whom Horace elsewhere describes as having learned his art from the Old Comedy.
33. Venusia was the birthplace of Horace.

O *Jupiter*, let it with rust be eaten,
Before it touch, or insolently threaten
The life of any with the least disease;
So much I love, and woo a general peace.
But, he that wrongs me (better, I proclaim,
He never had assay'd to touch my fame.)
For he shall weep, and walk with every tongue
Throughout the city, infamously sung.
Servius, the *Prætor*, threats the laws, and urn,
If any at his deeds repine or spurn;
The witch, *Canidia*, that *Albucius* got,
Denounceth witchcraft, where she loveth not:
Thurius, the judge, doth thunder worlds of ill,
To such, as strive with his judical will;
"All men affright their foes in what they may,
"Nature commands it, and men must obey."
Observe with me; "The wolf his tooth doth use:
"The bull his horn. And, who doth this infuse,
"But nature?" There's luxurious *Scaeva; * Trust
His long-liv'd mother with him; His so just
And scrupulous right hand no mischief will;
No more, than with his heel a wolf will kill,
Or Ox with jaw: Marry, let him alone
With temper'd poison to remove the crone.
    But, briefly, if to age I destin'd be,
Or that quick death's black wings environ me;
If rich, or poor; at *Rome*; or fate command
I shall be banish'd to some other land;
What hue soever, my whole state shall bear,
I will write satires still, in spite of fear.

TREB. *Horace;* I fear, thou draw'st no lasting breath:
And that some great man's friend will be thy death.

HORA. What? when the man that first did *satirize*,
Durst pull the skin over the ears of vice;
And make, who stood in outward fashion clear,
Give place, as foul within; shall I forbear?
Did *Laelius*,[34] or the man, so great with fame,

---

34. Neither the noble consul Laelius nor his noble friend the younger Scipio objected when the satirist Lucilius attacked such prominent and powerful citizens as Metellus and Lupus. To the contrary, Laelius and Scipio esteemed Lucilius.

That from sack'd *Carthage* fetch'd his worthy name,
Storm, that *Lucilius* did *Metellus* pierce?
Or bury *Lupus* quick, in famous verse?
Rulers, and subjects, by whole tribes he check'd;
But virtue, and her friends did still protect:
And when from sight, or from the judgement seat,
The virtuous *Scipio*, and wise *Laelius* met,
Embrac'd, with him in all light sports, they shar'd;
Till, their most frugal suppers were prepar'd.
What e're I am, though both for wealth, and wit,
Beneath *Lucilius*, I am pleas'd to sit;
Yet, envy (spite of her empoisoned breast)
Shall say, I liv'd in grace here, with the best;
And, seeking in weak trash to make her wound,
Shall find me solid, and her teeth unsound:
'Less, learn'd *Trebatius'* censure disagree.

TREB. No, *Horace*, I of force must yield to thee;
Only, take heed, as being advis'd by me,
Lest thou incur some danger: Better pause,
Than rue thy ignorance of the sacred laws;
There's justice, and great action may be su'd
'Gainst such, as wrong men's fames with verses lewd.

HORA. Ye, with lewd verses; such as libels be,
And aim'd at persons of good quality.
I reverence and adore that just decree:
But if they shall be sharp, yet modest rimes
That spare men's persons, and but tax their crimes,
Such, shall in open court, find current pass;
Were *Caesar* judge, and with the maker's grace.

TREB. Nay, I'll add more; if thou thy self being clear,
Shalt tax in person a man, fit to bear
Shame, and reproach; his suit shall quickly be
Dissolv'd in laughter, and thou thence sit free.

REALISM AND SATIRE

When the poetasters, Demetrius and Crispinus, join Tucca in attacking the realism and contemporaneity of Horace's satire, Jonson means to ridicule rival playwrights of the public theaters such as Dekker and Marston by having them attack his comical satire where it is strongest. (Ibid., *IV.iii.104–123.)*

DEME. Alas, sir, *Horace*! he is a mere sponge; nothing but humours, and observation; he goes up and down sucking from every society, and when he comes home, squeezes himself dry again. I know him, I.

TUCC. Thou sayest true, my poor *poetical Fury*, he will pen all he knows. A sharp thorny-tooth'd *satyrical* rascal, fly him; he carries hay in his horn: he will sooner lose his best friend, than his least jest. What he once drops upon paper, against a man, lives eternally to upbraid him in the mouth of every slave tankard bearer, or waterman; not a bawd, or a boy that comes from the bakehouse, but shall point at him: 'tis all dog, and scorpion; he carries poison in his teeth, and a sting in his tail. Fough, body of *Jove*! I'll have the slave whipp'd one of these days for his *satires*, and his humours, by one cashier'd clerk, or another.

CRIS. We'll undertake him, Captain.

DEME. I, and tickle him i' faith, for his arrogance, and his impudence, in commending his own things; and for his translating: I can trace him i' faith. O, he is the most open fellow, living; I had as lief as a new suit, I were at it.

SATIRE AND LIBEL—THE DISTINCTION

*Virgil praises Caesar, who has just punished Lupus and Demetrius for maliciously interpreting an emblem created by Horace. (*Ibid.,*V.iii.135–144.)*

VIRG.   *Caesar* hath done like *Caesar*. Fair, and just
            Is his award, against these brainless creatures.
            'Tis not the wholesome sharp morality,
            Or modest anger of a *satiric* spirit,
            That hurts, or wounds the body of a state;
            But the sinister application
            Of the malicious, ignorant, and base
            Interpreter: who will distort, and strain
            The general scope and purpose of an author,
            To his particular, and private spleen.

SATIRE OF PERSONS AND SATIRE OF VICE
THE USES OF HISTORICAL MODELS AND AUTHORIAL RESPONSIBILITY

*In this apologia, Jonson attenuates a little the dangerous Old Comedy theory of harsh, personal satire—but not quite to the point of embracing the New Comedy theory of impersonal satire. (*Ibid., *Apologetical Dialogue appended to the play.)*

TO THE READER

If, by looking on what is past, thou hast deserv'd that name, I am willing thou should'st yet know more, by that which follows; an *apologetical Dialogue*: which was only once spoken upon the stage, and all the answer I ever gave, to sundry impotent libels then cast out (and some yet remaining) against me, and this Play. Wherein I take no pleasure to revive the times, but that Posterity may make a difference, between their manners that provok'd me then, and mine that neglected them ever. For, in these strifes, and on such persons, were as wretched to affect a victory, as it is unhappy to be committed with them. [It is not the gray hairs but the manners of age which must be praised.]35

The Persons

NASUTUS, POLYPOSUS, AUTHOR

I pray you let's go see him, how he looks
After these libels.   POLY.   O, vex'd vex'd, I warrant you.
NAS.   Do you think so? I should be sorry for him,
    If I found that.   POLY.   O, they are such bitter things,
    He cannot choose.   NAS.   But, is he guilty of 'hem?
POL.   Fuh! that's no matter.   NAS.   No?   POL.   No.
    Here's his lodging;
    We'll steal upon him: or, let's listen, stay.
    He has a humour oft to talk t' himself.
NAS.   They are your manners lead me, not mine own.
AUT.   The *Fates* have not spun him the coarsest thread
    That (free from knots of perturbation)
    Doth yet so live, although but to himself,
    As he can safely scorn the tongues of slaves;
    And neglect *Fortune*, more than she can him.
    It is the happiest thing, this not to be
    Within the reach of malice; it provides
    A man so well, to laugh off injuries:
    And never sends him farther for his vengeance
    Than the vex'd bosom of his enemy.
    Aye, now, but think, how poor their spite sets off.
    Who, after all their waste of sulphurous terms,
    And burst-out thunder of their charged mouths,
    Have nothing left, but the unsav'ry smoke
    Of their black vomit, to upbraid themselves:

35. *Non annorum canicies est laudanda, sed morum.*

    Whilst I, at whom they shot, sit here shot-free,
    And as unhurt of envy, as unhit.
POL.   I, but the Multitude, they think not so, sir,
    They think you hit, and hurt: and dare give out
    Your silence argues it, in not rejoining
    To this, or that late libel?   AUT.   'Las, good rout!
    I can afford them leave, to err so still:
    And, like the barking students of Bears' College,
    To swallow up the garbage of the time
    With greedy gullets, whilst my self sit by,
    Pleas'd, and yet tortur'd, with their beastly feeding.
    'Tis a sweet madness runs along with them,
    To think, all that are aim'd at, still are struck:
    Then, where the shaft still lights, make that the mark,
    And so, each fear, or fever-shaken fool
    May challenge *Teucer's* hand[36] in archery.
    Good troth, if I knew any man so vile,
    To act the crimes, these whippers reprehend,
    Or what their servile apes gesticulate,
    I should not then much muse, their shreds were lik'd;
    Since ill men have a lust t' hear others sins,
    And good men have a zeal to hear sin sham'd.
    But when it is all excrement, they vent,
    Base filth, and offal: or thefts, notable
    As *Ocean* piracies, or highway stands:
    And not a crime there tax'd, but is their own,
    Or what their own foul thoughts suggested to them,
    And, that in all their heat of taxing others,
    Not one of them, but lives himself (if known)
    [Worse than a sodomite writing satires].[37]
    What should I say, more? then turn stone with wonder!
NAS.   I never saw this play bred all this tumult.
    What was there in it could so deeply offend?
    And stir so many hornets?   AUT.   Shall I tell you?
NAS.   Yes, and ingenuously.   AUT.   Then, by the hope,
    Which I prefer unto all other objects,
    I can profess, I never writ [a][38] piece

36. Teucer was the greatest archer in the Trojan War.
37. *Improbior satyram scribente cinaedo.* (Juvenal *Satires* IV.106.)
38. Folio reads "*that.*"

More innocent, or empty of offence.
Some salt it had, but neither tooth, nor gall,
Nor was there in it any circumstance,
Which, in the setting down, I could suspect
Might be perverted by an enemy's tongue.
Only, it had the fault to be call'd mine.
That was the crime.   POL.   No? why, they say you tax'd
The Law, and Lawyers; Captains; and the Players
By their particular names.   AUT.   It is not so.
I us'd no name. My Books have still been taught
To spare the persons, and to speak the vices.
These are mere slanders, and enforc'd by such
As have no safer ways to men's disgraces,
But their own lies, and loss of honesty.
Fellows of practis'd, and most laxative tongues,
Whose empty and eager bellies, i' the year,
Compell their brains to many desp'rate shifts,
(I spare to name 'hem: for, their wretchedness,
Fury it self would pardon.) These, or such,
Whether of malice, or of ignorance,
Or itch, t'have me their adversary (I know not)
Or all these mix'd; but sure I am, three years,
They did provoke me with their petulant styles
On every stage: And I at last, unwilling,
But weary, I confess, of so much trouble,
Thought, I would try, if shame could win upon 'hem.
And therefore chose *Augustus Caesar's* times,
When wit, and arts were at their height in *Rome*,
To show that *Virgil, Horace,* and the rest
Of those great master-spirits did not want
Detractors, then, or practicers against them:
And by this line (although no *parallel*)
I hop'd at last they would sit down, and blush.
But nothing could I find more contrary.
And though the impudence of flies be great,
Yet this hath so provok'd the angry wasps,
Or as you said, of the next nest, the hornets;
That they fly buzzing, mad, about my nostrils:
And like so many screaming grasshoppers,
Held by the wings, fill every ear with noise.

And what? those former calumnies you mention'd.
First, of the Law. Indeed, I brought in *Ovid*,
Chid by his angry father, for neglecting
The study of the laws, for poetry:
And I am warranted by his own words.
[Often, Father said, "Why do you pursue a useless study?
   Maeonides himself left no wealth."][39]
And in far harsher terms elsewhere, as these:
[I do not learn the ill-written laws, nor have I
   Prostituted my voice before the carping bar].[40]
But how this should relate, unto our laws,
Or their just ministers, with least abuse,
I reverence both too much, to understand!
   Then, for the Captain; I will only speak
An *Epigram* I here have made: It is
Unto true Soldiers. That's the *lemma*. Mark it.
   Strength of my Country, whilst I bring to view
     Such as are miscall'd Captains, and wrong you,
   And your high names; I do desire, that thence,
     Be nor put on you, nor you take offence:[41]
   I swear by your true friend, my Muse, I love
     Your great profession, which I once did prove;
   And did not shame it with my actions, then,
     No more then I dare, now, do with my pen.
   He that not trusts me, having vow'd thus much,
     But's angry for the Captains, still: is such.
Now, for the Players, it is true, I tax'd 'hem,
And yet, but some; and those so sparingly,
As all the rest might have sat still, unquestion'd,
Had they but had the wit, or conscience,
To think well of themselves. But, impotent they
Thought each man's vice belong'd to their whole tribe:
And much good do't 'hem. What th' have done 'gainst me,
I am now mov'd with. If it gave 'hem meat,
Or got 'hem clothes. 'Tis well. That was their end.
Only amongst them, I am sorry for

39. *Saepe pater dixit, studium quid inutile tentas? | Maeonides nullas ipse reliquit opes.*
40. *Non me verbosas leges ediscere, non me | Ingrato voces prostituisse foro.*
41. Jonson hopes that neither the audience nor true military officers will misunderstand him: he has attacked would-be captains merely.

Some better natures, by the rest so drawn,
To run in that vile line.   POL. And is this all?
Will you not answer then the libels?   AUT. No.
POL. Nor the untrussers?   AUT. Neither.   POL. Y'are undone then.
AUT. With whom?   POL. The world.   AU. The bawd!
POL. It will be taken
To be stupidity, or tameness in you.
AUT. But, they that have incens'd me, can in soul
Acquit me of that guilt. They know, I dare
To spurn, or baffle 'hem; or squirt their eyes
With ink, or urine: or I could do worse,
Arm'd with *Archilochus'*[42] fury, write *Iambics*,
Should make the desperate lashers hang themselves,
Rime 'hem to death, as they do *Irish* rats[43]
In drumming tunes. Or, living, I could stamp
Their foreheads with those deep, and public brands,
That the whole company of *Barber-Surgeons*
Should not take off, with all their art, and plasters.
And these my prints should last, still to be read
In their pale fronts: when, what they write 'gainst me,
Shall like a figure, drawn in water, fleet,
And the poor wretched papers be employ'd
To cloth *tobacco*, or some cheaper drug.
This I could do, and make them infamous.
But, to what end? when their own deeds have mark'd 'hem,
And, that I know, within his guilty breast
Each slanderer bears a whip, that shall torment him,
Worse, than a million of these temporal plagues:
Which to pursue, were but a feminine humour,
And, far beneath the dignity of a man.
NAS. 'Tis true: for to revenge their injuries,
Were to confess you felt 'hem. Let 'hem go,
And use the treasure of the fool, their tongues,
Who makes his gain, by speaking worst, of best.
POL. O, but they lay particular imputations—
AUT. As what?   PO. That all your writing, is mere railing.

42. Archilochus lampooned Lycambes so bitterly in iambic verses that Lycambes hanged himself.

43. A popular analogy. It was said that in Ireland they killed rats with doggerel incantations.

AUT. Ha! If all the salt in the old *comedy*
    Should be so censur'd, or the sharper wit
    Of the bold *satire*, termed scolding rage,
    What age could then compare with those, for buffoons?
    What should be said of *Aristophanes*?
    Persius? or *Juvenal*? whose names we now
    So glorify in schools, at least pretend it.
    Ha' they no other?   POL. Yes: they say you are slow,
    And scarce bring forth a play a year.   AUT. 'Tis true.
    I would, they could not say that I did that,
    There's all the joy that I take i' their trade,
    Unless such Scribes as they might be proscrib'd
    Th' abused theaters. They would think it strange, now,
    A man should take but coltsfoot,[44] for one day,
    And, between whiles, spit out a better *poem*
    Then e're the master of art, or giver of wit,
    Their belly made. Yet, this is possible,
    If a free mind had but the patience,
    To think so much, together, and so vile.[45]
    But, that these base, and beggarly conceits
    Should carry it, by the multitude of voices,
    Against the most abstracted work, oppos'd
    To the stuff'd nostrils of the drunken rout!
    O, this would make a learn'd, and liberal soul,
    To rive his stained quill, up to the back,
    And damn his long-watch'd labours to the fire;
    Things, that were born, when none but the still night,
    And his dumb candle saw his pinching throes:
    Were not his own free merit a more crown
    Unto his travails, than their reeling claps.
    This 'tis, that strikes me silent, seals my lips,
    And apts me, rather to sleep out my times,
    Than I would waste it in contemned strifes,
    With these vile *Ibides*,[46] these unclean birds,

44. Coltsfoot leaves were smoked to relieve asthma. Jonson's scurrilous suggestion is that he can "cough up" better stuff by smoking coltsfoot than the poetasters can "make" in their bowels.

45. I.e., the result would be better (see preceding footnote), but it would still be vile.

46. Ibises. Pliny is Jonson's authority for saying that ibises use their bills for enemas.

That make their mouths their clysters, and still purge
From their hot entrails. But, I leave the monsters
To their own fate. And, since the *Comic Muse*
Hath prov'd so ominous to me, I will try
If *Tragedy* have a more kind aspect.
Her favours in my next I will pursue,
Where, If I prove the pleasure but of one,
So he judicious be; He shall b' alone
A Theater unto me: Once, I'll say,[47]
To strike the ear of time, in those fresh strains,
As shall, beside the cunning of their ground,
Give cause to some of wonder, some despair,
And unto more, despair, to imitate their sound.
I, that spend half my nights, and all my days,
Here in a cell, to get a dark, pale face,
To come forth worth the ivy, or the bays,
And in this age can hope no other grace—
Leave me. There's something come into my thought,
That must, and shall be sung, high, and aloof,
Safe from the wolf's black jaw, and the dull ass's hoof.

NAS. I reverence these raptures, and obey 'hem.

47. Essay.

IV
COMEDY

In this prefatory poem from Thomas Wright's The Passions of the Mind in General *(fourth edition, 1621; first published 1602), Jonson praises what may well be the "psychological" source book for his theory of humour characterization in comedy.*

To the Author
In Picture, they which truly understand,
Require (besides the likeness of the thing)
Light, Posture, Height'ning, Shadow, Coloring,
All which are parts commend the cunning hand;
And all your Book (when it is thoroughly scann'd)
Will well confess; presenting, limiting,
Each subt'lest Passion, with her source, and spring,
So bold, as shows, your Art you can command.
But now, your Work is done, if they that view
The several figures, languish in suspense,
To judge which Passion's false, and which is true,
Between the doubtful sway of Reason', and sense;
'Tis not your fault, if they shall sense prefer,
Being told there, Reason cannot, Sense may err.

The Discipline of Poetry and Comedy

The dedication from the 1616 folio of Volpone, or The Fox. *In dedicating his first great comedy to Oxford and Cambridge, both of which had granted Jonson honorary Master of Arts degrees, Jonson takes the opportunity to denounce contemporary abuses in comedy and to announce his program for reform —to restore the art to its classical purity and greatness.*

TO THE * * * TWO FAMOUS UNIVERSITIES * * *

Never (most equal *sisters*) had any man a wit so presently excellent, as that it could raise itself; but there must come both matter, occasion, commenders, and favourers to it: If this be true, and that the fortune of all writers doth daily prove it, it behoves the careful to provide, well, toward these accidents; and, having acquir'd them, to preserve that part of reputation most tenderly, wherein the benefit of a friend is also defended. Hence is it, that I now render myself grateful, and am studious to justify the bounty of your act: to which, though your mere authority were satisfying, yet, it being an age, wherein *Poetry*, and the Professors of it hear so ill, on all sides, there will a reason be look'd for in the subject. It is certain, nor can it with any forehead be oppos'd, that the too-much licence of *Poetasters*, in this time, hath much deform'd their Mistress; that, every day, their manifold, and manifest ignorance, doth stick unnatural reproaches upon her: But for their petulancy, it were an act of the greatest injustice, either to let the learned suffer; or so divine a skill (which indeed should not be attempted with unclean hands) to fall, under the least contempt. For, if men will impartially, and not asquint, look toward the offices, and function of a Poet, they will easily conclude to themselves, the impossibility of any man's being the good Poet, without first being a good man. He that is said to be able to inform young men to all good disciplines, inflame grown men to all great virtues, keep old men in their best and supreme state, or as they decline to child-hood, recover them to their first strength; that comes forth the interpreter, and arbiter of nature, a teacher of things divine, no less than human, a master in manners; and can alone (or with a few) effect the business of mankind: this, I take him, is no subject for pride, and ignorance to exercise their railing rhetoric upon. But, it will here be hastily answer'd, that the writers of these days are other things; that, not only their manners, but their natures are inverted; and nothing remaining with them of the dignity of Poet, but the abused name, which every Scribe usurps: that now, especially in *dramatic*, or (as they term it) stage-*poetry*, nothing but ribaldry, profana-tion, blasphemy, all licence of offence to god, and man, is practis'd. I dare not deny a great part of this (and am sorry, I dare not) because in some men's abortive features (and would they had never boasted the light) it is over-true: But, that all are embark'd in this bold adventure for hell, is a most uncharitable thought, and, utter'd, a more malicious slander. For my particular, I can (and from a most clear conscience) affirm, that I have ever trembled to think toward the least prophaneness; have loathed the use of such foul, and unwash'd bawdr'y, as is now made the food of the *scene*. And, howsoever I cannot escape, from some, the imputation of sharpness, but that they will say I have taken a pride, or lust, to be bitter, and not my youngest infant but hath come into the world with all his teeth; I would ask of these supercilious politics, what nation, society, or general order, or state I have provok'd? what public person? whether I have not (in all these) preserv'd their dignity, as mine own person, safe? My works are read, allow'd, (I speak of those that are entirely mine) look into them: what broad reproofs have I us'd? Where have I been particular? Where personal? except to a mimic, cheater, bawd, or buffoon, creatures (for their insolen-

cies) worthy to be tax'd? Yet, to which of these so pointingly, as he might
not, either ingenuously have confes'd or wisely dissembled his disease? But
it is not rumour can make man guilty, much less entitle me, to other men's
crimes. I know, that nothing can be so innocently writ, or carried, but may
be made obnoxious to construction; marry, whil'st I bear mine innocence
about me, I fear it not. Application, is now, grown a trade with many; and
there are, that profess to have a key for the deciphering of every thing: but
let wise and noble persons take heed how they be too credulous, or give
leave to these invading interpreters, to be over-familiar with their fames,
who cunningly, and often, utter their own virulent malice, under other
men's simplest meanings. As for those, that will (by faults which charity
hath rak'd up, or common honesty conceal'd) make themselves a name
with the multitude, or (to draw their rude, and beastly claps) care not whose
living faces they entrench, with their petulant styles; may they do it,
without a rival, for me: I choose rather to live grav'd in obscurity, than
share with them, in so preposterous a fame. Nor can I blame the wishes of
those severe, and wiser patriots, who providing the hurts these licentious
spirits may do in a state, desire rather to see fools, and devils, and those
antique relics of barbarism retriev'd,[1] with all other ridiculous, and ex-
ploded follies: than behold the wounds of private men, of princes, and
nations. For, as *Horace* makes *Trebatius* speak, among these
   —[Each is afraid, though untouched, and hates you.][2]
And men may justly impute such rages, if continu'd, to the writer, as his
sports. The increase of which lust in liberty, together with the present trade
of the stage, in all their misc'line *enterludes*,[3] what learned or liberal soul doth
not already abhor? where nothing but the filth of the time is utter'd, and
that with such impropriety of phrase, such plenty of *solecisms*, such dearth
of sense, so bold *prolepses*,[4] so racked *metaphors*, with brothelry, able to violate
the ear of a pagan, and blasphemy, to turn the blood of a Christian to
water. I cannot but be serious in a cause of this nature, wherein my fame,
and the reputation of divers honest, and learned are the question; when a
Name,[5] so full of authority, antiquity, and all great mark, is (through their

1. An allusion to the preference of some for the cruder but less pointed drama
of the 1580's and 1590's. Jonson satirizes this preference in the induction to
Bartholomew Fair, in the choruses of *The Staple of News*, and elsewhere.
2. *Sibi quisque timet, quanquam est intactus, & odit.* (*Satires* II.I.23.)
3. From the Latin *ludi miscelli*: mere variety shows.
4. Anachronisms.
5. The name of Poetry.

insolence) become the lowest scorn of the age: and those men subject to the petulancy of every vernaculous Orator, that were wont to be the care of Kings, and happiest Monarchs. This it is, that hath not only 'rapp'd me to present indignation, but made me studious, heretofore; and, by all my actions, to stand off, from them: which may most appear in this my latest work (which you, most learned Arbitresses, have seen, judg'd, and to my crown, approv'd) wherein I have labour'd, for their instruction, and amendment, to reduce, not only the ancient forms, but manners of the *scene*, the easiness, the propriety, the innocence, and last the doctrine, which is the principal end of *poesy*, to inform men, in the best reason of living. And though my *catastrophe* may, in the strict rigour of *comic* law, meet with censure, as turning back to my promise; I desire the learned, and charitable critic to have so much faith in me, to think it was done of industry: For, with what ease I could have varied it, nearer his scale (but that I fear to boast my own faculty) I could here insert. But my special aim being to put the snaffle in their mouths, that cry out, we never punish vice in our *enterludes*, &c. I took the more liberty; though not without some lines of example, drawn even in the ancients themselves, the goings out of whose *comedies* are not always joyful, but oft-times, the bawds, the servants, the rivals, yes, and the masters are mulcted: and fitly, it being the office of a *comic Poet*, to imitate justice, and instruct to life, as well as purity of language, or stir up gentle affections. To which, I shall take the occasion elsewhere to speak. For the present (most reverenced *Sisters*) as I have car'd to be thankful for your affections past, and here made the understanding acquainted with some ground of your favours; let me not despair their continuance, to the maturing of some worthier fruits: wherein, if my *Muses* be true to me, I shall raise the despis'd head of *poetry* again, and stripping her out of those rotten and base rags, wherewith the Times have adulterated her form, restore her to her primitive habit, feature, and majesty, and render her worthy to be embraced, and kiss'd, of all the great and master-*spirits* of our world. As for the vile, and slothful, who never affected an act, worthy of celebration, or are so inward with their own vicious natures, as they worthily fear her; and think it a high point of policy, to keep her in contempt with the declamatory, and windy injectives: she shall out of just rage incite her servants (who are *genus irritabile*) to spout ink in their faces, that shall eat, farther than their marrow, into their fames; and not *Cinnamus* the barber,[6] with his art, shall be able to take out the brands, but they shall live, and be read, till the wretches die, as things worst deserving of themselves in chief, and then of all mankind.

6. From Martial *Epigrams* VI.lxiv.

The Laws of Comedy Restored: "Volpone"

Jonson, having turned from "comical satire" to comedy, offers Volpone *as
an example of comedy such as it has been defined by the best classical critics;
he warns his audience not to expect the usual contemporary indecorums. (*Ibid.,
Prologue.)

PROLOGUE

Now, luck yet send us, and a little wit
    Will serve, to make our play hit;
(According to the palates of the season)
    Here is rhyme, not empty of reason:
This we were bid to credit, from our *Poet*,
    Whose true scope, if you would know it,
In all his *poems*, still, hath been this measure,
    To mix profit, with your pleasure;
And not as some (whose throats their envy failing)
    Cry hoarsely, all he writes, is railing:
And, when his plays come forth, think they can flout them,
    With saying, he was a year about them.
To these there needs no lie, but this his creature,
    Which was, two months since, no feature;
And, though he dares give them five lives to mend it,
    'Tis known, five weeks fully penn'd it:
From his own hand, without a co-adjutor,
    Novice, journey-man, or tutor.
Yet, thus much I can give you, as a token
    Of his play's worth, no eggs are broken;
Nor quaking custards with fierce teeth affrighted,[7]
    Wherewith your rout are so delighted;
Nor hales he in a gull, old ends reciting,
    To stop gaps in his loose writing;
With such a deal of monstrous, and forc'd action:
    As might make *Bet'lem* a faction:
Nor made he'his play, for jests, stolen from each table,
    But makes jests, to fit his fable.
And, so presents quick *comedy*, refined,

7. Jonson promises that his play will not rely on such hackneyed low-comedy
conventions as hauling in a frightened fool with chattering teeth (?) or a clown
who can do nothing but parrot bits of poetry stolen from others.

As best Critics have designed,
The laws of time, place, persons he observeth,
From no needful rule he swerveth.
All gall, and copperas,[8] from his ink, he draineth,
Only, a little salt remaineth;
Wherewith, he'll rub your cheeks, till (red with laughter)
They shall look fresh, a week after.

THE UNIVERSAL, THE PARTICULAR, AND THE APPLICATION OF MODELS

From the 1616 folio of The Alchemist, *the prologue. Comedy attacks universal vices, not particular men, in order to cure them, not merely to rail at them. But as in classical comedy, so here: the dramatist finds his universal types by observing contemporary society. The goal is "realism," not "journalism."*

PROLOGUE

Fortune, that favors fools, these two short hours
  We wish away; both for your sakes, and ours,
Judging Spectators: and desire in place,
  To th'Author justice, to our selves but grace.
Our *Scene* is *London,* 'cause we would make known,
  No country's mirth is better than our own.
No clime breeds better matter, for your whore,
  Bawd, squire, imposter, many persons more,
Whose manners, now call'd humours, feed the stage:
  And which have still been subject, for the rage
Or spleen of *comic* writers. Though this pen
  Did never aim to grieve, but better men;
Howe'er the age, he lives in, doth endure
  The vices that she breeds, above their cure.[9]
But, when the wholesome remedies are sweet,
  And, in their working, gain, and profit meet,
He hopes to find no spirit so much diseas'd,
  But will, with such fair correctives, be pleas'd.
For here, he doth not fear, who can apply.
  If there be any, that will sit so nigh

8. Copperas or green vitriol, used in making ink.
9. The syntax is confusing: His is a subject that has been treated with rage and spleen, but ("though") he means to better men, not simply to vent his spleen— in spite of the fact that ("Howe'er") the age does not want to be made better.

Unto the stream, to look what it doth run,
They shall find things, they'ld think, or wish, were done;
They are so natural follies, but so shown,
As even the doers may see, and yet not own.

The Laws of Stagecraft: Comedy as a Realistic Moral Mirror

The prologue from the 1616 folio of Every Man in His Humour. *Jonson distinguishes between true comedy, which is realistic in subject and in treatment, and what he conceives to be the mindless grotesqueries of contemporary "romanticists"— including perhaps Shakespeare in his history plays.*

PROLOGUE

Though need make many *Poets*, and some such
As art, and nature have not bettered much;
Yet ours, for want, hath not so lov'd the stage,
As he dare serve th'ill customs of the age:
Or purchase your delight at such a rate,
As, for it, he himself must justly hate.
To make a child, now swaddled, to proceed
Man, and then shoot up, in one beard, and weed,
Past three score years: or, with three rusty swords,
And help of some few foot-and-half-foot words,
Fight over *York*, and *Lancaster's* long jars:
And in the tiring-house bring wounds, to scars.
He rather prays, you will be pleas'd to see
One such, today, as other plays should be.
Where neither *Chorus* wafts you o'er the seas;
Nor creaking throne comes down, the boys to please;
Nor nimble squib is seen, to make afear'd
The gentlewomen; nor roll'd bullet heard
To say, it thunders; nor tempestuous drum
Rumbles, to tell you when the storm doth come;
But deeds, and language, such as men do use:
And persons, such as *Comedy* would choose,
When she would show an Image of the times,
And sport with human follies, not with crimes.
Except, we make them such by loving still
Our popular errors, when we know th'are ill.

I mean such errors, as you'll all confess
By laughing at them, they deserve no less:
Which when you heartily do, there's hope left, then,
You, that have so grac'd monsters, may like men.

THE COMIC FICTION AS ARGUMENTUM AND ITS RELATION
TO THE FUNCTION OF COMEDY

From the 1616 folio of Epĭcoene, or The Silent Woman, *the second prologue. Renaissance critics sometimes distinguish among three different types of dramatic fiction: the* historia, *a plot which is both true-seeming and true— the traditional mode of tragic fictions; the* argumentum, *a plot which is true-seeming but not true—the mode of fiction which Jonson always favors for comedy; and the* fabula, *which is neither true-seeming nor true. Jonson's conception of the comical satire fiction sometimes suggested the* historia. *Here, he is worried that the audience will mistake his comic* argumentum *for satirical* historia—*a pervasive worry in Jonson's discussions of realistic comedy. He has only contempt for that comedy whose central fiction is the* fabula; *much of his contempt for contemporary comedy—including, it would seem, some of Shakespeare's—stems from Jonson's conviction that comedy must deal with deeds and language such as men do use: the* argumentum.

ANOTHER[10]

The ends of all, who for the *Scene* do write,
    Are, or should be, to profit, and delight.
And still 't hath been the praise of all best times,
    So persons were not touch'd to tax the crimes.
Then, in this play, which we present tonight,
    And make the object of your ear, and sight,
On forfeit of your selves, think nothing true:
    Lest so you make the maker to judge you.
For he knows, *Poet* never credit gain'd
    By writing truths, but things (like truths) well feign'd.
If any, yet, will (with particular slight
    Of application) wrest what he doth write;
And that he meant or him, or her, will say:
    They make a libel, which he made a play.

10. Jonson's note: "Occasioned by some persons' impertinent exception."

On Obscenity in Comedy

From the 1616 folio, Epigram **XLIX**.

to play-wright

Play-wright me reads, and still my verses damns,
 He says, I want the tongue of *Epigrams*;
I have no salt: no bawdry he doth mean.
 For witty, in his language, is obscene.
Play-write, I loath to have thy manners known
 In my chaste book: profess them in thine own.

Laughter and Shame in Comedy

From the 1616 folio of The Devil Is an Ass, *V.viii.169–174. As the play concludes, Manly comments on life—and also on the lenient comic* catastrophe. *The principle expressed is more typical than that in Jonson's better-known defense of the harsh comic* catastrophe *in* Volpone.

  It is not manly to take joy, or pride
  In human errors (we do all ill things,
  They do 'hem worst that love 'hem, and dwell there,
  Till the plague comes). The few that have the seeds
  Of goodness left, will sooner make their way
  To a true life, by shame, than punishment.

Comedy: The Argumentum

The prologue from the 1631 folio of The Staple of News.

the prologue for the court

A Work not smelling of the Lamp, tonight,
 But fitted for your *Majesty's* disport,
 And writ to the *Meridian* of your *Court*,
We bring; and hope it may produce delight:
The rather, being offered, as a *Rite*,
 To *Scholars*, that can judge, and fair report
 The sense they hear, above the vulgar sort
Of Nutcrackers, that only come for sight.
Wherein, although our *Title*, Sir, be *News*,

We yet adventure, here, to tell you none;
But show you common follies, and so known,
That though they are not truths, th'innocent *Muse*
Hath made so like, as Phant'sy could them state,
Or *Poetry*, without scandal, imitate.

COMIC STRUCTURE: THE EPITASIS AND THE CATASTROPHE

From the 1631 octavo of The New Inn, *the Argument. In a prefatory plot summary, Jonson calls attention in passing to certain aspects of the five-act structure.*

THE ARGUMENT

* * * *Here begins, at the* third Act, *the* Epitasis, *or business of the* Play. * * *
The fifth, and last *Act* is the *Catastrophe*, or knitting up of all, * * *

A GOOD PLAY

From the 1640 folio of The Magnetic Lady, or Humours Reconciled, *the induction.*

THE INDUCTION; OR, CHORUS
Two Gentlemen entering upon the Stage,
MR. PROBEE and MR. DAMPLAY.
A BOY of the house,
meets them.

BOY.   What do you lack, Gentlemen? what is't you lack? any fine Fancies, Figures, Humours, Characters, Ideas, Definitions of Lords, and Ladies? Waiting-women, Parasites, Knights, Captains, Courtiers, Lawyers? what do you lack?

PRO.   A pretty prompt Boy for the Poetic Shop.

DAM.   And a bold! where's one o' your Masters, Sirrah, the Poet?

BOY.   Which of 'hem? Sir, we have divers that drive that trade, now: Poets, Poet'accios, Poetasters, Poetito's—

DAM.   And all Haberdashers of small wit, I presume: we would speak with the Poet o' the day, *Boy.*

BOY.   Sir, he is not here. But, I have the dominion of the Shop, for this time, under him, and can show you all the variety the Stage will afford for the present.

PRO.   Therein you will express your own good parts, *Boy*.

DAM.   And tire us two, to you, for the gentle office.

PRO.   We are a pair of public persons (this Gentleman, and my self) that are sent, thus coupled unto you, upon state-business.

BOY.   It concerns but the state of the Stage, I hope!

DAM.   O, you shall know that by degrees, *Boy*. No man leaps into a business of state, without fording first the state of the business.

PRO.   We are sent unto you, indeed, from the people.

BOY.   The people! which side of the people?

DAM.   The Venison side,[11] if you know it, *Boy*.

BOY.   That's the left side. I had rather they had been the right.

PRO.   So they are. Not the *Faeces*, or grounds of your people, that sit in the oblique caves and wedges of your house, your sinful six-penny Mechanics—

DAM.   But the better, and braver sort of your people! Plush and Velvet-outsides! that stick your house round like so many eminences—

BOY.   Of clothes, not understandings? They are at pawn. Well, I take these as a part of your people though; what bring you to me from these people?

DAM.   You have heard, *Boy*, the ancient Poets had it in their purpose, still to please this people.

PRO.   Aye their chief aim was—

DAM.   [To please the people] (if he understands so much.)

BOY.   [Is the art of the stage.][12] I understand that, sin' I learn'd *Terence*, i' the third form at *Westminster*: go on Sir.

PRO.   Now, these people have employed us to you, in all their names, to intreat an excellent Play from you.

DAM.   For they have had very mean ones, from this shop of late, the Stage as you call it.

BOY.   Troth, Gentlemen, I have no wares, which I dare thrust upon the people with praise. But this, such as it is, I will venture with your people, your gay gallant people: so as you, again, will undertake for them, that they shall know a good *Play* when they hear it; and will have the conscience, and ingenuity beside, to confess it.

PRO.   We'll pass our words for that: you shall have a brace of us to engage ourselves.

BOY.   You'll tender your names, *Gentlemen*, to our book then?

DAM.   Yes, here's Mr. *Probee*; A man of most powerful speech, and parts to persuade.

PRO.   And Mr. *Damplay*, will make good all he undertakes.

11. A pun on "heart" and "hart."
12. *Populo ut placerent | quas fecissent fabulas.* (Terence, *Andria*, Prologue.)

BOY.   Good Mr. *Probee*, and Mr. *Damplay*! I like your securities: whence do you write your selves?

PRO.   Of *London*, Gentlemen: but Knights' brothers, and Knights' friends, I assure you.

DAM.   And Knights' fellows too. Every Poet writes Squire now.

BOY.   You are good names! very good men, both of you! I accept you.

DAM.   And what is the Title of your *Play*, here? *The Magnetic Lady*?

BOY.   Yes, Sir, an attractive title the Author has given it.

PRO.   *A Magnet*, I warrant you.

DAM.   O, no, from *Magnus, Magna, Magnum*.[13]

BOY.   This Gentleman hath found the true magnitude—

DAM.   Of his portal, or entry to the work, according to *Vitruvius*.

BOY.   Sir, all your Work is done without a Portal—or *Vitruvius. In For*,[14] as a true Comedy should be. And what is concealed within, is brought out, and made present by report.

DAM.   We see not that always observ'd, by your Authors of these times: or scarce any other.

BOY.   Where it is not at all known, how should it be observ'd? The most of those your people call *Authors*, never dreamt of any *Decorum*, or what was proper in the *Scene*; but grope at it, i' the dark, and feel, or fumble for it; I speak it, both with their leave, and the leave o' your people.

DAM.   But, why *Humours reconcil'd*? I would fain know.

BOY.   I can satisfy you there, too: if you will. But, perhaps you desire not to be satisfied.

DAM.   No? why should you conceive so, *Boy*?

BOY.   My conceit is not ripe, yet: I'll tell you that anon. The *Author*, beginning his studies of this kind, with *Every Man in His Humour*; and after, *Every Man Out of His Humour*: and since, continuing in all his *Plays*, expecially those of the *Comic* thread, whereof the *New-Inn* was the last, some recent humours still, or manners of men, that went along with the times, finding himself now near the close, or shutting up of his Circle, hath phantasied to himself, in *Idea*, this *Magnetic Mistress*. A Lady, a brave bountiful House-keeper, and a virtuous Widow: who having a young Niece, ripe for a man and marriageable, he makes that his Center attractive, to draw thither a diversity of Guests, all persons of different humours to make up his *Perimeter*. And this he hath call'd *Humors reconcil'd*.

13. Damplay is Inigo Jones. Jonson satirizes his bad Latin, his worship of Vitruvius' dicta on architecture, etc.

14. In open court, the classical stage set.

PRO.   A bold undertaking! and far greater, than the reconciliation of both Churches, the quarrel between humours having been much the ancienter, and in my poor opinion, the root of all Schism, and Faction, both in Church and Commonwealth.

BOY.   Such is the opinion of many wise men, that meet at this shop still; but how he will speed in it, we cannot tell, and he himself (it seems) less cares. For he will not be entreated by us, to give it a *Prologue*. He has lost too much that way already, he says. He will not woo the gentle ignorance so much. But careless of all vulgar censure, as not depending on common approbation, he is confident it shall super-please judicious Spectators, and to them he leaves it to work with the rest, by example, or otherwise.

DAM.   He may be deceived in that, *Boy*: Few follow examples now, especially, if they be good.

BOY.   The *Play* is ready to begin, *Gentlemen*, I tell you, lest you might defraud the expectation of the people, for whom you are Delegates! Please you take a couple of Seats, and plant yourselves, here, as near my standing as you can: Fly every thing (you see) to the mark, and censure it; freely. So, you interrupt not the *Series*, or thread of the Argument, to break or pucker it, with unnecessary questions. For, I must tell you, (not out of mine own *Dictamen*, but the *Author's*,) A good *Play*, is like a skein of silk: which, if you take by the right end, you may wind off, at pleasure, on the bottom, or card of your discourse, in a tale or so; how you will: But if you light on the wrong end, you will pull all into a knot, or elf-lock; which nothing but the shears, or a candle will undo, or separate.

DAM.   Stay! who be these, I pray you?

BOY.   Because it is your first question, (and these be the prime persons) it would in civility require an answer: but I have heard the Poet affirm, that to be the most unlucky *Scene* in a *Play*, which needs an Interpreter; especially, when the *Auditory* are awake: and such are you, he presumes. *Ergo*.

COMEDY: COMIC STRUCTURE AND ITS PURPOSE

*(*Ibid., *Chorus after Act I.)*

CHORUS

BOY.   Now, *Gentlemen*, what censure you of our *Protasis*, or first *Act*.

PRO.   Well, *Boy*, it is a fair Presentment of your *Actors*. And a handsome promise of somewhat to come hereafter.

DAM.   But, there is nothing done in it, or concluded: Therefore I say, no Act.

BOY.   A fine piece of Logic! Do you look, Mr. *Damplay*, for conclusions in a *Protasis*. I thought the Law of *Comedy* had reserv'd them to the *Catastrophe*: and that the *Epitasis*, (as we are taught) and the *Catastasis*, had been intervening parts, to have been expected. But you would have all come together, it seems: The Clock should strike five, at once, with the Acts.

DAM.   Why, if it could do so, it were well, *Boy*.

BOY.   Yes, if the nature of a Clock were to speak, not strike. So, if a Child could be born, in a *Play*, and grow up to a man, i' the first Scene, before he went off the Stage: and then after to come forth a Squire, and be made a Knight: and that Knight to travel between the Acts, and do wonders i' the holy land, or elsewhere; kill Paynims, wild Boars, dun Cows, and other Monsters; beget him a reputation, and marry an Emperor's Daughter for his Mistress; convert her Father's Country; and at last come home, lame, and all to be laden with miracles.

DAM.   These miracles would please, I assure you: and take the *People*! For there be of the *People*, that will expect miracles, and more than miracles from this Pen.

BOY.   Do they think this Pen can juggle? I would we had *Hokos-pokos* for 'hem then, your *People*; or *Travitanto Tudesko*.

DAM.   Who's that, *Boy*.

BOY.   Another Juggler, with a long name. Or that your expectors would be gone hence, now, at the first Act; or expect no more hereafter, than they understand.

DAM.   Why so, my peremptory Jack?

BOY.   My name is *John*, indeed—Because, who expect what is impossible, or beyond nature, defraud themselves.

PRO.   Nay, there the *Boy* said well: They do defraud themselves indeed.

BOY.   And therefore, Mr. *Damplay*, unless like a solemn Justic of wit, you will damn our *Play*, unheard, or unexamin'd; I shall intreat your Mrs. Madam *Expectation*, if she be among these Ladies, to have patience, but a pissing while: give our Springs leave to open a little, by degrees! A Source of ridiculous matter may break forth anon, that shall steep their temples, and bathe their brains in laughter, to the fomenting of Stupidity itself, and the awaking any velvet Lethargy in the House.

PRO.   Why do you maintain your Poet's quarrel so with velvet, and good clothes, *Boy*? we have seen him in indifferent good clothes, ere now.

BOY.   And may do in better, if it please the King (his Master) to say Amen to it, and allow it, to whom he acknowledgeth all. But his clothes shall never be the best thing about him, though; he will have somewhat beside, either of humane letters, or severe honesty, shall speak him a man though he went naked.

PRO. He is beholden to you, if you can make this good, *Boy*.

BOY. Himself hath done that, already, against Envy.

DAM. What's your name Sir? or your Country?

BOY. *John Try-gust* my name: A *Cornish* youth, and the Poet's Servant.

DAM. West-country breed, I thought, you were so bold.

BOY. Or rather saucy: to find out your palate, Mr. *Damplay*. Faith we do call a Spade, *a Spade*, in *Cornwall*. If you dare damn our *Play*, i' the wrong place, we shall take heart to tell you so.

PRO. Good *Boy*.

COMIC TYPES AND THE EPITASIS AND CATASTROPHE

*Jonson uses his boy to conduct his most extensive consideration of the five-act structure. (*Ibid., *Choruses after Act II, Act III, and Act IV.)*

CHORUS [AFTER ACT II]

DAM. But whom doth your Poet mean now by this—Mr. *Bias*? what Lord's Secretary, doth he purpose to personate, or perstringe?

BOY. You might as well ask me, what *Alderman*, or *Alderman's* Mate, he meant by Sir *Moth Interest*? or what eminent Lawyer, by the ridiculous Mr. *Practise*? who hath rather his name invented for laughter, than any offence, or injury it can stick on the reverend Professors of the Law: And so the wise ones will think.

PRO. It is an insidious Question, Brother *Damplay*! Iniquity itself would not have urg'd it. It is picking the Lock of the Scene; not opening it the fair way with a Key. A *Play*, though it apparel, and present vices in general, flies from all particularities in persons. Would you ask of *Plautus*, and *Terence*, (if they both liv'd now) who were *Davus*, or *Pseudolus* in the Scene? who *Pyrgopolinices*, or *Thraso*? who *Euclio* or *Menedemus*?

BOY. Yes, he would: And enquire of *Martial*, or any other *Epigrammatist*, whom he meant by *Titius*, or *Seius* (the common *John à Noke*, or *John à Style*) under whom they note all vices, and errors taxable to the *Times*? As if there could not be a name for a Folly fitted to the *Stage*, but there must be a person in nature, found out to own it.

DAM. Why, I can phantasy a person to my self *Boy*, who shall hinder me?

BOY. And, in not publishing him, you do no man an injury. But if you will utter your own ill meaning on that person, under the *Authors* words, you make a Libel of his *Comedy*.

DAM.   O, he told us that in a *Prologue*, long since.

BOY.   If you do the same reprehensible ill things, still the same reprehension will serve you, though you heard it afore: They are his own words. I can invent no better, nor he.

PRO.   It is the solemn vice of interpretation, that deforms the figure of many a fair *Scene*, by drawing it awry; and indeed is the civil murder of most good *Plays*: If I see a thing vively[15] presented on the *Stage*, that the Glass of custom (which is *Comedy*) is so held up to me, by the Poet, as I can therein view the daily examples of men's lives, and images of Truth, in their manners, so drawn for my delight, or profit, as I may (either way) use them: and will I, rather (than make the true use) hunt out the *Persons* to defame, by my malice of misapplying? and imperil the innocence, and candor of the *Author*, by his calumny? It is an unjust way of hearing, and beholding *Plays*, this, and most unbecoming a *Gentleman* to appear malignantly witty in another's *Work*.

BOY.   They are no other but narrow, and shrunk natures; shriveled up, poor things, that cannot think well of themselves, who dare to detract others. That *Signature* is upon them, and it will last. A half-witted *Barbarism*! which no Barber's art, or his balls, will ever expunge or take out.

DAM.   Why, Boy? This were a strange Empire, or rather a Tyranny, you would entitle your Poet to, over Gentlemen, that they should come to hear, and see *Plays*, and say nothing for their money.

BOY.   O, yes; say what you will: so it be to purpose, and in place.

DAM.   Can anything be out of purpose at a *Play*? I see no reason, if I come here, and give my eighteen pence, or two shillings for my Seat, but I should take it out in censure, on the *Stage*.

BOY.   Your two shilling worth is allow'd you: but you will take your ten shilling worth, your twenty shilling worth, and more: And teach others (about you) to do the like, that follow your leading face; as if you were to cry up or down every *Scene*, by confederacy, be it right or wrong.

DAM.   Who should teach us the right, or wrong at a *Play*.

BOY.   If your own science can not do it, or the love of Modesty, and Truth; all other entreaties, or attempts—are vain. You are fitter *Spectators* for the *Bears*, than us, or the Puppets.[16] This is a popular ignorance indeed, somewhat better apparel'd in you, than the People: but a hard-handed, and stiff ignorance, worthy a Trowel, or a Hammer-man; and not only fit to be scorn'd, but to be triumph'd o'er.

15. Lively.

16. I.e., you are fitter spectators for bear-baiting or the primitive puppet shows than for the drama.

DAM. By whom, *Boy*?

BOY. No particular, but the general neglect, and silence. Good Master *Damplay*, be your self still, without a second: Few here are of your opinion today, I hope; tomorrow, I am sure there will be none, when they have ruminated this.

PRO. Let us mind what you come for, the *Play*, which will draw on to the *Epitasis* now.

CHORUS [AFTER ACT III]

DAM. This was a pitiful poor shift o' you Poet, Boy, to make his prime woman with child, and fall in labour, just to compose a quarrel.

BOY. With whose borrowed ears, have you heard, Sir, all this while, that you can mistake the current of our *Scene* so? The stream of the *Argument*,[17] threatened her being with child from the very beginning, for it presented her in the first of the second *Act*, with some apparent note of infirmity, or defect: from knowledge of which, the Auditory were rightly to be suspended by the *Author*, till the quarrel, which was but the accidental cause, hastened on the discovery of it, in occasioning her affright; which made her fall into her throes presently, and within that compass of time allow'd to the *Comedy*, wherein the Poet express'd his prime Artifice, rather than any error, that the detection of her being with child, should determine the quarrel, which had produc'd it.

PRO. The Boy is too hard for you. Brother *Damplay*, best mark the *Play*, and let him alone.

DAM. I care not for marking the *Play*: I'll damn it, talk, and do that I come for. I will not have *Gentlemen* lose their privilege, nor I myself my prerogative, for ne'er an overgrown, or superannuated Poet of 'hem all. He shall not give me the Law; I will censure, and be witty, and take my Tobacco, and enjoy my *Magna Charta* of reprehension, as my Predecessors have done before me.

BOY. Even to license, and absurdity.

PRO. Not now, because the *Gentlewoman* is in travail: and the Midwife may come on the sooner, to put her and us out of our pain.

DAM. Well, look to your business afterward, *Boy*, that all things be clear, and come properly forth, suited, and set together; for I will search what follows severely and to the nail.

BOY. Let your nail run smooth then, and not scratch: lest the *Author* be bold to pare it to the quick, and make it smart: you'll find him as severe as your self.

17. Plot.

DAM.   A shrewd Boy! and has me everywhere. The Midwife is come, she has made haste.

CHORUS [AFTER ACT IV]

DAM.   Troth, I am one of those that labour with the same longing,[18] for it is almost pucker'd, and pull'd into that knot, by your Poet, which I cannot easily, with all the strength of my imagination, untie.

BOY.   Like enough, nor is it in your office to be troubled or perplexed with it, but to sit still, and expect. The more your imagination busies itself, the more it is entangled, especially if (as I told, in the beginning) you happen on the wrong end.

PRO.   He hath said sufficient, Brother *Damplay*; our parts that are the Spectators, or should hear a *Comedy*, are to await the process, and events of things, as the *Poet* presents them, not as we would corruptly fashion them. We come here to behold *Plays*, and censure them, as they are made, and fitted for us; not to beslaver our own thoughts, with censorious spittle tempering the *Poet's* clay, as we were to mold every *Scene* anew: That were a mere Plastic, or Potter's ambition, most unbecoming the name of a *Gentleman*. No, let us mark, and not lose the business on foot, by talking. Follow the right thread, or find it.

DAM.   Why, here his *Play* might have ended, if he would ha' let it; and have spar'd us the vexation of a *fifth Act* yet to come, which every one here knows the issue of already, or may in part conjecture.

BOY.   That conjecture is a kind of Figure-flinging, or throwing the Dice,[19] for a meaning was never in the *Poet's* purpose perhaps. Stay, and see his last *Act*, his *Catastrophe*, how he will perplex that, or spring some fresh cheat, to entertain the *Spectators*, with a convenient delight, till some unexpected, and new encounter break out to rectify all, and make good the *Conclusion*.[20]

PRO.   Which, ending here, would have shown dull, flat, and unpointed; without any shape, or sharpness, Brother *Damplay*.

DAM.   Well, let us expect then: And wit be with us, o' the *Poet's* part.[21]

18. I.e., longing for knowledge of how the plot will be worked out. The tying and untying of the knot is, of course, a traditional metaphor in discussions of plot structure.

19. Trying to outguess the author as to how the plot will be resolved is as much a matter of chance as casting an astrological figure or casting dice.

20. The boy defines here Jonson's conception of the *catastasis*. Cf. Cordatus' discussion of the function of the fifth act in the chorus after Act IV of *Every Man Out* (p. 87 in this collection).

21. For the sake of the poet?

Masque Elements in Comedy

The epilogue from the 1640 folio of A Tale of a Tub. *In this late statement, Jonson calls attention to the fact that he has succumbed to the popular demand for fabulous fictions as opposed to realistic ones—even to the point of including a sort of masque, as Shakespeare had done, to Jonson's disgust, in some of his late plays.*

EPILOGUE: SQUIRE TUB
This Tale of me, the *Tub* of *Totten-Court*,
A Poet, first invented for your sport.

* * *

Got In-and-In, to get you in a *Masque:*
That you be pleased, who come to see a *Play*,
  With those that hear, and mark what we say.
Wherein the Poet's fortune is, I fear,
  Still to be early up, but n'er the near'.

V

TRAGEDY

THE LAWS OF TRAGEDY AND THE TRAGIC AESTHETIC

The preface from the 1616 folio of Sejanus.

TO THE READERS

The following, and voluntary Labours of my Friends, prefix'd to my Book, have relieved me in much, whereat (without them) I should necessarily have touch'd: Now, I will only use three or four short, and needful Notes, and so rest.

First, if it be objected, that what I publish is no true *Poem*; in the strict Laws of *Time*. I confess it: as also in the want of a proper *Chorus*, whose Habit, and Moods are such, and so difficult, as not any, whom I have seen since the *Ancients*, (no, not they who have most presently affected Laws) have yet come in the way off. Nor is it needful, or almost possible, in these our Times, and to such Auditors, as commonly Things are presented, to observe the old state, and splendour of *Dramatic Poems*, with preservation of any popular delight. But of this I shall take more seasonable cause to speak; in my Observations upon *Horace* his *Art* of *Poetry*,[1] which (with the Text translated) I intend, shortly to publish. In the meantime, if in truth of Argument, dignity of Persons, gravity and height of Elocution, fullness and frequency of Sentence, I have discharg'd the other offices of a *Tragic* writer, let not the absence of these *Forms* be imputed to me, wherein I shall give you occasion hereafter (and without my boast) to think I could better prescribe, than omit the due use, for want of a convenient knowledge.

The next is, lest in some nice nostril, the *Quotations* might savour affected, I do let you know, that I abhor nothing more; and have only done it to show my integrity in the *Story*, and save my self in those common Torturers, that bring all wit to the Rack: whose Noses are ever like Swine spoiling, and rooting up the *Muses'* Gardens, and their whole Bodies, like Moles, as blindly working under Earth to cast any, the least, hills upon *Virtue*.

Whereas, they are in *Latin* and the work in *English*, it was presuppos'd, none but the Learned would take the pains to confer[2] them,

---

1. Jonson's critical essay on the *Ars Poetica* perished in the fire of 1623.
2. Consult.

the Authors themselves being all in the learned *Tongues,* save one, with whose English side I have had little to do: To which it may be required, since I have quoted the Page, to name what Edition I follow'd. * * *

Lastly I would inform you, that this Book, in all numbers, is not the same with that which was acted on the public Stage, wherein a second Pen had good share: in place of which I have rather chosen, to put weaker (and no doubt less pleasing) of mine own, than to defraud so happy a *Genius* of his right, by my loathed usurpation.

Fare you well. And if you read farther of me, and like, I shall not be afraid of it though you praise me out.

[Nor am I so callous][3]

But that I should plant my felicity, in your general saying *Good,* or *Well,* &c. were a weakness which the better sort of you might worthily contemn, if not absolutely hate me for.

Fear and Tragedy

From the 1605 quarto of Sejanus, the concluding paragraph of the Argument. Jonson interprets the tragic catastrophe for his readers.

This[4] do we advance as a mark of Terror to all *Traitors,* & *Treasons;* to show how just the *Heavens* are in pouring and thundering down a weighty vengeance on their unnatural intents, even to the worst *Princes:* Much more to those, for guard of whose Piety and Virtue, the Angels are in continual watch, and *God* himself miraculously working.

Pity and Fear

From the 1616 folio of Sejanus, final scene, lines 833–903. Arruntius, the Nuntius, Lepidus, and Terentius form a chorus of sorts as they comment on the action that has just concluded. The villainous protagonist, Sejanus, has been

3. I.e., so callous as to be insensitive to praise. *Neque enim mihi cornea fibra est.*
4. The horrible death of the villainous protagonist, Sejanus.

*slaughtered; so have his innocent young children. Jonson uses this final chorus,
in part at least, to make clear the function of tragic pity and tragic fear,
emotions traditionally stirred and purged by tragedies.*

ARRUNTIUS, NUNTIUS, TERENTIUS

More of Sejanus? NUN. Yes. LEP. What can be added?
We know him dead. NUN. Then, there begin your pity.
There is enough behind, to melt ev'n *Rome*,
And Caesar into tears: (since never slave
Could yet so highly' offend, but tyranny,
In torturing him, would make him worth lamenting.)
A son, and daughter, to the dead *Sejanus*,
(Of whom there is not now so much remaining
As would give fast'ning to the hangman's hook)
Have they drawn forth for farther sacrifice;
Whose tenderness of knowledge, unripe years,
And childish silly innocence was such,
As scarce would lend them feeling of their danger:
The girl so simple, as she often asked,
Where they would lead her? for what cause they dragg'd her?
Cry'd, *she would do no more. That she could take
Warning with beating.* And because our laws
Admit no virgin immature to die,
The wittily, and strangely cruel *Macro*,
Deliver'd her to be deflower'd, and spoil'd,
By the rude lust of the licentious hangman,
Then, to be strangled with her harmless brother.
LEP. O, act, most worthy hell, and lasting night,
To hide it from the world! NUN. Their bodies thrown
Into the *Gemonies*,5 (I know not how,
Or by what accident return'd) the mother,
Th'expulsed *Apicata*, finds them there;
Whom when she saw lie spread on the degrees,
After a world of fury on her self,
Tearing her hair, defacing of her face,
Beating her breasts, and womb, kneeling amaz'd,
Crying to heaven, then to them; at last
Her drowned voice got up above her woes:

5. Steps leading to the Tiber; the bodies of criminals were taken there.

And with such black, and bitter execrations,
(As might affright the gods and force the sun
Run back-ward to the east, nay, make the old
Deformed *Chaos* rise again, t' o'erwhelm
Them, us, and all the world) she fills the air:
Upbraids the heavens with their partial dooms,
Defies their tyrannous powers, and demands,
What she, and those poor innocents have transgress'd,
That they must suffer such a share in vengeance,
Whilst *Livia*, *Lygdus*, and *Evdemus* live,
Who (as she says, and firmly vows, to prove it
To *Caesar*, and the *Senate*) poison'd *Drusus*?

LEP.   Confederates with her husband?   NUN.   Aye.   LEP.   Strange
act!

ARR.   And strangely open'd: what says now my monster,
The multitude? they reel now? do they not?

NUN.   Their gall is gone, and now they 'gin to weep
The mischief they have done.   ARR.   I thank 'hem, rogues!

NUN.   Part are so stupid, or so flexible,
As they believe him innocent; all grieve:
And some, whose hands yet reek with his warm blood,
And grip the part which they did tear off him,
Wish him collected, and created new.

LEP.   How fortune plies her sports, when she begins
To practice 'hem! pursues, continues, adds!
Confounds, with varying her empassion'd moods!

ARR.   Do'st thou hope, Fortune, to⁶ redeem thy crimes?
To make amends, for thy ill placed favours,
With these strange punishments? Forbear, you things,
That stand upon the pinnacles of state,
To boast your slippery height; when you do fall,
You pash your selves in pieces, ne'er to rise:
And he that lends you pity, is not wise.

TER.   Let this example move the 'insolent man,
Not to grow proud, and careless of the gods:
It is an odious wisdom, to blaspheme,
Much more to slighten, or deny their powers.
For, whom the morning saw so great, and high,
Thus low, and little, 'fore the 'even doth lie.

6. My emendation; the original reads "hope fortune to."

HISTORY AND PLAYS

From the 1616 folio of The Devil Is an Ass, *II.iv.8–15. The traditional theory that the fiction of tragedy is true-seeming and true is so well known that even Squire Fitzdottrel, Meercraft, and Engine allude to it. The discussion stems from Fitzdottrel's not wishing to have anything to do with the name of Gloucester, three dukes of which were subjects of early English tragedies.*

FIT.   I know not that, Sir. But *Thomas* of *Woodstock,*
  I'm sure, was *Duke,* and he was made away,
  At *Calice;*[7] as *Duke Humphrey* was at *Bury*:
  And *Richard* the third, you know what end he came to.
MER.   By my 'faith you are cunning i' the *Chronicle,* Sir.
FIT.   No, I confess I ha't from the *Play-books,*
  And think they'are more *authentic.* ENG.   That's sure, Sir.

 7. Calais.

VI

MASQUE

THE REQUIREMENTS OF MASQUE SYMBOLOGY

From the 1604 quarto of The King's Entertainment at Fen-Church.

* * * The nature and property of these Devices being, to present always some one entire body, or figure, consisting of distinct members, and each of those expressing itself, in the own active sphere, yet all, with that general harmony so connexed, and disposed, as no one little part can be missing to the illustration of the whole: where also is to be noted, that the *Symbols* used, are not, neither ought to be, simply *Hieroglyphics, Emblems,* or *Impresas,*[1] but a mixed character, partaking somewhat of all, and peculiarly apted to these more magnificent inventions: wherein, the garments and ensigns deliver the nature of the person, and the word the present office. Neither was it becoming, or could it stand with the dignity of these shows (after the most miserable and desperate shift of the Puppets) to require a Truchman,[2] or (with the ignorant Painter) one to write, *This is a Dog*; or, *This is a Hare*; but so to be presented, as upon the view, they might, without cloud, or obscurity, declare themselves to the sharp and learned: And for the multitude, no doubt but their grounded judgements did gaze, said it was fine, and were satisfied.

THE MEANING OF MASQUE: THE SOUL AND BODY OF SYMBOL

The preface from the 1616 folio of Hymenaei. *This is the central statement in Jonson's criticism of the masque as a serious art form.*

It is a noble and just advantage, that the things subjected to *understanding* have of those which are objected to *sense,* that the one sort are but momentary, and merely taking; the other impressing, and lasting: Else the glory of all these *solemnities* had perish'd like a blaze, and gone out, in the *beholders*' eyes. So short-liv'd are the bodies of all things, in comparison of their *souls*. And, though *bodies* oft-times have

---

1. Hieroglyphics: technically, trees or animals used as symbols; emblems: pictures accompanied by a short verse expressing the conceit; impresas: symbolic devices, usually with a motto. Jonson's own impresa was a broken compass with the motto "That is missing which would complete the circle [*Deest quod duceret orbem*]."

2. Interpreter; here the equivalent of a moralization.

143

the ill luck to be sensually preferr'd, they find afterwards, the good fortune (when souls live) to be utterly forgotten. This it is hath made the most royal *Princes*, and greatest *persons* (who are commonly the *personaters* of these *actions*) not only studious of riches, and magnificence in the outward celebration, or show; (which rightly becomes them) but curious after the most high, and hearty *inventions*, to furnish the inward parts: (and those grounded upon *antiquity*, and solid *learnings*) which, though their *voice* be taught to sound to present occasions, their *sense*, or doth, or should always lay hold on more remov'd *mysteries*. And, howsoever some may squeamishly cry out, that all endeavour of *learning*, and *sharpness* in these transitory *devices*[3] especially, where it steps beyond their little, or (let me not wrong 'hem) no brain at all, is superfluous; I am contented, these fastidious *stomachs* should leave my full tables, and enjoy at home, their clean empty trenchers, fittest for such airy tastes: where perhaps a few *Italian* herbs, pick'd up, and made into a *salad*, may find sweeter acceptance, than all, the most nourishing, and sound meats of the world.

For these men's palates, let not me answer, *O Muses*. It is not my fault, if I fill them out *Nectar*, and they run to *Metheglin*.

[Let them drink rotgut if it pleases them].[4]

All the courtesy I can do them, is to cry, again;

[Let them pass it by if something doesn't suit their stomachs].[5]

As I will, from the thought of them, to my better subject.

ALLEGORY AND MASQUE: REASON AND THE HUMOURS

*Jonson allegorizes his moral theory of humours. He explains the allegory in a footnote: unless reason controls man's humours and their accompanying passions, man becomes "immoral," "sacrilegious." (*Ibid., *ll. 109–160.)*

Here out of a Microcosm, *or* Globe, *(figuring Man) with a kind of contentious Music, issued forth the first* Masque, *of eight men.*

3. I.e., masques.
4. *Vaticana bibant, si delectentur.*
5. *Praetereant, si quid non facit ad stomachum.*

These represented the four Humours,[6] *and four* Affections, *all gloriously attired, distinguish'd only by their several* Ensigns *and* Colours; *and, dancing out on the Stage, in their return, at the end of their dance, drew all their swords, offered to encompass the* Altar, *and disturb the* Ceremonies. *At which,* Hymen *troubled, spake:*

HYMEN

Save, save the *virgins*; keep your hallow'd lights
Untouch'd; and with their flame defend our *Rites*.
The four untemp'red *Humours* are broke out.
And, with their wild *affections*, go about
To ravish all Religion. If there be
A Power, like *Reason*, left in that huge Body,
Or little *world of man*, from whence these came,
Look forth, and with thy bright and numerous flame
Instruct their darkness, make them know, and see,
In wronging these, they have rebell'd 'gainst thee.

Hereat, Reason, *seated in the top of the* Globe *(as in the brain, or highest part of* Man *) figur'd in a venerable* personage, *her hair white, and trailing to her waist, crowned with lights, her garments blue, and semined with stars, girded unto her with a white band, fill'd with* Arithmetical *figures, in one hand bearing a* Lamp, *in the other a bright* Sword, *descended, and spake:*

REASON

Forbear your rude attempt; what ignorance
Could yield you so profane, as to advance
One thought in act, against these *mysteries*?
Are *Union's orgies* of so slender price?

6. Jonson's note: "And for the Allegory, though here it be very clear, and such as might well escape a candle, yet because there are some, must complain of darkness, that have but thick eyes, I am contented to hold them this Light. First, as in *natural bodies*, so likewise in *minds*, there is no disease, or distemperature, but is caused either by some abounding *humour*, or perverse *affection;* after the same manner, in *politic bodies* (where *Order, Ceremony, State, Reverence, Devotion,* are parts of the *Mind*) by the difference, or predominant will of what we (*metaphorically*) call *Humours*, and *Affections*, all things are troubled and confused. These, therefore, were *trop*[*olog*]*ically* brought in, before *Marriage*, as disturbers of that *mystical body*, and the *rites*, which were *soul* unto it; that afterwards, in *Marriage*, being dutifully tempered by her *power*, they might more fully celebrate the happiness of such as live in that sweet *union*, to the harmonious laws of Nature and Reason."

> She that makes *souls*, with *bodies*, mix in love,
> Contracts the *world* in one, and therein *Jove*:
> Is *spring*, and *end* of all things: yet, most strange!
> Herself nor suffers *spring*, nor *end*, nor *change*.
> No wonder, they were you, that were so bold;
> For none but *Humours* and *Affections* would
> Have dar'd so rash a venture. You will say
> It was your zeal, that gave your powers the sway;
> And urge the *masqued*, and disguis'd pretence,
> Of saving blood, and succ'ring innocence?
> So want of *knowledge*, still, begetteth jars,
> When *humourous* earthlings will control the stars.
> Inform yourselves, with safer reverence,
> To these mysterious *rites*, whose mystic sense,
> *Reason* (which all things, but itself, confounds)
> Shall clear unto you, from th'authentic grounds.

At this, the Humours *and* Affections *sheathed their swords, and retired amazed to the sides of the stage, while* Hymen *began to rank the* Persons, *and order the* Ceremonies: * * *

The Function of Masque as Tribute

From the 1616 folio of The Haddington Masque, *the preface.*

The worthy custom of honouring worthy *marriages*, with these noble *solemnities*, hath, of late years, advanc'd itself frequently with us; to the reputation no less of our *court*, than *nobles*: expressing besides (through the difficulties of expense, and travel, with the cheerfulness of under-taking) a most real affection in the *personators*, to those, for whose sake they would sustain these *persons*. It behooves then us, that are trusted with a part of their honor, in these *celebrations*, to do nothing in them, beneath the dignity of either. With this proposed part of judgement, I adventure to give that abroad, which in my first conception I intended honorably fit: and (though it hath labour'd since, under censure) I, that know *Truth* to be always of one stature, and so like a rule, as who bends it the least way, must needs do an injury to the right, cannot but smile at their tyrannous ignorance, that will offer to slight me (in these things being an *artificer*) and give themselves a peremptory licence to judge, who have never touch'd so much as to the bark, or utter shell of any *knowledge*. But, their daring dwell, with them. They have found a place, to pour out their follies, and I a seat, to sleep out the passage.

The Antimasque, Function and Conception: "The Masque of Queens"

From the 1616 folio of The Masque of Queens, *lines 1–42. Jonson recalls the origin of an antimasque.*

It increasing, now, to the third time of my being us'd in these services to her Majesty's personal presentations, with the Ladies whom she pleaseth to honor;[7] it was my first, and special regard, to see that the Nobility of the Invention should be answerable to the dignity of the persons. For which reason, I chose the Argument, to be, *A Celebration of honorable, & true Fame, bred out of Virtue :* observing that rule of the best Artist,[8] to suffer no object of delight to pass without his mixture of profit, & example.

And because her Majesty (best knowing, that a principal part of life in these *Spectacles* lay in their variety) had commanded me to think on some *Dance,* or show, that might precede hers, and have the place of a foil, or false-*Masque*; I was careful to decline not only from others, but mine own steps in that kind, since the last year[9] I had an *Anti-Masque* of Boys: and therefore, now, devis'd that twelve Women, in the habit of *Hags,* or Witches, sustaining the persons of *Ignorance, Suspicion, Credulity,* &c. the opposites to good *Fame,* should fill that part; not as a *Masque,* but a spectacle of strangeness, producing multiplicity of Gesture, and not unaptly sorting with the current, and whole fall of the Device.

First, then, his Majesty being set, and the whole Company in full expectation, that which presented it self was an ugly *Hell*; which, flaming beneath, smoked unto the top of the Roof. And, in respect all *Evils* are (*morally*) said to come from *Hell* * * * These Witches, with a kind of hollow and infernal music, came forth from thence

7. The masques were personal gifts from the Queen to her court, especially to honor certain of her ladies, who performed in the masques.

8. Jonson's note: "Horace in his *Ars Poetica.*"

9. Jonson's note: "In the Haddington Masque."

* * * all differently attir'd; some, with rats on their heads; some, on their shoulders; others with ointment pots at their girdles; All with spindles, timbrels, rattles, or other *venefical*[10] instruments, making a confused noise, with strange gestures. The device of their attire was *Mr. Jones his*, with the Invention and *Architecture* of the whole *Scene*, and Machine. Only, I prescrib'd them the *properties*, of vipers, snakes, bones, herbs, roots, and other ensigns of their *Magic*, out of the authority of ancient, & late *Writers*. Wherein the faults are mine, if there be any found; and for that cause I confess them.

The Art of Hinting Allegory: "The Masque of Queens"

Just before Ate reveals that the witches of the antimasque are actually the "opposites to Fame, *&* Glory"—*Ignorance, Suspicion, Falsehood, Slander, etc.*—*Jonson justifies the need for such subtle revelations in highly symbolic or allegorical scenes. A little later, in a note to line 132, he adds: "Here again, by way of irritation, I make the* Dame *pursue the purpose of the coming, and discover their natures more largely which had been nothing if not done, as doing another thing." (* Ibid., *ll. 95–110.)*

At this, the *Dame* [Ate, or Mischief][11] entered to them, naked arm'd, barefooted, her frock tuck'd, her hair knotted, and folded with vipers; In her hand, a Torch made of a dead Man's arm, lighted; girded with a snake. To whom they all did reverence, and she spake, uttering, by way of question, the end wherefore they came: which, if it had been done either before, or otherwise, had not been so natural. For, to have made themselves their own decipherers, and each one to have told, upon their entrance, *what they were, and whether they would*, had been a most piteous hearing, and utterly unworthy any quality of a *Poem*: wherein a *Writer* should always trust somewhat to the capacity of the *Spectator*, especially at these *Spectacles*; Where Men, beside inquiring eyes, are understood to bring quick ears, and not those sluggish ones of Porters, and Mechanics, that must be bor'd through, at every act, with Narrations.

10. Used in black magic.
11. Jonson's note: "This dame I make to bear the person of Ate, or Mischief, (for so I interpret it) out of Homer's description of her in the *Iliad*."

THE HISTORICAL AND THE MORAL: THEIR FUSION IN MASQUE

Jonson implies that the appeal of the masque is twofold—it appeals to the spectator's love for moral symbols and to his love for classical learning. Thus, Jonson's Dame is, tropologically, the opposite of fame and glory. More specifically, she is a type of the witch, as that type has been defined in classical literature. More specifically still, she is the classical archetype of witchery, Ate, the goddess of fatal fury and its punishment. Jonson underlines the same theory in a note to line 368 where he explains that the moral ideal of masculine virtue is fused with the classical figure of Perseus, armed, as Jonson points out, as he is described in Hesiod. (Ibid., ll. 205-217, note to l. 368.)

Here the *Dame* put her self into the midst of them, and began her following invocation; wherein she took occasion to boast all the power attributed to witches by the *Ancients*: of which every *Poet* (or the most) doth give some. *Homer* * * * *Theocritus* * * * *Virgil* * * * *Ovid* * * * *Tibullus* * * * *Horace* * * * *Seneca* * * * *Petr(onius) Arbiter* * * * And *Claudius* to his *Megaera* * * * who takes the habit of a Witch as these do, and supplies that *historical* part in the *Poem*, beside her *moral* person of a *Fury*. Confirming the same drift, in ours.

The Ancients expressed a brave, and masculine *virtue*, in three figures. (Of *Hercules*, *Perseus*, and *Bellerophon*) of which I chose that of *Perseus*, armed, as I have him described out of *Hesiod*.

THE ANTIMASQUE

From the 1640 folio of The Masque of Augurs, *lines 250-269. Just before the second antimasque, Jonson satirizes the inartistic use of the antimasque by making the poetaster Van-Goose theorize to the Groom of the Revels. In the original, Van-Goose's lines are set in black letter.*

VAN.   Pilgrim? now yow talk of de Pilgrim, it come in my head, Ick vill shew yow all de whole brave pilgrim o' de Vorld: de Pilgrim dat go now, now at de instant, two, dre towsand Mile to de great *Mahomet*, at de *Mecha*, or here, dere, every where, make de fine Labyrints, and shew all de brave error in de world.

* * *

GRO.   I would try him, but what has all this to do with our Masque?

VAN.   O Sir, all de better, vor an Antick-masque, de more absurd it be, and vrom de purpose, it be ever all de better. If it go from de *Nature* of de ting, it is de more *Art:* for dear[12] is *Art*, and dear is *Nature;* yow sall see. *Hochos-pochos, Paucos Palabros.*

THE QUARREL WITH INIGO JONES

From the 1756 edition, An Expostulation with Inigo Jones, *lines 1–17, 29–65, 85–104. In this satire on the famous architect and masque designer, Jonson indulges in invective, but also summarizes the central theoretical difference between the two greatest contributers to the magnificence of the Jacobean form. In Jonson's view, the invention of the poet is the soul of the masque; staging, costuming, machinery, all that appeals to the eye of the beholder must be subordinated to the poet's invention.*

> Mr Surveyor, you that first began
> From thirty pound in pipkins, to the Man
> You are; from them leapt forth an Architect,
> Able to talk of Euclid, and correct
> Both him & Archimede; damn Architas[13]
> The noblest Engineer that ever was!
> Control Ctesibius:[14] overbearing us
> With mistook Names out of Vitruvius!
> Drawn Aristotle on us! & thence shown
> How much Architectonics is your own!
> Whether the building of the Stage or Scene!
> Or making of the Properties it mean?
> Vizors or Antics? or it comprehend
> Something your Sirship doth not yet intend!
> By all your Titles, & whole style at once
> Of Tire-man, Mountebank & Justice Jones,
> I do salute you! * * *
>
>   * * *
>
> What is the cause you pomp it so? I ask,
> And all men echo you have made a Masque.
> I chime that too: And I have met with those
> That do cry up the Machine, & the Shows!
> The majesty of Juno in the Clouds,

12. There.
13. Archytas, the inventor of analytical geometry.
14. Ctesibius was celebrated for his mechanical inventions.

And peering forth of Iris in the Shrouds!
Th'ascent of Lady Fame which none could spy
Not they that sided her, Dame Poetry,
Dame History, Dame Architecture too,
And Goody Sculpture, brought with much ado
To hold her up. O Shows! Shows! Mighty Shows!
The Eloquence of Masques! What need of prose
Or Verse, or Sense t'express Immortal you?
You are the Spectacles of State! 'Tis true
Court Hieroglyphics! & all Arts afford
In the mere perspective of an Inch board!
You ask no more than certain politic Eyes,
Eyes that can pierce into the Mysteries
Of many colors! read them! & reveal
Mythology there painted on slit deal!
Oh, to make Boards to speak! There is a task:
Painting & Carpentry are the Soul of Masque.
Pack with your peddling Poetry to the Stage,
This is the money-get, Mechanic Age!
To plant the Music where no ear can reach!
Attire the Persons as no thought can teach
Sense, what they are! which by a specious fine
Term of the Architect's is called Design!
But in the practiced truth Destruction is
Of any Art, beside what he calls his!
Whither? oh, whither will this Tireman grow?
His name is [Stage Mechanic][15] we all know,
The maker of the Properties! in sum
The Scene! the Engine! but he now is come
To be the Music Master! Fabler too!
He is, or would be the main Dominus do[16]
All in the Work! * * *

                   * * *

Oh wise Surveyor! wiser Architect!
But wisest Inigo! who can reflect
On the new priming of thy old Sign posts

15. Σκενοποιος. Jonson takes the term from *Poetics* VI.19, where Aristotle speaks of spectacle as the least artistic part of poetry—it depends more for its effects on the art of the stage mechanic than on that of the poet.

16. Dominus Fac Totem; i.e., Mr. Know-it-all.

Reviving with fresh colors the pale Ghosts
Of thy dead Standards: or (with miracle) see
Thy twice conceived, thrice paid for Imagery?
And not fall down before it? and confess
Almighty Architecture? who no less
A Goddess is, than painted Cloth, Deal boards,
Vermilion, Lake, or Cinnopar[17] affords
Expression for! with that unbounded line
Aim'd at in thy omnipotent Design!
What Poesy ere was painted on a wall
That might compare with thee? what story shall
Of all the Worthies hope t'outlast thy one,
So the Materials be of Purbeck stone!
Live long the feasting Room.[18] And ere thou burn
Again, thy Architect to ashes turn!
Whom not ten fires, nor a Parliament can
With all Remonstrance make an honest man.

17. Crimson.
18. At Whitehall, scene of many masques staged by Inigo Jones; it burned in 1619 and was rebuilt by Jones.

VII
CONTEMPORARY POETS AND
PLAYWRIGHTS

On Kyd's "Spanish Tragedy"

From the 1616 folio of Every Man in His Humour, *I.iii.126–142. The gull Matthew and the braggart soldier Bobadil, the former having no taste and the latter having a natural taste for inflated language, are made to prefer Kyd to more disciplined playwrights.*

BOB.   What new book have you there? what? *Go by Jieronimo.*[1]

MAT.   Aye, did you ever see it acted? is't not well penn'd?

BOB.   Well penn'd: I would fain see all the Poets of our time pen such another play as that was; they'll prate and swagger, and keep a stir of art and devices, when (by God's so) they are the most shallow pitiful fellows that live upon the face of the earth again.

MAT.   Indeed, here are a number of fine speeches in this book: *Oh eyes, no eyes but fountains fraught with tears;*[2] there's a conceit: Fountains fraught with tears. *Oh life, no life, but lively form of death:* is't not excellent? *Oh world, no world, but mass of public wrongs;* O God's me: *confus'd and fill'd with murder and misdeeds.* Is't not simply the best that ever you heard? Ha, how do you like it?

BOB.   Tis good.

The Conventions of the Popular Stage: Its Specious Rhetoric

From the 1616 folio of Poetaster, *III.iv.187–274, 317–369. The reprobate Captain Tucca, a likely candidate for Old Comedy satirization, accosts an actor and a playwright from the public theaters for performing comical satires. They hasten to explain that Tucca must be thinking of the private theaters— that their plays are inconsequential. Demetrius (Dekker) and Tucca are then shown admiring the various corrupt styles Jonson associates with the poetasters —primarily doggerel and bombast. Kyd and Peele are the main authors parodied.*

TUCC.   And what matters have you now afoot, sirrah? ha? I would fain come with my cockatrice one day, and see a play; if I knew when there were a good bawdy one: but they say, you ha' nothing but *humours, revels,* and *satires,* that gird, and fart at the time, you slave.

1. I.e., *The Spanish Tragedy.*
2. Matthew is quoting *The Spanish Tragedy,* III.ii.1–4. He does not misquote. Perhaps Jonson thinks the lines turgid enough as they stand in the original.

HIST.   No, I assure you, Captain, not we. They are on the other side of
Tiber:[3] we have as much ribaldry in our plays, as can be, as you would
wish, Captain: All the sinners, i' the suburbs, come, and applaud our
action, daily.

TUCC.   I hear, you'll bring me o' the stage there; you'll play me, they say:
I shall be presented by a sort of copper-lac'd scoundrels of you: life of
Pluto, and you stage me, stinkard; your mansions shall sweat for't, your
tabernacles, varlets, your *Globes*, and your *Triumphs*.[4]

HIST.   Not we, by *Phoebus*, Captain: do not do us imputation without desert.

TUCC.   I wu' not, my good two-penny rascal: reach me thy neufe.[5] Do'st
hear? What wilt thou give me a week, for my brace of beagles, here, my
little point-trussers?[6] you shall ha' them act among yee. Sirrah, you, pronounce. Thou shalt hear him speak, in king *Darius'* doleful strain.

1. PYR.   *O doleful days! O direful deadly dump!*
 O wicked world! and worldly wickedness!
 How can I hold my fist from crying, thump,
 In rue of this right rascal wretchedness!

TUCC.   In an amorous vein now, sirrah, peace.

1. PYR.   *O, she is wilder, and more hard, withall,*[7]
 Than beast, or bird, or tree, or stony wall.
 Yet might she love me, to uprear her state:
 I, but perhaps, she hopes some nobler mate.
 Yet might she love me, to content her sire:
 I, but her reason masters her desire.
 Yet might she love me as her beauteous thrall:
 I, but I fear, she cannot love at all.

TUCC.   Now, the horrible fierce Soldier, you, sirrah.

1. PYR.   *What? will I brave thee? I, and beard thee too.*
 A roman *spirit scorns to bear a brain.*
 So full of base pusillanimity.

DEMET. HIST.   Excellent.

---

3. The private theaters were on the north side of the Thames; the public, on
the south bank. The speaker is an actor (Histrio) from the public theaters.

4. "Globes," would-be theaters such as the Globe; "*triumphs*" are pageants.
Tucca's references are not always completely logical.

5. Fist.

6. Tucca has two boy pages. He calls them his *pyrgi* (dice boxes) because he
uses them to cast for his fortune. Here he is wondering whether they might make
good boy actors.

7. Quoted more or less accurately from *The Spanish Tragedy*, I.ii.9 ff.

TUCC.   Nay, thou shalt see that, shall ravish thee anon: prick up thine ears, stinkard: the Ghost, boys.

1. PYR.   *Vindicta.*[8]

2. PYR.   *Timoria.*

1. PYR.   *Vindicta.*

2. PYR.   *Timoria.*

1. PYR.   *Veni.*

2. PYR.   *Veni.*

TUCC.   Now, thunder, sirrah, you, the rumbling player.

2. PYR.   I, but some body must cry (*murder*) then, in a small voice.

TUCC.   Your fellow-sharer, there, shall do't; Cry, sirrah, cry.

1. PYR.   *Murder, murder.*

2. PYR.   *Who calls out murder? lady, was it you?*[9]

DEMET.   HIST.   O, admirable good, I protest.

TUCC.   Sirrah, boy, brace your drum a little straighter, and do the t'other fellow there, he in the—what sha' call him—and yet, stay too.

2. PYR.   *Nay, and thou dalliest, then I am thy foe,*[10]
    And fear shall force, what friendship cannot win;
    Thy death shall bury what thy life conceals,
    Villain! thou diest, for more respecting her—

1. PYR.   *O, stay my Lord.*

2. PYR.   *Then me: yet speak the truth, and I will guerdon thee: But if thou dally once again, thou diest.*

TUCC.   Enough of this, boy.

2. PYR.   *Why then lament therefore: damn'd be thy guts*
    Unto king Pluto's *hell, and princely* Erebus;
    For sparrows must have food.

HIST.   Pray, sweet Captain, let one of them do a little of a lady.

TUCC.   O! he will make thee eternally enamour'd of him, there: do, sirrah, do: 'twill allay your fellow's fury a little.

1. PYR.   *Master, mock on: the scorn thou givest me,*
    Pray Jove, *some lady may return on thee.*

2. PYR.   No: you shall see me do the *Moor:*[11] Master, lend me your scarf a little.

8. The Latin tags suggesting Revenge and Horror are apparently typical tags from revenge plays.

9. Quoted from Chapman's *The Blind Beggar of Alexandria;* why Jonson quotes it in this context is not clear.

10. Quoted from *The Spanish Tragedy*, II.i.67–75.

11. Muly Mahamet in Peele's *The Battle of Alcazar.*

TUCC.   Here, 'tis at thy service, boy.

2. PYR.   You, master *Minos*, hark hither a little. [*They withdraw to make themselves ready.*]

* * *

TUCC.   Stay, thou shalt see the *Moor*, ere thou goest: what's he, with the half-arms there, that salutes us out of his cloak, like a *motion*? ha?

HIST.   O, sir, his doublet's a little decayed; he is otherwise a very simple honest fellow, sir, one *Demetrius*, a dresser of plays about the town, here; we have hired him to abuse *Horace*, and bring him in, in a play, with all his gallants: as, *Tibullus, Maecenas, Cornelius Gallus*, and the rest.

TUCC.   And: why so, stinkard?

HIST.   O, it will get us a huge deal of money (Captain) and we have need on't; for this winter has made us all poorer, than so many starv'd snakes: No body comes at us; not a gentleman, nor a—

TUCC.   But, you know nothing by him, do you, to make a play of?

HIST.   Faith, not much, Captain: but our Author will devise, that, that shall serve in some sort.

TUCC.   Why, my *Parnassus*, here, shall help him, if thou wilt: Can thy Author do it impudently enough?

HIST.   O, I warrant you, Captain, and spitefully enough, too; he has one of the most overflowing rank wits, in *Rome*. He will slander any man that breathes, if he disgust him.

TUCC.   I'll know the poor, egregious, nitty rascal, and he have these commendable qualities, I'll cherish him (stay, here comes the *Tartar*) I'll make a gathering for him, I: a purse, and put the poor slave in fresh rags. Tell him so, to comfort him: well said, boy. [*The boy comes in on Minos' shoulders, who stalks, as he acts.*]

2. PYR.   *Where are thou, boy? where is* Calipolis?[12]
    Fight earth-quakes, in the entrails of the earth,
    And eastern whirlwinds in the hellish shades;
    Some foul contagion of th'infected heavens
    Blast all the trees; and in their cursed tops
    The dismal night raven, and tragic owl
    Breed, and become forerunners of my fall.

TUCC.   Well, now fare thee well, my honest penny-biter: Commend me to seven-shares-and-a-half,[13] and remember tomorrow—if you lack a service, you shall play in my name, rascals, but you shall buy your own cloth, and I'll ha' two shares for my countenance. Let thy author stay with me.

12. Quoted from *Battle of Alcazar*, ll. 512, 516–521.
13. The theater manager.

DEME. Yes, sir.

TUCC. 'Twas well done, little *Minos*, thou didst stalk well; forgive me that I said thou stunkst, *Minos*: 'twas the savour of a *poet*, I met sweating in the street, hangs yet in my nostrils.

CRIS. Who? *Horace?*

TUCC. Aye, he; do'st thou know him?

CRIS. O, he forsook me most barbarously, I protest.

TUCC. Hang him fusty *satyr*, he smells all goat; he carries a ram, under his arm-holes, the slave: I am the worse when I see him. * * *

THE CONTEMPORARY ABUSE OF SATIRE

*The trial of Crispinus (Marston) and Demetrius (Dekker) begins after they plead not guilty to the charge of turning the art of satire into the crime of calumny by attacking the irreproachable Horace (Jonson). Horace and Virgil distinguish between true satire and libelous invective. The passage opens as Tibullus reads the first piece of evidence against the poetasters—an example of Crispinus' style. (*Ibid., V.iii.274–378.)

VIRG. Read them aloud.

TIBU. *Ramp up, my genius; be not retrograde:*
But boldly nominate a spade, a spade.
What, shall thy lubrical and glibber Muse
Live, as she were defunct, like punk in stews?
          (TUCC. Excellent!)
Alas! That were no modern consequence,
To have cothurnal buskins frightened hence.
No; teach thy incubus *to poetize;*
And throw abroad thy spurious snotteries,
Upon that puff'd-up lump of barmy froth.
          (TUCCA. Ah, ha!)
Or clumsy chil-blain'd judgement; that, with oath,
Magnificates his merit; and bespawles
The conscious time, with humorous foam, and brawls,
As if his organons *of sense would crack*
The sinews of my patience. Break his back,
O Poets *all, and some: For now we list*
Of strenuous vengeance to clutch the fist.
        Subscri. CRIS.

TUCC. Aye marry, this was written like a *Hercules* in *poetry*, now.

CAES. Excellently well threatened!

VIRG. I, and as strangely worded, *Caesar*.

CAES. We observe it.

VIRG. The other, now.

TUCC. This's a fellow of a good prodigal tongue too; this'll do well.

TIBU. *Our Muse is in mind for th'untrussing a poet,*
 I slip by his name; for most men do know it:
 A critic, *that all the world bescumbers*
 With satirical *humours, and* lyrical *numbers:*
     (TUCC. Art thou there, boy?)
 And for the most part, himself doth advance
 With much self-love, and more arrogance.
     (TUCC. Good again.)
 And (but that I would not be thought a prater)
 I could tell you, he were a translator.
 I know the authors from whence he has stole,
 And could trace him too, but that I understand 'hem
        not full and whole.
  (TUCC. That line is broke loose from all his fellows:
    chain him up shorter, do.)
 The best note I can give you to know him by,
 Is, that he keeps gallants' *company;*
 Whom I would wish, in time should him fear,
 Lest after they buy repentence too dear.
     Subscri. DEME. FAN.

TUCC. Well said. This carries palm with it.

HORA. And why, thou motley gull? why should they fear?
 When hast thou known us wrong, or tax a friend?
 I dare thy malice, to betray it. Speak.
 How thou curl'st up, thou poor, and nasty snake,
 And shrink'st thy pois'nous head into thy bosom:
 Out viper, thou that eat'st thy parents, hence.
 Rather, such speckled creatures, as thy self,
 Should be eschew'd, and shunned: such, as will bite
 And gnaw their absent friends, not cure their fame,
 Catch at the loosest laughters, and affect
 To be thought jesters, such, as can devise
 Things never seen, or heard, t' impair men's names,
 And gratify their credulous adversaries,

Will carry tales, do basest offices,
Cherish divided fires, and still increase
New flames, out of old embers, will reveal
Each secret that's committed to their trust,
These be black slaves: *Romans*, take heed of these.

TUCC. Thou twang'st right, little *Horace*: they be indeed a couple of chap-fallen curs. Come, We of the bench, let's rise to the *Urn*, and condemn 'hem, quickly.

VIRG. Before you go together (worthy *Romans*)
We are to tender our opinion;
And give you those instructions, that may add
Unto your even judgement in the cause:
Which thus we do commence. First, you must know
That where there is a true, and perfect merit,
There can be no dejection; and the scorn
Of humble baseness, oftentimes, so works
In a high soul upon the grosser spirit,
That to his bleared, and offended sense,
There seems a hideous fault blaz'd in the object;
When only the disease is in his eyes.
Here-hence it comes, our *Horace* now stands tax'd
Of impudence, self-love, and arrogance,
By these, who share no merit in themselves;
And therefore, think his portion is as small.
For they, from their own guilt, assure their souls,
If they should confidently praise their works,
In them it would appear inflation:
Which, in a full, and well-digested man,
Cannot receive that foul abusive name,
But the fair title of erection.
And, for his true use of translating men,
It still hath been a work of as much palm
In clearest judgements, as t' invent, or make.
His sharpness, that is most excusable;
As being forc'd out of a suffering virtue,
Oppressed with the license of the time:
And howsoever fools, or jerking *pedants*,
Players, or such like *buffon*, barking wits,
May with their beggerly, and barren trash,
Tickle base vulgar ears, in their despite;

This (like *Jove's* thunder) shall their pride control,
"The honest *Satire* hath the happiest soul."
Now, Romans, you have heard our thoughts. Withdraw when you
please.

The Italians and the English

From the 1616 folio of Volpone, *III.iv.76–112. Volpone is no match for the chattering Lady Politic Would-be, an English literary lady, who is here made to epitomize the English rage for Italian literature. Perhaps Jonson means to allude to Daniel as the poet who plagiarized from Guarini's pastoral. The lady's somewhat confusing summary of Jonson's theory of humours concludes the scene—she knows a little bit about all of the literary fads.*

VOLP.   The Poet,
     As old in time, as *Plato*, and as knowing,
     Says that your highest female grace is silence.
LAD.   Which o' your Poets? *Petrarch?* or *Tasso?* or *Dante? Guarini? Ariosto?*
     Aretine?
     Cieco di Hadria?[14] I have read them all.
VOLP.   Is everything a cause, to my destruction?
LAD.   I think, I ha' two or three of 'hem, about me.
VOLP.   The sun, the sea will sooner, both, stand still,
     Than her eternal tongue! nothing can 'scape it.
LAD.   Here's *Pastor Fido*—   VOLP.   Profess obstinate silence,
     That's, now, my safest.   LAD.   All our *English* writers,
     I mean such, as are happy in th'*Italian*,
     Will deign to steal out of this author, mainly;
     Almost as much, as from *Montaigne*;
     He has so modern, and facile a vein,
     Fitting the time, and catching the court ear.
     Your *Petrarch* is more passionate, yet he,
     In days of something, trusted 'hem, with much:
     Dante is hard, and few can understand him.
     But, for a desperate wit, there's *Aretine*!
     Only, his pictures are a little obscene—[15]
     You mark me not?   VOLP.   Alas, my mind's perturb'd.
LAD.   Why, in such cases, we must cure our selves,
     Make use of our philosophy—   VOLP.   O'y me.

14. "The blind man of Adria," Luigi Groto, poet and dramatist, sixteenth century.

15. The reference is to poems Aretino, sixteenth century, wrote for a collection of obscene designs.

LAD. And, as we find our passions do rebel,
  Encounter 'hem with reason; or divert 'hem,
  By giving scope unto some other humour
  Of lesser danger: as, in politic bodies,
  There's nothing, more, doth overwhelm the judgement,
  And clouds the understanding, than too much
  Settling, and fixing, and (as't were) subsiding
  Upon one object. For the incorporating
  Of these same outward things, into that part,
  Which we call mental, leaves some certain *faeces*,
  That stop the organs, and, as *Plato* says,
  Assassinates our knowledge. * * *

In Defense of Fletcher's "Faithful Shepherdess"

From the 1610 edition of The Faithful Shepherdess, *prefatory poem. Jonson thought Fletcher's pastoral tragicomedy a good play; here he argues that it was not the fault of the play that it was not well received by contemporary playgoers.*

To the worthy Author
MR. JOHN FLETCHER

  The wise, and many-headed *Bench*, that sits
    Upon the Life, and Death of *Plays*, and *Wits*,
  (Compos'd of *Gamester*, *Captain*, *Knight*, *Knight's man*,
    Lady, or *Pusil*,[16] that wears mask, or fan,
  Velvet, or *Taffeta* cap, rank'd in the dark
    With the shop's *Foreman*, or some such *brave spark*,
  That may judge for his *sixpence*) had, before
    They saw it half, damn'd thy whole play, and more;
  Their motives were, since it had not to do
    With vices, which they look'd for, and came to.[17]
  I, that am glad, thy Innocence was thy Guilt,
    And wish that all the *Muses*' blood were spilt,
  In such a *Martyrdom*; to vex their eyes,
    Do crown thy murdered *Poem*: which shall rise
  A glorified work to Time, when Fire,
    Or Moths shall eat, what all these Fools admire.

16. Slut.
17. I.e., came to see.

Beaumont

From the 1616 folio, Epigram LV.

to francis beaumont

How I do love thee *Beaumont,* and thy *Muse,*
    That unto me dost such religion use!
How I do fear my self, that am not worth
    The least indulgent thought thy pen drops forth!
At once thou mak'st me happy, and unmak'st;
    And giving largely to me, more thou tak'st.
What fate is mine, that so it self bereaves?
    What art is thine, that so thy friend deceives?
When even there, where most thou praisest me,
    For writing better, I must envy thee.

On Plagiarism and the Writing of Plays

*Poet-Ape steals from contemporaries; his thefts are conspicuous in that they are the only decent things in his plays. When Jonson himself adapted the ancients, the process involved the laborious discipline of so imitating the style of the original that one could not tell what was original and what was adapted. In William Drummond's phrase, Jonson "quintessenced" the ancients. (*Ibid., Epigram LVI.*)*

on poet-ape

Poor *Poet-Ape,* that would be thought our chief,
    Whose works are e'en the frippery of wit,
From brocage[18] is become so bold a thief,
    As we, the robb'd, leave rage, and pity it.
At first he made low shifts, would pick and glean,
    Buy the reversion of old plays; now grown
To'a little wealth, and credit in the *scene,*
    He takes up all, makes each man's wit his own.
And, told of this, he slights it. Tut, such crimes
    The sluggish gaping auditor devours;
He marks not whose 'twas first: and aftertimes
    May judge it to be his, as well as ours.
Fool, as if half eyes will not know a fleece
    From locks of wool, or shreds from the whole piece?

18. Illicit dealing in old things.

SHAKESPEARE

*Commendatory poem from the first folio of Shakespeare, 1623. Jonson's great
tribute to Shakespeare in the folio carefully points out that Shakespeare owed
his preeminence to art as well as to genius. This statement should be compared
with Jonson's remark to Drummond that Shakespeare wanted art, and to the
statement in* Discoveries, *where Jonson suggests that Shakespeare's friends
praised him where he was weakest when they claimed that he never blotted a
line.*

To the memory of my beloved,
The AUTHOR
MR. WILLIAM SHAKESPEARE:
AND
what he hath left us
To draw no envy (*Shakespeare*) on thy name,
    Am I thus ample to thy Book, and Fame:
While I confess thy writings to be such,
    As neither *Man*, nor *Muse*, can praise too much.
'Tis true, and all men's suffrage. But these ways
    Were not the paths I meant unto thy praise:
For silliest Ignorance on these may light,
    Which, when it sounds at best, but echoes right;
Or blind Affection, which doth ne'er advance
    The truth, but gropes, and urgeth all by chance;
Or crafty Malice, might pretend this praise,
    And think to ruin, where it seem'd to raise.
These are, as some infamous Bawd, or Whore,
    Should praise a Matron. What could hurt her more?
But thou art proof against them, and indeed
    Above th'ill fortune of them, or the need.
I, therefore will begin. Soul of the Age!
    The applause! delight! and wonder of our Stage!
My *Shakespeare*, rise; I will not lodge thee by
    Chaucer, or *Spenser*, or bid *Beaumont* lie
A little further, to make thee a room:
    Thou art a Monument, without a tomb,
And art alive still, while thy Book doth live,
    And we have wits to read, and praise to give.
That I not mix thee so, my brain excuses;

I mean with great, but disproportion'd *Muses:*
For, if I thought my judgement were of years,
    I should commit thee surely with thy peers,
And tell, how far thou didst our *Lyly* outshine,
    Or sporting *Kyd,* or *Marlowe's* mightly line.
And though thou hadst small *Latin,* and less *Greek,*
    From thence to honour thee, I would not seek
For names; but call forth thund'ring *Aeschylus,*
    Euripides, and *Sophocles* to us,
Pacuvius, Accius, him of *Cordoba* dead,[19]
    To life again, to hear thy Buskin tread,
And shake a Stage: Or, when thy Socks were on,
    Leave thee alone, for the comparison
Of all, that insolent *Greece,* or haughty *Rome*
    Sent forth, or since did from their ashes come.
Triumph, my *Britain,* thou hast one to show,
    To whom all Scenes of *Europe* homage owe.
He was not of an age, but for all time!
    And all the *Muses* still were in their prime,
When like *Apollo* he came forth to warm
    Our ears, or like a *Mercury* to charm!
Nature herself was proud of his designs,
    And joy'd to wear the dressing of his lines!
Which were so richly spun, and woven so fit,
    As, since, she will vouchsafe no other Wit.
The merry *Greek,* tart *Aristophanes,*
    Neat *Terence,* witty *Plautus,* now not please;
But antiquated, and deserted lie
    As they were not of Nature's family.
Yet must I not give Nature all: Thy Art,
    My gentle *Shakespeare,* must enjoy a part.
For though the *Poet's* matter, Nature be,
    His Art doth give the fashion. And, that he,
Who casts to write a living line, must sweat,
    (Such as thine are) and strike the second heat
Upon the *Muses'* anvil: turn the same,
    (And himself with it) that he thinks to frame;
Or for the laurel, he may gain a scorn,

19. Pacuvius and Accius are mentioned by Horace; "him of Cordoba" is
Seneca the tragedian.

For a good *Poet's* made, as well as born.
And such wert thou. Look how the father's face
    Lives in his issue, even so, the race
Of *Shakespeare's* mind, and manners brightly shines
    In his well turned, and true-filed lines:
In each of which, he seems to shake a Lance,
    As brandish'd at the eyes of Ignorance.
Sweet Swan of *Avon*! what a sight it were
    To see thee in our waters yet appear,
And make those flights upon the banks of *Thames*,
    That so did take *Eliza*, and our *James*!
But stay, I see thee in the *Hemisphere*
    Advanc'd, and made a Constellation there!
Shine forth, thou Star of *Poets*, and with rage,
    Or influence, chide, or cheer the drooping Stage;
Which, since thy flight from hence, hath mourn'd like night,
    And despairs day, but for thy Volume's light.

RICHARD BROME

Commendatory poem from the 1632 edition of The Northern Lass.
*Brome was Jonson's servant as a young man; later, a writer of Jonsonian
comedies.*

To my old Faithful Servant: and (by
his continu'd Virtue) my loving Friend:
the Author of this Work, Mr. RICH[ARD] BROME

I Had you for a Servant, once, *Dick Brome*;
    And you perform'd a Servant's faithful parts:
Now, you are got into a nearer room,
    Of *Fellowship*, professing my old Arts.
And you do do them well, with good applause,
    Which you have justly gained from the *Stage*,
By observation of those Comic Laws
    Which I, your *Master*, first did teach the Age.
You learn'd it well; and for it, serv'd your time
    Apprenticeship: which few do nowadays.
Now each Court-Hobby-horse will wince in rhyme;
    Both learned, and unlearned, all write *Plays*.
It was not so of old: Men took up trades
    That knew the Crafts they had been bred in, right:

     An honest *Bilbo*-Smith[20] would make good blades,
      And the *Physician* teach men spew, or shite;
        The *Cobbler* kept him to his nall;[21] but, now
        He'll be a *Pilot*, scarce can guide a Plough.

Joseph Rutter

Commendatory poem from the 1635 edition of The Shepherd's Holiday:
A Pastoral Tragi-Comedy.

To my dear Son, and right-learned Friend,
Master JOSEPH RUTTER

    You look, my *Joseph*, I should something say
    Unto the *world*, in praise of your *first Play*:
    And truly, so I would, could I be heard.
    You know, I never was of Truth afeard,
    And less asham'd; not when I told the crowd
    How well I lov'd *Truth*: I was scarce allow'd
    By those deep-gounded, understanding men,
    That sit to censure *Plays*, yet know not when,
    Or why to like; they found, it all was new,
    And newer, then could please them, because true.
    Such men I met withal, and so have you.
    Now, for mine own part, and it is but due,
    (You have deserv'd it from me) I have read,
    And weigh'd your *Play*: untwisted ev'ry thread,
    And know the woof, and warp thereof; can tell
    Where it runs round, and even: where so well,
    So soft, and smooth it handles, the whole piece,
    As it were spun by nature, off the fleece:
    This is my censure. Now there is a new
    Office of Wit, a Mint,[22] and (this is true)

20. Bilbao in Spain was famous for its excellent sword blades. In the old days, it was a point of pride for a man to know his craft, the craft of sword-making or any other. Now, young men expect to be admitted overnight even to the craft of poetry, the highest craft of all.

21. Awl.

22. Though Jonson may have particular individuals in mind, this cryptic denunciation of a new "Office" of critics has never been satisfactorily explicated. Perhaps Jonson scoffs simply at the growing number or nonprofessionals who feel qualified to make judgements about plays.

Cried up of late: Whereto there must be first
A *Master-worker* call'd, th'old standard burst
Of wit, and a new made: a *Warden* then,
And a *Comptroller*, two most rigid men
For order, and for governing the pyx,
A *Say-master*, hath studied all the tricks
Of *Fineness*, and *alloy*: follow his hint,
Yo'have all the *Mysteries* of *Wit's new Mint*,
The *valuations*, *mixtures*, and the same
Concluded from a *Carat* to a *dram*.

OF ANCIENTS AND CONTEMPORARIES:
CONVERSATIONS WITH DRUMMOND

From the transcript of Sir Robert Sibbald in the National Library of Scotland—Sibbald's "Adversaria," MS 33. 3. 19. Jonson's nineteenth-century editor William Gifford interrupts his survey of the Conversations *to lament (*Works *[Boston: Crosby and Co., 1860], p.42), "Such are the remarks of Jonson on his contemporaries: set down in malice, abridged without judgement, and published without shame." Drummond's cryptic notes, taken during Jonson's visit with him in Scotland in 1619, will disappoint most modern students of Jonson more because of their disorder and brevity than because they occasionally reveal that Drummond was not taken with the master's authoritarian air. Anecdote, reminiscence, gossip, and literary criticism seem to be mixed here in about equal parts—nor is it always easy to tell which is which. Drummond presumably tells us* what *Jonson said, but he does not always fill in the context (which can be everything). With this caveat in mind, readers will find the* Conversations *interesting and illuminating reading.*

1. That he had an intention to perfect an Epic Poem entitled *Heroologia*, of the worthies of his country roused by fame, and was to dedicate it to his country; it is all in couplets, for he detesteth all other rhymes. Said he had written a discourse of Poesy both against Campion and Daniel, especially this last, where he proves couplets to be the bravest sort of verses, especially when they are broken, like Hexameters; and that cross rhymes and stanzas (because the purpose would lead him beyond 8 lines to conclude) were all forced.

2. He recommended to my reading Quintilian (who (he said) would tell me the faults of my verses as if he had lived with me) and Horace, Plinius

Secundus' Epistles, Tacitus, Juvenal, Martial, whose Epigram "[The things which make life better],"[23] etc., he hath translated.

3. His censure of the English Poets was this: That Sidney did not keep a Decorum in making everyone speak as well as himself. Spenser's stanzas pleased him not, nor his matter, the meaning of which allegory he had delivered in papers to Sir Walter Raleigh. Samuel Daniel was a good honest man, had no children, but no poet.

That Michael Drayton's *Polyalbion* (if he had performed what he promised to write, the deeds of all the worthies) had been excellent; his long verses pleased him not.

That Silvester's translation of Du Bartas was not well done, and that he wrote his verses before it ere he understood to confer.

Nor that of Fairfax's.[24]

That the translations of Homer and Virgil in long Alexandrines were but prose.

That John Harrington's Ariosto, under all translations, was the worst.

* * *

That Donne's *Anniversary* was profane and full of blasphemies.

That he told Mr. Donne, if it had been written of the Virgin Mary, it had been something. To which he answered that he described the Idea of a woman and not as she was. That Donne for not keeping of accent deserved hanging.

That Shakespeare wanted Art.

That Sharpham, Day, Dekker were all rogues, and that Minishew was one.[25]

That Abram Francis in his English hexameters was a fool.

That next himself, only Fletcher and Chapman could make a Masque.

4. His judgement of Stranger Poets was that he thought not Bartas a poet but a verser, because he wrote not fiction.[26]

He cursed Petrarch for redacting verses to sonnets, which he said were like that Tyrant's bed, where some who were too short were racked, others too long cut short.

23. *Vitam quae faciunt Beatiorem.* (X.47).

24. That is, his translation of Tasso's *Jerusalem Delivered.*

25. Edward Sharpham, a writer of farces; John Day, playwright for the Children's Revels; Thomas Dekker; John Minsheu; Abram Fraunce, distinguished lawyer and writer of hexameters, a member of Gabriel Harvey's school.

26. It was sometimes said that Lucan and Tasso wrote history, not poetry, because they did not mix the fabulous and the historical. Jonson applies this criticism to Bartas—he wrote truths, not things like truths well feigned.

That Guarini in his *Pastor Fido* kept not decorum in making shepherds speak as well as himself could.

That Lucan taken in parts was good, divided; read altogether merited not the name of a Poet.

* * *

That the best pieces of Ronsard were his Odes.

All this was to no purpose, for he neither
doth understand French nor Italian.

* * *

5. To me he read the Preface of his *Art of Poesy*, upon Horace's *Art of Poesy*, where he hath an apology of a play of his, *Saint Bartholomew's Fair*; by Criticus[27] is understood Dr. Donne. There is an Epigram of Sir Edward Herbert's before it. The [translation] he said he had done in my Lord Aubigny's house 10 years since, anno 1604.[28]

The most commonplace of his repetition was a dialogue Pastoral between a shepherd & shepherdess about singing.

* * *

6. His censure of my verses was that they were all good, especially my epitaph of the Prince, save that they smelled too much of the schools and were not after the fancy of the time. For a child, says he, may write after the fashion of the Greeks & Latin verses in running;[29] yet that he wished, to please the King, that piece of *Forth Feasting* had been his own.

7. He esteemeth John Donne the first poet in the world in some things. His verses of the Lost Chain,[30] he hath by heart; and that passage of *The Calm*:[31] that dust and feathers do not stir, all was so quiet. Affirmeth Donne to have written all his best pieces ere he was 25 years old. Sir Edward Wotton's verses of a happy life[32] he hath by heart, and a piece of Chapman's translation of the 13 of the *Iliad*, which he thinketh well done.

That Donne said to him he wrote that *Epitaph on Prince Henry* (Look to me, faith) to match Sir Edward Herbert in obscureness.

27. The character Criticus in Jonson's dialogue preface to Horace's *Ars Poetica*, now lost.

28. Jonson wrote his apology for *Bartholomew Fair* in 1614; he had translated the *Ars Poetica* ten years earlier.

29. Campion favored rhymeless imitations of classical meters; Daniel favored irregular rhymes or cross-rhymes; Jonson thought iambic pentameter couplets the bravest sort of verse.

30. Elegy XI, "The Bracelet."

31. In *Letters to Several Personages*.

32. Henry Wotton's "How happy is he born, or taught."

He hath by heart some verses of Spenser's *Calendar*, about wine, between Colin and Pierce.[33]

* * *

9. That Petronius, Plinius Secundus, Tacitus speak best Latin; that Quintilian's 6. 7. 8. books were not only to be read but altogether digested. Juvenal, Persius, Horace, Martial for delight, & so was Pindar. For health, Hippocrates. Of their nation, Hooker's *Ecclesiastical History* (whose children now beggars) for church matters. * * *

* * *

10. For a heroic poem, he said there was no such ground as King Arthur's fiction, & that Sir Philip Sidney had an intention to have transformed all his *Arcadia* to the stories of King Arthur.

11. His acquaintance & behavior with poets living with him.

Daniel was at jealousies with him.

That Francis Beaumont loved too much himself & his own verses.

That Sir John Roe loved him, & when they two were ushered by my Lord Suffolk from a Masque, Roe wrote a moral epistle to him, which began that next to plays the Court and the State were the best.

God threateneth Kings, Kings Lords, and Lords do us.

He beat Marston and took his pistol from him.

* * *

Ned Field was his scholar & he had read to him the satires of Horace and some epigrams of Martial.

That Markham[34] (who added his *English Arcadia*) was not of the number of the Faithful (*i.e.*, Poets) and but a base fellow.

That such were Day and Middleton.

That Chapman and Fletcher were loved of him.

Overbury[35] was first his friend, then turn'd his mortal enemy.

12. Particulars of the actions of other poets, and apothegms.

* * *

That in that paper Sir Walter Raleigh had of the allegories of his [Spenser's] *Fairie Queene*, by the Blatant Beast the Puritans were understood; by the false Duessa, the Queen of Scots.

That Southwell was hanged; yet, so he had written that piece of his *The Burning Babe*, he would have been content to destroy many of his.

* * *

33. In the "October" eclogue, wine is praised for its powers of inspiration.

34. Gervase Markham, an indefatigable poetaster, who wrote a conclusion to Sidney's *Arcadia*.

35. Sir Thomas Overbury.

That Donne himself, for not being understood, would perish.

That Sir Walter Raleigh esteemed more of fame than conscience: the best wits of England were employed for making of his history; Ben himself had written a piece to him of the Punic War, which he altered and set in his book.

* * *

Marston wrote his father-in-law's preaching, & his father-in-law his comedies.

Shakespeare in a play brought in a number of men saying they had suffered shipwreck in Bohemia, where there is no sea near by some 100 miles.

Daniel wrote *Civil Wars*, and yet hath not one battle in his book.

* * *

Owen[36] is a poor pedantic Schoolmaster, sweeping his living from the posteriors of little children, and hath no thing good in him; his epigrams being bare narrations.

* * *

Fletcher and Beaumont, ten years since, hath written *The Faithful Shepherdess*, a tragicomedy well done.

* * *

13. Of his own life, education, birth, actions.

* * *

He was delated by Sir James Murray to the King for writing something against the Scots in a play *Eastward Hoe* & voluntarily imprisoned himself with Chapman and Marston, who had written it amongst them. The report was that they should then had their ears cut & noses. After their delivery, he banqueted all his friends: there was Camden, Selden,[37] and others. * * *

He had many quarrels with Marston, beat him & took his pistol from him, wrote his *Poetaster* on him; the beginning of them were that Marston represented him in the stage.

In his youth, given to venery.

* * *

Northampton was his mortal enemy for brawling on a St. George's day [with] one of his attenders. He was called before the Council for his *Sejanus* & accused of Popery and treason by him.

* * *

36. John Owen, headmaster of King Henry VIII's school, Warwick, published several collections of epigrams.

37. William Camden was a famous scholar and Jonson's mentor. John Selden was a famous juror and scholar of the seventeenth century. Jonson was proud to call such men his friends.

He hath a mind to be a churchman, and so he might have favor to make one sermon to the King, he careth not what thereafter should befall him: for he would not flatter though he saw Death.

* * *

15. His opinion of verses.

That he wrote all his first in prose, for so his master Camden had learned him.

That verses stood by sense without either colors or accent, which yet other times he denied.

A great many epigrams were ill, because they expressed in the end what should have been understood by what was said.

* * *

16. Of his works.

That the half of his comedies were not in print. He hath a pastoral entitled *The May Lord*;[38] his own name is Alkin. * * * In his first story, Alkin cometh in mending his broken pipe. Contrary to all other pastorals, he bringeth the Clowns making mirth and foolish sports.

He hath intention to write a fisher or pastoral play & set the stage of it in the Lowmond Lake.

* * *

A play of his upon which he was accused, *The Devil Is an Ass*: according to Comedia Vetus in England, the devil was brought in either with one Vice or other; the play done, the devil carried away the Vice. He brings in the devil so overcome with the wickedness of this age that [he] thought himself an ass.

* * *

He hath commented & translated Horace's *Art of Poesy*; it is in dialogue ways: by Criticus he understandeth Dr. Donne.

The old book that goes about (*The Art of English Poesy*)[39] was done 20 years since & kept long in writ as a secret.

He had an intention to have made a play like Plautus' *Amphitrio*, but left it off, for that he could never find two so like others that he could persuade the spectators they were one.[40]

* * *

38. Nothing is known of Jonson's *The May Lord*.

39. Puttenham's, published anonymously in 1587.

40. In Plautus' play, Zeus impersonates Amphitruo and Mercury impersonates the slave Sosia; the real Amphitruo and Sosia arrive, and the greatest confusion ensues.

18. Miscellaneous.

* * *

Lucan, Sidney, Guarini make every man speak as well as themselves, forgetting decorum; for Dametas[41] sometimes speaks grave sentences.

Lucan taken in parts excellent; altogether, naught.

He disuaded me from Poetry, for that she had beggared him, when he might have been a rich lawyer, physician, or merchant.

* * *

He was better versed & knew more in Greek and Latin than all the poets in England and quintessenced their brains.

* * *

41. The type of the rustic clown in Sidney's *Arcadia*.

VIII

CONTEMPORARY ACTORS AND AUDIENCES

The Audience as Stage Critic

From the 1616 folio of Every Man Out of His Humour, *I.ii.55–65.*
Carlo Buffone gives the clown Sogliardo satiric advice on how to behave as a
gentleman of the times.

SOG. I warrant you, sir.

CAR. I, and sit o'the stage, and flout: provided, you have a good suit.

SOG. O, I'll have a suit only for that, sir.

CAR. You must [if you are to be a gentleman] endeavour to feed cleanly at
your Ordinary,[1] sit melancholy, and pick your teeth when you cannot speak:
and when you come to Plays, be humorous, look with a good starch'd face,
and ruffle your brow like a new boot; laugh at nothing but your own jests,
or else as the Noblemen laugh. That's a special grace you must observe.

The Derivative and the Revived and the Audience as Stage Critic

From the 1616 folio of Cynthia's Revels, Induction, *lines 168–218. The*
third boy actor takes the role of a critical auditor; the second boy, the role of
Jonson's "attorney."

2. * * * if you please to confer with our Author, by attorney, you may,
sir: our proper self here, stands for him.

3. Troth, I have no such serious affair to negotiate with him, but what may
very safely be turn'd upon thy trust. It is in the general behalf of this fair
society here, that I am to speak, at least the more judicious part of it,
which seems much distasted with the immodest and obscene writing of
many, in their plays. Besides, they could wish, your *Poets* would leave to
be promoters of other men's jests, and to waylay all the stale *apothegms*, or
old books they can hear of (in print, or otherwise) to farce their *Scenes*
withal. That they would not so penuriously glean wit, from every laun-
dress, or hackney-man, or derive their best grace (with servile imitation)
from common stages, or observation of the company they converse with;
as if their invention liv'd wholly upon another man's trencher. Again, that
feeding their friends with nothing of their own, but what they have twice or
thrice cook'd, they should not wantonly give out how soon they had
dressed it; nor how many coaches came to carry away the broken meat,
besides hobby-horses, and foot-cloth nags.

1. Boarding house.

2.   So, sir, this is all the reformation you seek?

3.   It is: do not you think it necessary to be practic'd, my little wag?

2.   Yes, where any such ill-habited custom is receiv'd.

3.   O (I had almost forgot it too) they say, the *umbrae*, or ghosts of some three or four plays, departed a dozen years since, have been seen walking on your stage here: take heed, boy, if your house be haunted with such *hobgoblins*, 'twill fright away all your spectators quickly.

2.   Good, sir, but what will you say now, if a *Poet* (untouched with any breath of this disease) find the tokens upon you, that are of the auditory? As some one civet-wit among you, that knows no other learning, than the price of satin and velvets; nor other perfection than the wearing of a neat suit; and yet will censure as desperately as the most profess'd *critic* in the house: presuming, his clothes should bear him out in't. Another (whom it hath pleas'd nature to furnish with more beard, than brain) prunes his mustaccio, lisps, and (with some score of affected oaths) swears down all that sit about him; *That the old Jieronimo,* (as it was first acted) *was the only best, and judiciously penned play of Europe.* A third great-bellied juggler talks of twenty years since, and when *Monsieur* was here,[2] and would enforce all wits to be of that fashion, because his doublet is still so. A fourth miscalls all by the name of fustian, that his grounded capacity cannot aspire to. A fifth, only shakes his bottle-head, and out of his cork brain, squeezeth out a pitiful-learned face, and is silent.

3.   By my faith, Jack, you have put me down * * *.

THE POPULAR THEATER AND POPULAR AND CAVALIER CRITICS

From the 1616 folio of The Case Is Altered, *I.ii.28–82. The work of Antonio Balladino (Anthony Munday) is satirized as the epitome of public drama—stale poetry and extravagant plots. Onion the clown is Jonson's satiric version of the penny groundlings who support the romantic extravagances of the popular stage.*

ANTO.   My name is *Antonio Balladino.*

ONI.   *Balladino?* you are not *Pageant* Poet to the City of *Milan* sir, are you?

ANTO.   I supply the place sir: when a worse cannot be had sir.

ONI.   I cry you mercy sir, I Love you the better for that sir, by Jesu you must pardon me, I knew you not, but I'ld pray to be better acquainted with you sir, I have seen of your works.

ANTO.   I am at your service good Master *Onion,* but concerning this maiden that you love sir? what is she?

2.   The Duke d'Alençon, suitor to Elizabeth and visitor to England in the 1570's.

ONI.   O did my fellow *Juniper* tell you? marry sir, she is as one may say, but a poor man's child indeed, and for mine own part I am no Gentleman born I must confess, but *my mind to me a kingdom is*[3] truly.

ANTO.   Truly a very good saying.

ONION.   'Tis somewhat stale, but that's no matter.

ANTO.   O 'tis the better, such things ever are like bread, which the staler it is, the more wholesome.

ONION.   This is but a hungry comparison in my judgement.

ANTO.   Why, I'll tell you, *M. Onion*, I do use as much stale stuff, though I say it my self, as any man does in that kind I am sure. Did you see the last *Pageant*, I set forth?

ONION.   No faith sir, but there goes a huge report on't.

ANTO.   Why, you shall be one of my *Maecen-assess*,[4] I'll give you one of the books, O you'll like it admirably.

ONI.   Nay that's certain, I'll get my fellow *Juniper* to read it.

ANTO.   Read it sir, I'll read it to you.

ONION.   Tut then, I shall not choose but like it.

ANTO.   Why look you sir, I write so plain, and keep that old *Decorum*,[5] that you must of necessity like it; marry you shall have some now (as for example, in plays) that will have every day new tricks, and write you nothing but humours: indeed this pleases the Gentlemen: but the common sort they care not for't, they know not what to make on't, they look for good matter, they, and are not edified with such toys.

ONION.   You are in the right, I'll not give a halfpenny to see a thousand on 'hem. I was at one the last Term, but & ever I see a more roguish thing, I am a piece of cheese, & no *onion*, nothing but kings & princes in it, the fool came not out a jot.

ANTO.   True sir, they would have me make such plays, but as I tell 'hem, and they'll give me twenty pound a play, I'll not raise my vein.

ONION.   No, it were a vain thing, and you should sir.

ANTO.   Tut give me the penny, give me the penny, I care not for the Gentlemen I, let me have a good ground, no matter for the pen, the plot shall carry it.

ONION.   Indeed that's right, you are in print already for the best plotter.[6]

ANTO.   I, I might as well have been put in for a dumb show too.

ONI.   I marry sir, I marvel you were not, stand aside sir a while.

3. Quoted from an old song by Sir Edward Dyer.
4. Maecenas, patron of Horace and Virgil; the type of the patron of literature.
5. The old-fashioned "decorum" of early English drama.
6. In Francis Meres' *Paladis Tamia*.

The State of Dramatic Art:
The Polished and the Copious

From the 1616 folio of The Alchemist, *the preface.*

TO THE READER

If thou beest more, thou art an understander, and then I trust thee. If thou art one that tak'st up, and but a Pretender, beware at what hands thou receiv'st thy commodity; for thou wert never more fair in the way to be coz'ned (than in this Age) in *Poetry*, especially in Plays: wherein, now, the Concupiscence of Dances, and Antiques[7] so reigneth, [that] to run away from Nature, and be afraid of her, is the only point of art that tickles the *Spectators*. But how out of purpose, and place, do I name Art? when the Professors are grown so obstinate contemners of it, and presumers on their own Naturals, as they are deriders of all diligence that way, and, by simple mocking at the terms, when they understand not the things, think to get off wittily with their Ignorance. Nay, they are esteem'd the more learned, and sufficient for this, by the Many, through their excellent vice of judgement. For they commend Writers, as they do Fencers, or Wrestlers; who if they come in robustuously, and put for it with a great deal of violence, are receiv'd for the braver fellows: when many times their own rudeness is the cause of their disgrace, and a little touch of their Adversary gives all that boisterous force the foil. I deny not, but that these men, who always seek to do more than enough, may sometime happen on something that is good, and great; but very seldom: And when it comes it doth not recompense the rest of their ill. It sticks out perhaps, and is more eminent, because all is sordid, and vile about it: as lights are more discern'd in a thick darkness, than a faint shadow. I speak not this, out of a hope to do good on any man, against his will; for I know, if it were put to the question of theirs, and mine, the worse would find more suffrages: because the most favour common errors. But I give thee this warning, that there is a great difference between those, that (to gain the opinion of Copy) utter all they can, how ever unfitly; and those that use election, and a mean. For it is only the disease of the unskillful, to think rude things greater than polish'd: or scatter'd more numerous than compos'd.

7. Jonson objects to the introduction of masque elements into comedy. Perhaps he alludes to Shakespeare's *Winter's Tale*. Cf. the induction to *Bartholomew Fair* where similar attacks are made with Shakespeare in mind.

THE ARTIST AND THE AUDIENCE AGAIN

The prologue from the 1616 folio of Epicoene. *Here Jonson disdains mere coterie playwrighting in the name of a truly universal drama which will satisfy all types of auditors—the "people" and the "cunning palates." The Horatian orthodoxy of the opening statement should be noted.*

PROLOGUE

Truth says, of old, the art of making plays
Was to content the people; & their praise
   Was to the *Poet* money, wine, and bays.
But in this age, a sect of writers are,
   That, only, for particular likings care,
   And will taste nothing that is popular.
With such we mingle neither brain, nor breasts;
   Our wishes, like to those (make public feasts)
   Are not to please the cook's tastes, but the guests'.
Yet, if those cunning palates hither come,
   They shall find guest entreaty, and good room;
   And though all relish not, sure, there will be some,
That, when they leave their seats, shall make 'hem say,
   Who wrote that piece, could so have wrote a play:[8]
   But that, he knew, this was the better way.
For, to present all custard, or all tart,
   And have no other meats, to bear a part,
   Or to want bread, and salt, were but course-art.
The *Poet* prays you then, with better thought
   To sit; and, when his cakes are all in brought,
   Though there be none forfeit, there will dear-bought
Be fit for ladies: some for lords, knights, squires,
   Some for your waiting wench, and city-wires,
   Some for your men, and daughters of *White-Friars*.
Nor is it, only, while you keep your seat
Here, that his feast will last; but you shall eat
A week at ord'naries, on his broken meat:
      If his *Muse* be true,
      Who commends her to you.

8. I.e., he who wrote part of the play in a certain fashion could have written all of it so, if he had not had better things in mind.

EDWARD ALLEYN

From the 1616 folio, Epigram **LXXXIX.** *A tribute to one of the great actors of the age, a rival of Richard Burbage, famous for such roles as that of Marlowe's Faustus.*

TO EDWARD ALLEYN

If *Rome* so great, and in her wisest age,
    Fear'd not to boast the glories of her stage,
As skilfull *Roscius*, and grave *Æsope*,[9] men,
    Yet crown'd with honors, as with riches, then;
Who had no less a trumpet of their name,
    Than *Cicero*, whose every breath was fame:
How can so great example die in me,
    That, *Alleyn*, I should pause to publish thee?
Who both their graces in thy self hast more
    Outstripp'd, than they did all that went before:
And present worth in all dost so contract,
    As others speak, but only thou dost act.
Wear this renown. 'Tis just, that who did give
    So many *Poets* life, by one should live.

SALOMON PAVY

Jonson's famous tribute to one of the child actors. (Ibid., Epigram **CXX.**)

EPITAPH ON S[ALOMON] P[AVY]
A CHILD OF Q. EL[IZABETH'S] CHAPEL

Weep with me all you that read
    This little story:
And know, for whom a tear you shed,
    Death's self is sorry.
'Twas a child, that so did thrive
    In grace, and feature,
As *Heaven* and *Nature* seem'd to strive
    Which own'd the creature.
Years he numbered scarce thirteen
    When *Fates* turn'd cruel,
Yet three fill'd *Zodiacs* had he been
    The stage's jewel;

9. Roscius and Aesope were Roman actors of comedy and tragedy, respectively.

And did act (what now we moan)
    Old men so duly,
As, sooth, the *Parcæ* thought him one,
    He play'd so truly.
So, by error, to his fate
    They all consented;
But viewing him since (alas, too late)
    They have repented.
And have sought (to give new birth)
    In baths to steep him;
But, being so much too good for earth,
    Heaven vows to keep him.

THE POPULAR STAGE AND THE ARTIST: THE AUDIENCE AS CRITIC

From the 1631 folio of Bartholomew Fair, *the induction. Jonson calls attention to what is in many cases a sophistication of earlier dramatic conventions by having the stage-keeper lament the passing of the good old days; he also tries once again to teach his audience something about its true function as critic.*

STAGE-KEEPER

Gentlemen, have a little patience, they are e'en upon coming, instantly. He that should begin the Play, Master *Littlewit,* the *Proctor,* has a stitch new fallen in his black silk stocking; 'twill be drawn up ere you can tell twenty. He plays one o' the *Arches,*[10] that dwells about the *Hospital,* and he has a very pretty part. But for the whole *Play,* will you ha' the truth on't? (I am looking, lest the *Poet* hear me, or his man, Master *Brome,* behind the Arras) it is like to be a very conceited scurvy one, in plain English. When 't comes to the *Fair,* once: you were e'en as good go to *Virginia,* for any thing there is of *Smithfield.* He has not hit the humours, he does not know 'hem; he has not convers'd with the *Bartholmew*-birds, as they say; he has ne'er a Sword, and Buckler man in his *Fair,* nor a little *Davy,*[11] to take toll o' the Bawds there, as in my time, nor a *Kind-heart,* if anybody's teeth should chance to ache in his *Play.* Nor a juggler with a well-educated Ape to come over the chain, for the *King* of *England,* and back again for the *Prince,* and sit still on his arse for the *Pope,* and the *King* of *Spain*! None o' these fine sights! Nor has he the

10. A proctor in the Court of Arches.
11. A little Davy is a roaring bully; a kind-heart is a tooth-drawer: types associated with the Smithfield Fair.

Canvas cut i' the night, for a Hobby-horseman to creep in to his she-neigh-
bour, and take his leap, there! Nothing! No, and some writer (that I know)
had had but the penning o' this matter, he would ha' made you such a *jig-
ajog* i' the booths, you should ha' thought an earthquake had been i' the
Fair! But these Master-*Poets*, they will ha' their own absurd courses; they will
be inform'd of nothing! He has (*sirreverence*) kick'd me three, or four times
about the Tiring-house, I thank him, for but offering to put in, with my
experience. I'll be judg'd by you, *Gentlemen*, now, but for one conceit of mine!
would not a fine Pump upon the Stage ha' done well, for a property now?
and a *Punk* set under upon her head, with her Stern upward, and ha' been
sous'd by my witty young masters o' the *Inns o' Court*? what think you o' this
for a show, now? he will not hear o' this! I am an Ass! I! and yet I kept the
Stage in Master *Tarleton's*[12] time, I thank my stars. Ho! and that man had
liv'd to have play'd in *Bartholmew Fair*, you should ha' seen him ha' come in,
and ha' been cozened i' the Cloth-quarter, so finely! And *Adams*,[13] the Rogue,
ha' leap'd and caper'd upon him, and ha' dealt his vermin about, as though
they had cost him nothing. And then a substantial watch to ha' stolen in
upon 'hem, and taken 'hem away, with mistaking words,[14] as the fashion is,
in the *Stage*-practice.

Book-holder: Scrivener. To him.

BOOK.   How now? what rare discourse are you fallin upon? ha? ha' you
found any familiars here, that you are so free? what's the business?
STA.   Nothing, but the understanding Gentlemen o' the ground here, ask'd
my judgement.
BOOK.   Your judgement, Rascal? for what? sweeping the *Stage*? or gathering
up the broken Apples for the bears[15] within? Away Rogue, it's come to a
fine degree in these *spectacles* when such a youth as you pretend to a judgement. And yet he may, i' the most o' this matter i'faith: For the *Author*
hath writ it just to his *Meridian*, and the *Scale* of the grounded judgements
here, his Play-fellows in wit. Gentlemen; not for want of a *Prologue*, but
by way of a new one, I am sent out to you here, with a Scrivener, and
certain Articles drawn out in haste between our *Author*, and you; which
if you please to hear, and as they appear reasonable, to approve of; the
Play will follow presently. Read, *Scribe*, gi' me the Counterpane.

12. Richard Tarlton, leading comic actor until his death in 1588.
13. John Adams, one of Tarlton's fellow actors.
14. For example, perhaps, Dogberry in Shakespeare's *Much Ado About Nothing*.
15. The Hope Theatre was a combination theater and bear garden used for
bear baiting.

SCR. *Articles* of Agreement, indented, between the *Spectators* or *Hearers*, at the *Hope* on the Bank side, in the County of *Surrey* on the one party; And the *Author of Bartholmew Fair* in the said place, and County on the other party: the one and thirtieth day of *Octob.* 1614. and in the twelfth year of the Reign of our Sovereign Lord, *James* by the grace of God *King of England, France, & Ireland*; Defender of the faith. And of *Scotland* the seven and fortieth.

INPRIMIS, It is covenanted and agreed, by and between the parties abovesaid, and the said *Spectators*, and *Hearers*, as well the curious and envious, as the favouring and judicious, as also the grounded judgements and understandings, do for themselves severally Covenant, and agree to remain in the places, their money or friends have put them in, with patience, for the space of two hours and an half, and somewhat more. In which time the *Author* promiseth to present them by us, with a new sufficient Play called *BARTHOLMEW FAIR*, merry, and as full of noise, as sport: made to delight all, and to offend none. Provided they have either, the wit, or the honesty to think well of themselves.

It is further agreed that every person here, have his or their free will of censure, to like or dislike at their own charge, the *Author* having now departed with his right: It shall be lawful for any man to judge his six pen'orth, his twelve pen'orth, so to his eighteen pence, 2. shillings, half a crown, to the value of his place: Provided always his place get not above his wit. And if he pay for half a dozen, he may censure for all them too, so that he will undertake that they shall be silent. He shall put in for *Censures* here, as they do for *lots* at the *lottery*: marry, if he drop but six pence at the door, and will censure a crown's worth, it is thought there is no conscience, or justice in that.

It is also agreed, that every man here, exercise his own judgement, and not censure by *Contagion*, or upon *trust*, from another's voice, or face, that sits by him, be he never so first, in the *Commission of Wit*: As also, that he be fixed and settled in his censure, that what he approves, or not approves today, he will do the same tomorrow, and if tomorrow, the next day, and so the next week (if need be:) and not to be brought about by any that sits on the *Bench* with him, though they indict, and arraign *Plays* daily. He that will swear, *Jeronimo,* or *Andronicus*[16] are the best plays, yet, shall pass unexcepted at, here, as a man whose judgement shows it is constant, and hath stood still, these five and twenty, or thirty years. Though it be an *Ignorance*, it is a virtuous and stay'd ignorance; and next to *truth*, a confirm'd error does well; such a one, the *Author* knows where to find him.

16. *Titus Andronicus*, published in 1594.

It is further covenanted, concluded and agreed, that how great soever the expectation be, no person here, is to expect more than he knows, or better ware than a *Fair* will afford: neither to look back to the sword and buckler-age of *Smithfield*, but content himself with the present. In stead of a little *Davy*, to take toll o' the Bawds, the *Author* doth promise a strutting *Horse-courser*, with a *leer*-Drunkard, two or three to attend him, in as good *Equipage* as you would wish. And then for *Kind-heart*, the Tooth-drawer, a fine oily *Pig-woman* with her *Tapster*, to bid you welcome, and a consort of *Roarers* for music. A wise *Justice* of *Peace meditant*, in stead of a *Juggler*, with an *Ape*. A civil *Cutpurse searchant*. A sweet *Singer* of new Ballads *allurant*: and as fresh an *Hypocrite*,[17] as ever was broach'd, *rampant*. If there be never a *Servant-monster* i'the *Fair*,[18] who can help it? he says; nor a nest of *Antiques*?[19] He is loath to make Nature afraid in his *Plays*, like those that beget *Tales*, *Tempests*, and such like *Drolleries*, to mix his head with other men's heels, let the concupiscence of *Jigs* and *Dances*, reign as strong as it will amongst you: yet if the *Puppets* will please anybody, they shall be entreated to come in.

In *consideration of which*, it is finally agreed, by the foresaid hearers, and *spectators*, that they neither in themselves conceal, nor suffer by them to be concealed any *State-decipherer*, or politic *Picklock* of the *Scene*, so solemnly ridiculous, as to search out, who was meant by the *Gingerbread-woman*, who by the *Hobby-horse-man*, who by the *Costard-monger*, nay, who by their *Wares*. Or that will pretend to affirm (on his own *inspired ignorance*) what *Mirror of Magistrates* is meant by the *Justice*, what great *Lady* by the *Pig-woman*, what *conceal'd States-man*, by the *Seller* of *Mouse-traps*, and so of the rest. But that such person, or persons so found, be left discovered to the mercy of the *Author*, as a forfeiture to the *Stage*, and your laughter, aforesaid. As also, such as shall so desperately, or ambitiously, play the fool by his place aforesaid, to challenge the *Author* of scurrility, because the language somewhere savours of *Smithfield*, the Booth, and the Pig-broth, or of profaneness, because a *Mad-man* cries, *God quit you*, or *bless you*. In *witness* whereof, as you have preposterously put to your Seals already (which is your money) you will now add the other part of suffrage, your hands. The *Play* shall presently begin. And though the *Fair* be not kept in the same Region, that some here, perhaps, would have it, yet think, that therein the *Author* hath observ'd a special *Decorum*, the place being as dirty as *Smithfield*, and as stinking every whit.

17. Puritan.
18. A reference to Caliban in Shakespeare's *The Tempest*.
19. A reference to the dance of satyrs in *The Winter's Tale*.

Howsoever, he prays you to believe, his *Ware* is still the same, else you will make him justly suspect that he that is so loath to look on a *Baby*, or an *Hobby-horse*, here, would be glad to take up a *Commodity* of them, at any laughter, or loss, in another place.[20]

COMIC TYPES AND THE POPULAR AUDIENCE:
THE AUDIENCE AS CRITIC

From the 1631 folio of The Staple of News, *Intermeans after Acts I, II, III, and IV. Again Jonson satirizes popular tastes, this time by making the Gossips—Mirth, Tattle, Expectation, and Censure—misconstrue the comedy, yearn for the conventions and comic types of an earlier day, and inadvertently call attention to what is actually going on.*

THE FIRST INTERMEAN AFTER THE FIRST ACT
* * *

TATTLE.   I would fain see the *Fool*, gossip, the *Fool* is the finest man i' the company, they say, and has all the wit: He is the very *Justice* o' *Peace* o' the Play, and can commit whom he will, and what he will, error, absurdity, as the toy takes him, and no man say, black is his eye, but laugh at him.

MIRTH.   But they ha' no *Fool* i' this Play, I am afraid, gossip.

TATTLE.   It's a wise Play, then.

EXPECTATION.   They are all fools, the rather, in that.

CENSURE.   Like enough.

TATTLE.   My husband, (*Timothy Tattle*, God rest his poor soul) was wont to say, there was no Play without a *Fool*, and a *Devil* in't; he was for the *Devil* still, God bless him. The *Devil* for his money, would he say, I would fain see the *Devil*. And why would you so fain see the *Devil*? would I say. Because he has horns, wife, and may be a cuckold as well as a *Devil*, he would answer: You are e'en such another, husband, quoth I. Was the *Devil* ever married? where do you read, the *Devil* was ever so honorable to commit *Matrimony*? The Play will tell us that, says he, we'll go see't to-morrow, the *Devil is an Ass*. He is an errant learn'd man, that made it, and can write, they say, and I am foully deceiv'd, but he can read too.

MIRTH.   I remember it gossip, I went with you, by the same token, *Mrs. Trouble Truth* dissuaded us, and told us, he was a profane *Poet*, and all his Plays had *Devils* in them. That he kept school upo' the *Stage*, could conjure there, above the *School* of *Westminster*, and *Doctor Lamb*[21] too: not a Play

20. I.e., anyone with the poor taste to disapprove of Jonson's fictitious fair may be presumed to have the poor taste to enjoy real fairs.

21. A notorious astrologer of the day.

he made, but had a *Devil* in it. And that he would learn us all to make our
husbands Cuckolds at Plays: by another token, that a young married wife
i'the company, said, she could find in her heart to steal thither, and see a
little o'the vanity through her mask, and come practice at home.

TATTLE.   O, it was, *Mistress*—

MIRTH.   Nay, Gossip, I name no body. It may be 'twas my self.

EXPECTATION.   But was the *Devil* a proper man, Gossip?

MIRTH.   As fine a gentleman, of his inches, as ever I saw trusted to the *Stage*,
or any where else: and lov'd the common wealth, as well as e'er a *Patriot*
of 'hem all: he would carry away the *Vice* on his back, quick to *Hell*, in
every Play where he came, and reform abuses.

EXPECTATION.   There was the *Devil* of *Edmonton*,[22] no such man, I warrant
you.

CENSURE.   The *Conjurer* cozen'd him with a candle's end, he was an Ass.

MIRTH.   But there was one *Smug*, a Smith, would have made a horse laugh,
and broke his halter, as they say.

TATTLE.   O, but the poor man had got a shrewd mischance, one day.

EXPECTATION.   How, Gossip?

TATTLE.   He had dressed a Rogue i'the morning, that had the *Staggers*, and
had got such a spice of 'hem himself, by noon, as they would not away all
the Play time, do what he could, for his heart.

MIRTH.   'Twas his part, Gossip, he was to be drunk, by his part.

TATTLE.   Say you so? I understood not so much.

EXPECTA.   Would we had such an other part, and such a man in this play,
I fear 'twill be an excellent dull thing.

CENSURE.   Expect, intend it.

THE SECOND INTERMEAN AFTER THE SECOND ACT

CENSURE.   Why, this is duller and duller! intolerable! scurvy! neither *Devil*
nor *Fool* in this Play! pray God, some on us be not a *witch*, Gossip, to fore-
speak the matter thus.

MIRTH.   I fear we are all such, and we were old enough: But we are not all
old enough to make one *witch*. How like you the *Vice* i'the Play?

EXPECTATION.   Which is he?

MIR.   Three or four: old *Covetousness*, the sordid *Penny-boy*, the *Money-bawd*,
who is a flesh-bawd too, they say.

TATTLE.   But here is never a *Fiend* to carry him away. Besides, he has never
a wooden dagger! I'ld not give a rush for a *Vice*, that has not a wooden
dagger to snap at every body he meets.

22. A famous old play, anonymous.

MIRTH.   That was the old way, Gossip, when *Iniquity* came in like *Hokos-Pokos*, in a Juggler's jerkin, with false skirts, like the *Knave* of *Clubs*! but now they are attir'd like men and women o' the time, the *Vices*, male and female! *Prodigality* like a young heir, and his *Mistress Money* (whose favours he scatters like counters) pranked up like a prime *Lady*, the *Infanta* of the *Mines*.

CEN.   Aye, therein they abuse an honorable *Princess*, it is thought.

MIRTH.   By whom is it so thought? or where lies the abuse?

CEN.   Plain in the styling her *Infanta*, and giving her three names.

MIRTH.   Take heed, it lie not in the vice of your interpretation: what have *Aurelia, Clara, Pecunia* to do with any person? do they any more, but express the property of *Money*, which is the daughter of earth, and drawn out of the Mines? Is there nothing to be call'd *Infanta*, but what is subject to exception? Why not the *Infanta* of the Beggars? or *Infanta* o'the Gypsies? as well as *King* of Beggars, and *King* of Gypsies?

CEN.   Well, and there were no wiser then I, I would sew him in a sack, and send him by sea to his *Princess*.

MIRT.   Faith, and he heard you *Censure*, he would go near to stick the Ass's ears to your high dressing, and perhaps to all ours for harkening to you.

TATTLE.   By'r *Lady*, but he should not to mine, I would harken, and harken, an censure, if I saw cause, for th'other *Princess*' sake *Pokahontas*, surnam'd the blessed, whom he has abus'd indeed (and I do censure him, and will censure him) to say she came forth of a Tavern, was said like a paltry *Poet*.

MIRTH.   That's but one Gossip's opinion, and my Gossip *Tattle's* too! but what says *Expectation*, here, she sits sullen and silent.

EXP.   Troth, I expect their *Office*, their great *Office*! the Staple, what it will be! they have talk't on't, but we see't not open yet; ∗ ∗ ∗.

THE THIRD INTERMEAN AFTER THE THIRD ACT

∗ ∗ ∗

CEN.   For my part, I believe it:[23] and there were no wiser than I, I would have ne'er a cunning *School-Master* in *England*. I mean a *Cunning-Man*, a *School-Master*; that is a *Conjuror*, or a *Poet*, or that had any acquaintance with a *Poet*. They make all their scholars *Play-boys*! Is't not a fine sight, to see all our children made *Interluders*? Do we pay our money for this? we send them to learn their *Grammar*, and their *Terence*, and they learn their *play-books*? well, they talk, we shall have no more Parliaments (God bless

23. Gossip Censure believes the foolish story of black magic which Gossip Tattle has just told her, then proceeds to attack poets for their "magic," and plays and playwrights too.

us) but an' we have, I hope, *Zeal-of-the-land-Busy*, and my Gossip, *Rabby Trouble-Truth*[24] will start up, and see we shall have painful good Ministers to keep School, and *Catechise* our youth, and not teach 'hem to speak *Plays*, and act *Fables* of false news, in this manner, to the super-vexation of Town and Country, with a wanion.

THE FOURTH INTERMEAN AFTER THE FOURTH ACT

TATTLE.   Why? This was the worst of all! the *Catastrophe*![25]

CEN.   The matter began to be good, but now: and he has spoil'd it all, with his Beggar there!

MIRT.   A beggarly *Jack* it is, I warrant him, and a kin to the *Poet*.

TAT.   Like enough, for he had the chiefest part in his play, if you mark it.

EXP.   Absurdity on him, for a huge overgrown *Play-maker*! why should he make him live again, when they, and we all thought him dead? If he had left him to his rags, there had been an end of him.

TAT.   I, But set a beggar on horse-back, he'll never linne[26] till he be agallop.

CEN.   The young heir grew a fine *Gentleman*, in this last Act!

EXP.   So he did, *Gossip*: and kept the best company.

CEN.   And feasted 'hem, and his *Mistress*!

TAT.   And show'd her to 'hem all! was not jealous!

MIRTH.   But very communicative, and liberal, and began to be *magnificent*, if the churl his father would have let him alone.

CEN.   It was spitefully done o'the *Poet*, to make the Chuff take him off in his height, when he was going to do all his brave deeds!

THE AUDIENCE OF THE PLAY "THE NEW INN"

The dedication from the 1631 octavo of The New Inn. *Jonson was not happy with the poor reception the play received in the theater.*

THE DEDICATION, TO THE READER

If thou be such, I make thee my Patron, and dedicate the Piece to thee: If not so much, would I had been at the charge of thy better literature. Howsoever, if thou canst but spell, and join my sense; there is more hope of thee, than of a hundred fastidious *impertinents*, who were there present the first day,

24. Puritan hypocrites.

25. The gossips here dramatize Jonson's use of the five-act structure. They are upset by the *epitasis* which concludes Act Four (Tattle calls it the *catastrophe*)— the false *catastrophe* of the *epitasis* will be remedied in Act Five by the *catastasis* and the *catastrophe*.

26. Stop.

yet never made piece of their prospect the right way. What did they come for, then? thou wil't ask me. I will as punctually answer: To see, and to be seen. To make a general muster of themselves in their clothes of credit: and possess the Stage, against the Play. To dislike all, but mark nothing. And by their confidence of rising between the Acts, in oblique lines, make *affidavit* to the whole house, of their not understanding one Scene. Arm'd, with this prejudice, as the *Stage* furniture, or *Arras* cloths, they were there, as Spectators, away. For the faces in the hangings, and they beheld alike. So I wish, they may do ever. And do trust my self, and my Book, rather to thy rustic candor, than all the pomp of their pride, and solemn ignorance, to boot. Fare thee well, and fall too. Read.

THE ARTIST AND POPULAR TASTE

*(*Ibid., *Prologue.)*

THE PROLOGUE

You are welcome, welcome all, to the *new Inn*;
Though the old house, we hope our cheer will win
Your acceptation: we ha' the same Cook,
Still, and the fat, who says, you sha' not look
Long, for your bill of fare, but every dish
Be serv'd in, i' the time, and to your wish:
If any thing be set to a wrong taste,
'Tis not the meat, there, but the mouth's displac'd,
Remove but that sick palate, all is well. ∗ ∗ ∗

THE AUDIENCE OF THE PLAY

*(*Ibid., *Second Epilogue.)*

ANOTHER EPILOGUE ∗ ∗ ∗ MADE FOR THE PLAY IN THE POET'S DEFENCE ∗ ∗ ∗
A *Jovial Host*, and Lord of the new *Inn*,
    Clep't the Light Heart, with all that past therein,
Hath been the subject of our *Play* tonight,
    To give the *King*, and *Queen*, and *Court* delight:
But, then we mean, the *Court* above the stairs,
    And past the guard; men that have more of ears,
Than eyes to judge us: Such as will not hiss
    Because the Chambermaid was named *Cis*.
We think, it would have serv'd our *Scene* as true,

> If, as it is, at first we had call'd her *Pru*,
> For any mystery we there have found,
>   Or magic in the letters, or the sound.
> She only meant was, for a girl of wit,
>   To whom her *Lady* did a Province fit:
> Which she would have discharg'd, and done, as well,
>   Had she beene christ'ned *Joyce, Grace, Doll*, or *Nell*.

THE AUDIENCE OF PLAYS: FINAL STATEMENT

*(*Ibid., Ode to Himself, *appended to* The New Inn*)*.

The just indignation the *Author* took at the vulgar censure of his *Play*,
by some malicious spectators, begat this following *Ode* to himself.

> Come leave the loathed stage,
> And the more loathsome age:
> Where pride, and impudence (in faction knit)
>   Usurp the chair of wit!
> Indicting, and arraigning every day
>   Something they call a Play.
> Let their fastidious, vain
> Commission of the brain[27]
> Run one, and rage, sweat, censure, and condemn:
> They were not made for thee, less, thou for them.
>
>   Say, that thou pour'st them wheat,
>   And they will acorns eat:
> 'Twere simple fury, still, thy self to waste
>   On such as have no taste!
> To offer them a surfeit of pure bread,
>   Whose appetites are dead!
>   No, give them grains their fill,
>   Husks, draff to drink, and swill.
> If they love lees, and leave the lusty wine,
> Envy them not, their palate's with the swine.
>
>   No doubt some mouldy tale,
>   Like *Pericles*; and stale
> As the Shrieve's crusts, and nasty as his fish-
>   scraps, out of every dish,
> Thrown forth, and rak'd into the common tub,
>   May keep up the *Play-club*:

27. Self-appointed critics, satirized also in his commendatory poem to Joseph
Rutter (p. 168) and the induction to *Bartholomew Fair* (p. 187).

There, sweepings do as well
As the best order'd meal.[28]
For, who the relish of these guests will fit,
Needs set them, but, the alms-basket of wit.

And much good do't you then:
Brave *plush*, and *velvet*-men;
Can feed on orts: And safe in your stage-clothes,
Dare 'quit, upon your oaths,
The stagers, and the stage-wrights too (your peers)
Of larding[29] your large ears
With their foul *comic* socks;
Wrought upon twenty blocks:
Which, if they are torn, and turn'd, & patch'd enough,
The gamesters share your guilt, and you their stuff.

Leave things so prostitute,
And take the *Alcaic* Lute;
Or thine own *Horace*, or *Anacreon's* Lyre;
Warm thee, by *Pindar's* fire:
And though thy nerves be shrunk, and blood be cold,
Ere years have made thee old;
Strike that disdainful heat
Throughout, to their defeat:
As curious fools, and envious of thy strain,
May, blushing, swear no palsy's in thy brain.

But, when they hear thee sing
The glories of thy *King*,
His zeal to *God*, and his just awe o'er men;
They may, blood-shaken, then,
Feel such a flesh-quake to possess their powers:
As they shall cry, like ours
In sound of peace,[30] or wars,
No Harp e're hit the stars;
In tuning forth the acts of his sweet reign:
And raising *Charles* his chariot, 'bove his *Wain*.[31]

28. In an earlier version, this couplet read: "Brome's sweepings do as well /
There, as his Master's meal."

29. Garnishing.

30. I.e., they shall exclaim that there is no peaceful or martial sound equal to
Jonson's.

31. Jonson will raise Charles above his star, Boötes.

Selected Bibliography

Barish, Jonas. *Ben Jonson and the Language of Prose Comedy*. Cambridge, Mass.: Harvard University Press, 1960.

Campbell, Oscar James. *Comicall Satyre and Shakespeare's Troilus and Cresida*. San Marino, Calif.: Huntington Library, 1938.

Cunningham, Dolora. "The Jonsonian Masque as a Literary Form," *ELH*, XXII (June 1955), 108–124.

Enck, John J. *Jonson and the Comic Truth*. Madison: University of Wisconsin Press, 1957.

Jonson, Ben. *Ben Jonson*. Ed. C. H. Herford and Percy and Evelyn Simpson. 11 vols. Oxford: Clarendon Press, 1925–1952.

Knowlton, Edgar C. "The Plots of Ben Jonson," *MLN*, XLIV (February 1929), 77–86.

Partridge, Edward B. *The Broken Compass: A Study of the Major Comedies of Ben Jonson*. New York: Columbia University Press, 1958.

Trimpi, Wesley. *Ben Jonson's Poems: A Study of the Plain Style*. Stanford: Stanford University Press, 1962.

Acknowledgments

I should like to express here my gratitude to Professor G. E. Bentley of Princeton University, who first introduced me to Jonson the poet and critic, and my indebtedness to him for his scholarly guidance and example. I am also grateful to Mrs. Mae Chatterjee for helping with the typing of the manuscript, to Professors John Ambrose and Nathan Dane of Bowdoin College for helping me with the Greek and Latin, to Professor Paul Olson for his numerous shrewd editorial suggestions, and to the Bowdoin College Faculty Research Fund for a grant which helped defray clerical expenses. Needless to say, no student of Jonson can ever express strongly enough his indebtedness to the editors of the great Oxford edition of *Ben Jonson*.

Index

Accius, 166
Actors: child, 122–130, 156–159, 189–192; praise of, 184
Acts: *See* Plot
Adams, John, 186
Aeschylus, 166
Alcaeus, 32
Alcestis, 31
Alcibiades, 34
Allegory, 20–24, 148, 149. *See also* Symbolism
Alleyn, Edward, 184
Anacreon, 195
Ancients, authority of, xiii–xvi, 4–5, 10–13, 24–26, 26–37, 81. *See also* Art vs. Nature
Antimasque, lv–lvi, 57–58, 147, 149
Archilochus, 32, 107, 107 n.
Aretino, 162
Argumentum, 120, 121
Aristarchus, 53, 80
Aristophanes, xxxix, 37, 81–82, 108, 166
Aristotle, xv–xvi, xxx, xxxi–xxxii, xxxiv–xxxviii, xliii–l, 26, 28, 29, 30, 32–33, 34, 36, 37–40, 151
Ars Poetica, Jonson's preface to, xii, 135, 135 n., 171, 174. *See also* Horace *and* Jonson
Art vs. Nature, xiii–xvi, 4–5, 9–10, 10–13, 15, 20, 26–37, 119, 162, 164, 165–166, 167
Arthur, King, 172
Artist, ideal character of, 71
Audience, 6, 7, 8–9, 9–10, 58–59, 68, 75–81, 84, 89, 91, 92, 95, 102, 103, 104, 113–116, 120, 122–124, 147, 149, 163, 165–166, 179, 185–189, 189–192, 193, 194

Bacon, Sir Francis, 13, 26
Bacon, Sir Nicholas, 13
Bartas, Guillaume de Salluste, Seigneur du, 170
Beaumont, Francis, 164, 165, 172
Brome, Richard, xiii, 167–168, 185, 195

Callimachus, 64
Camden, William, 173, 174
Campion, Thomas, 169, 171
Catastasis: *See* Plot
Catastrophe: *See* Plot
Cato, Dionysius, 64
Cecillius, 82
Cestius, 8, 23
Chaerillus, 35
Chaloner, Sir Thomas, 13
Chapman, John, 170, 173
Characterization: *See* Humours
Characters, stock, 122–124, 185–189, 189–192
Chaucer, Geoffrey, 19, 22, 165
Chionides, 82
Chorus, xli, xlvi, 82, 135, 136–138
Chronicle plays, 139
Cicero, Marcus Tullius, xvii, xvii n., xxv, xliv–xlv, 8, 29, 32, 85
Comedy: defined, xxxiv—xxxix, xliv–xlvi, 33–37; ends of, 26–37, 66–67, 68, 75–81, 85–111, 117–120, 121–122, 123–130, 155–161, 185–189, 193, *see also* Poetry, ends of; similarity to rhetoric, 26–37; history of growth of, 75–82; laws of, 26–37, 75–82,

Comedy (*continued*)
113–118, 167; romantic, 85; satiric,
75–82, 85, 88, 90, 91, 92–111,
113–121, 127–131, 155–159, 159–
162, 183
Couplets, 169
Cratinus, 82
Criticism: aim of, xi–xii, 8, 18–20; a
faculty of the poet only, 26–37;
function of, 113–117
Custom, mistress of language, 20–24

Daniel, Samuel, liv, 169, 170, 172, 173
Dante, 162
Day, John, 170
Dekker, Thomas, xxxv, 155, 170
Demosthenes, 34
Devil of Edmonton, The, 190, 190 n.
Diction, xvi–xx, 4, 20–24, 64, 121;
organic theory of, 24–26; decorum of,
169–175, 182; types of, 10–13. *See
also* Language; Metaphor; *and* Style
Donatus, xxi
Donne, John, 19, 170, 173, 174
Drama, contemporary: attacked, 104–
111, 113–117; popular opinion of,
113–117
Drayton, Michael, 170
Drummond, William: *See* Jonson, *Con-
versations*
Dryden, John, xxiii–xxiv, xxix, xlix–l,
lii
Dyer, Edward, 181, 181 n.

Egerton, Thomas, Baron Ellesmere, 13
Eloquence, 7
Elyot, Sir Thomas, 13
Ennius, Quintus, 19, 64
Envy, 5–7
Epic, 37–40, 169, 170, 172
Epicharmus, 82
Episode, 37–40
Epitasis: *See* Plot
Erasmus, 27

Essex, Robert Devereux, Earl of, 13
Eupolis, 82
Euripides, 31, 34, 166

Fabianus, 23
Fable: *See* Plot
Fairfax, Edward, 170
Fame, 5
Farce, 117
Field, Nathaniel, 172
Five-act structure: *See* Plot
Fletcher, John, 163, 170
Fraunce, Abram, 170

Galen, xxix, xxix n.
Gardiner, Stephen, Bishop, 13
Gower, John, 19
Guarini, Giovanni Battista, 162, 171,
172

Harrington, John, 170
Haterius, 9
Heath, John, 8
Heinsius, Daniel, xxxi, xxxii, 35 n.
Herbert, Edward, 170
Hermetic books, 66–67
Hesiod, 64, 149
Historia: *See* Plot
Homer, 19, 39, 40, 64, 148 n., 170
Hooker, Richard, 13
Horace, xii, xxi, xxviii, xxxv, xxxvi,
xxxix, xxxix n., 16, 28, 31, 32–33, 35,
36, 41–53, 62, 98–101, 105, 115, 135,
147, 159–162, 169–170, 172, 183
Humours, xxiv–xxix, 51, 59, 75, 76–82,
83, 86, 87, 88, 90, 113, 118, 144–145,
155, 162, 180–181

Imitation, xxxiv–xxxviii, 15–17, 20,
26–37, 62–64, 75–82, 113–117, 118,
119, 121, 165–167, 179, 182, 185–189

Jerome, Saint, 27
Jones, Inigo, lv, 124, 131, 148, 150–152

Jonson, Ben:
 Alchemist, The, xiii, xxvii–xxviii, xxx, xxxiii, xxxvii–xxxviii, 118–119, 182;
 Ars Poetica, translated, 41–53;
 Bartholomew Fair, 115 n., 182 n., 185–189, 194 n.;
 Case Is Altered, The, 180–181;
 Catiline, xxxiii–xxxiv, xli;
 Conversations with Drummond, xii, xiv, xix, xliii, 169–175;
 Cynthia's Revels, xxxviii, xxxix, 58–60, 88 n., 89–94, 179;
 Devil Is an Ass, The, 121, 139, 174;
 Discoveries, xii, xiii n., xiv, xv–xvi, xvi–xx, xxi, xxx, xxxi, xxxv, xxxvi, xxxviii, xliii–xliv, xlvi, li–lii, 3–40;
 Epicoene, xxxvi, 120, 183;
 Every Man in His Humour, xx, xxx, xxxii, xxxiii, xxxviii, 57–58, 119–120, 155;
 Every Man Out of His Humour, xiv–xv, xxvi, xxvii, xxx, xxxii, xxxviii, xxxix, xl–xli, 75–89, 130 n., 179;
 "Expostulation with Inigo Jones," lv, 150–152;
 Haddington Masque, The, 146–147, 147 n.;
 Hymenaei, xxvi, liii–liv, lv, 143–146;
 King's Entertainment, The, liv, 143;
 Magnetic Lady, The, xxii–xxiv, xxviii, xxx, xxxvi, xxxviii, 122–130;
 Masque of Augurs, The, lv, 149–150;
 Masque of Queens, The, lv, 147–149;
 Neptune's Triumph, 66–68;
 New Inn, The, xxii, xxxvi, 122, 192–195; "Ode to Himself," 194–195;
 Poetaster, xxxv, xxxix, 60–65, 95–109, 155–162; "Apological Dialogue," xxxix, 102–109;
 Sad Shepherd, The, xxx, 69–71;
 Sejanus, xli–lii, 135–138;
 Shakespeare, commendatory poem from first folio of, 165–167;
 Staple of News, The, 68–69, 115 n., 121–122, 189–192;
 Tale of a Tub, A, xxxiv, 131;
 Timber: See Discoveries;
 Volpone, xii, xv–xvi, xxvii, xxix, xxx, xxxi, xxxii–xxxiii, xxxviii, xli, 113–118, 162–163

Johnson, Samuel, xi
Juvenal, xxxix, 104, 104 n., 108, 170, 172

Kyd, Thomas, 155–157, 166, 180, 187

Laberius, 35
Language: abuses of, xvi–xx, 64, 182; custom and, 20–24; ornamental, 20–24; realistic, 20–24, 119; ,shows the man, 24–26. See also Diction; Metaphor; and Style
Laughter, xxxviii–xxxix, xliii–xliv, 36–37, 76, 81, 88–89, 90–91, 117–118, 121, 126
Lipsius, Justus, 30
Livy, 19
Lucan, 171
Lucilius, Gaius, 35, 99, 101
Lucretius, 28
Lycophron, 64
Lyly, John, 166

Markham, Gervase, 170
Marlowe, Christopher, 166; Tamerlane, 12
Marston, John, 159–163, 172, 173
Martial, 8, 28, 68, 68 n., 116, 127, 169–170, 172
Masque: ends of, liii–lvi, 143, 147; indirection in, 148; in the drama, 131; magnificence of, 143; soul vs. body of, 143–144, 150–151; unity of, 143, 146, 147; variety in, 147; obscurity of, 150–151. See also Antimasque
Maximus, Valerius, 31
Menander, 36, 82

Meres, Francis, 181, 181 n.
Metaphor, 20–24
Middleton, Thomas, 172
Minsheu, John, 170
Minturno, xlii, xlvi, xlviii, l
Montaigne, Michel Eyquem de, 11, 162
More, Thomas, 13
Munday, Anthony, 180–181
Musaeus, 64
Music: *See* Masque, unity of

Naevius, Gnaeus, 34
New Comedy, xxxix, xli. *See also* Comedy; Plautus; *and* Terence

Old Comedy, xxxix–xli, xxxix n., 26–37, 75–82, 89, 98–102, 104–111. *See also* Aristophanes *and* Lucilius
Originality, 75–82, 89. *See also* Ancients *and* Art vs. Nature
Orpheus, 64
Overbury, Thomas, 172
Ovid, 30, 60–61, 95–96, 106, 106 n.

Pacuvius, 166
Passions, xxv–xxix, 3–4, 113, 144–146. *See also* Humours
Pastoral drama, 69–71, 162, 163, 168, 169, 174
Patronage, 4, 8–9, 61–62, 192
Pavy, Salomon, 184
Peele, George, 155
Pericles, 34
Pericles, 194
Persius, xxxix, 27, 108, 172
Petrarch, 162, 170
Petronius, Arbiter, Gaius, 172
Philemon, 82
Philosophy vs. Poetry, 26–37
Phormus, 82
Pindar, 64, 195
Plagiarism, 164, 179
Plato, 30, 163

Plautus, 19–20, 34–37, 64, 82, 86, 127, 166, 174
Players, 96–98. *See also* Actors
Pliny, 16, 108 n., 169–170
Plot, xx–xxiv, 26–37, 81–82, 83, 85, 86, 87, 88, 89, 90, 117, 119, 168, 180–181; defined, 37–39, 122–131; catastasis, xx–xxiv, 125–126, 127–131; catastrophe, xx–xxiv, xxx, 87–88, 121, 122, 125–131, 189–192; epitasis, xx–xxiv, 85, 122, 125–131; protasis, xx–xxiv, 86, 125–127
Plutarch, 15
Poem, defined, 26–37
Poet: art of, xii–xiv, 26–37; nature of, xii–xiv, 14, 57–58, 59, 60, 62–64, 66–69, 104–111, 113–117, 159–162; reputation of, 5–7; requirements of, 26–37; best critic, 26–37
Poetry, 8–9; and rhetoric, 26–37; compared to painting, 15–17; contemporary abuses of, 15–17; corrective aim of, 26–37; dramatic, satirized, 155–159; ends of, 57, 58, 61, 89, 113–117; subject not primary, 5–7
Posterity, xi, 5, 18, 109
Prologue, 122–125, 127–131
Protasis: *See* Plot
Puritans, 76, 184, 185, 192
Puttenham, George, xl, 174

Quintilian, xlv, 19, 21, 24, 35, 169–170, 172

Rabelais, François, 66–67
Raleigh, Sir Walter, 13, 170, 173
Realism: *See* Imitation
Rhetoric and poetry, xliv–xlv, 26–37
Ronsard, Pierre de, 171
Rutter, Joseph, 168, 194 n.
Rymer, Thomas, xi

Sallust, 19
Sandys, Edwin, 13

Satire, personal, xxxix–xli, 84, 88, 95, 98–102, 102–111, 113–117, 159–162, 185–189, 193. *See also* Comedy; Old Comedy; Aristophanes; Lucilius; *and* Horace

Saville, Henry, 13

Scaliger, Joseph, 31, 35

Scaliger, Julius Caesar, xxiii, xl, xlii, 31, 35

Selden, John, 173

Seneca, Lucius Annaeus, lii, 23, 30, 166

Shakespeare, William, xii, xiv, xxxiii, xli, lii, 9–10, 85, 119, 165–167, 170, 173, 182, 186–188, 194

Sharpham, Edward, 170

Sidney, Sir Philip, xix, xlvi, 1, 13, 19, 170, 172, 175

Silvester, Joshuah, 170

Simylus, 32

Smith, Thomas, 13

Socrates, xxviii–xxix, 16, 37

Sophocles, 34, 40, 166

Southwell, Robert, 172

Spectacle, xxxii–xxxiv, 68, 83, 90, 117, 119, 121, 131, 147, 150–151, 182

Spenser, Edmund, 19, 170, 172

Statius, Publius Papinius, 32

Stilo, Lucius Aelius, 34

Stobaeus, Joannes, 32

Style, xvi–xx, 4; decorum of, 20–24, 64, 169–175; excesses of, 9–10, 182; the natural, 7–8; necessity for variety of, 17–24; in pastoral, 69–71; perspicuity of, 18–20, 21–24; requirements for a good, 17–18; significance of, 13–14; two kinds of, 18–20; types of, 10–13, 20–24, 24–26. *See also* Diction; Language; *and* Metaphor

Suetonius, 23

Surrey, Henry, Earl of, 13

Susario, 82

Swinburne, Algernon, li

Symbolism, 65, 143–144, 147, 148, 149. *See also* Allegory

Tacitus, Cornelius, 22, 170

Tarlton, Richard, 186

Tasso, Tarquato, 170 n.

Taylor, John, 8

Terence, xli, 19–20, 64, 81, 123, 123 n., 127, 166

Theaters, public vs. private, 155–159, 179, 180–182

Theocritus, 64

Tragedy, defined, xli–1, 26–37, 135–139

Tragicomedy, 69–71, 85, 162, 163, 169–175

"Truth of Argument": *See* Tragedy

Tully: *See* Cicero

Unities, xxix–xxxii, 37–40, 69–71, 75–82, 83, 86, 87, 88, 113–117, 118–120, 122–125, 127–131, 135, 168

Varro, Marcus Terentius, 34

Vetus Comoedia: See Old Comedy

Vice, the, 174, 189–192

Virgil, xx, xxxi–xxxii, 19, 22, 23, 28, 32, 39, 40, 62–64, 105, 159, 170

Vitruvius, 16, 124

Vives, Juan Luis, 22 n.

Wit, types of, 10–13

Wotton, Edward, 170

Wright, Thomas, xxv–xxvi, 113

Wyatt, Sir Thomas, 13